GROWING UP IN

GROWING UP IN STEPFAMILIES

GILL GORELL BARNES
PAUL THOMPSON
GWYN DANIEL
and
NATASHA BURCHARDT

CLARENDON PRESS · OXFORD
1998

Oxford University Press, Great Clarendon Street, Oxford OX2 6DP

Oxford New York

Athens Auckland Bangkok Bogota Bombay
Buenos Aires Calcutta Cape Town Dar es Salaam
Delhi Florence Hong Kong Istanbul Karachi
Kuala Lumpur Madras Madrid Melbourne
Mexico City Nairobi Paris Singapore
Taipei Tokyo Toronto Warsaw

and associated companies in
Berlin Ibadan

Oxford is a trade mark of Oxford University Press

Published in the United States
by Oxford University Press Inc., New York

British Library Cataloguing in Publication Data

Data available

Library of Congress Cataloging in Publication Data

Growing up in stepfamilies/by Gill Gorell Barnes . . . [et al.].
Includes bibliographical references and index.
1. Stepchildren–Great Britain–Longitudinal studies.
2. Stepfamilies–Great Britain–Longitudinal studies. I. Barnes,
Gill Gorell.
HQ777.7.G76 1997   306.874–dc21   97-31184
ISBN 0-19-828097-1
ISBN 0-19-828096-3 (pbk.).

1 3 5 7 9 10 8 6 4 2

Typeset by J&L Composition Ltd, Filey, North Yorkshire
Printed in Great Britain
on acid-free paper by
Biddles Ltd, Guildford and King's Lynn

PREFACE

THE growth of stepfamilies has been one of the most dramatic changes in British and also American family life in recent decades. Britain today has the highest divorce rate in Europe, at almost twice the average, and it is currently estimated that up to a quarter of all newly-born children in Britain will experience parental separation before they are 16. The rate of remarriage has quadrupled in the last twenty years. By the early 1990s one in six children in the United States and one in twelve in Britain were already living in stepfamilies.[1] Calculations by Stepfamily (the National Stepfamily Association) predict 2.5 to 3 million children and young adults will be stepchildren by the year 2000.

In the past, stepfamilies formed by remarriage after death were a common experience, and references to them are widespread in literature, diaries and personal documents, and folklore—above all in the myth of the wicked stepmother. And more positively, many of the most important and creative figures in European culture were stepchildren: among them Isaac Newton, John Donne, Descartes, Spinoza, Michelangelo, and Leonardo da Vinci. Perhaps the most famous of all stepchildren was Jesus Christ, the ramifications of whose step-relationships were explored through medieval myths and in Byzantine mosaics such as those in Chora, Istanbul. But in the first half of this century, as parental death became unusual, stepfamilies became unfamiliar rarities and much of the common understanding of their dynamics was lost. The recent very rapid growth in divorce and remarriage has exposed millions of adults and children to life situations which are surprisingly little understood, either at the level of common wisdom, or through research.

It is widely assumed that a very high proportion of children who are referred to social and health professionals come from broken or reconstituted families: according to some figures, over half. But this has created a further difficulty in understanding the typical processes of stepfamily experience. Until relatively recently the interpretation of the post-divorce and stepfamily experience of children was dominated by analyses of clinic data and clients, and even today probably the most publicized research project has been

Judith Wallerstein's Californian study of children after divorce. Her research is based on families using her clinic, and in evaluating long-term consequences she therefore focuses above all on those whose difficulties proved most intransigent.[2] Wallerstein's influence has been crucial in some of the more recent changes in law and practice following divorce in Britain. Nevertheless, when the children of stepfamilies are compared with those of intact families in large-scale studies based on random samples, their differences are not startling, and it is clear that—as in the past—many stepchildren prove extremely successful in their lives. There is clearly important variety within stepfamily experience. Yet there is astonishingly little reliable research on the differences between those stepfamilies which are 'good enough' for the children who live in them and those stepfamilies which are not. Exploring these differences has been one of the principal objectives of our own research.

Internationally there are now three well-developed research studies based on reliable samples which have helped to provide a firmer framework for understanding stepfamilies: those of Hetherington and of Furstenberg and Spanier in the USA, and of Ochiltree in Australia.[3] In Britain the best study of stepfamily life so far published, Burgoyne and Clark's *Making a Go of It*, was based on a local Sheffield project without a reliable sample base.[4] It is also written from the viewpoint of parents rather than of children. More recently a small but largely statistical study of children now at school, taken from different types of family household has been carried out in Exeter.[5] Our own study is the first in Britain which examines the long-term outcome experience of stepfamily life through the evidence of children selected on the basis of a reliable sample.

For our project we have carried out interviews with fifty children who were all born in a single week in 1958, and have been followed from birth with structured survey questionnaire interviews by the National Child Development Study. We chose for interview those who had been recorded as entering stepfamilies between the ages of 7 and 16, so that there was a good chance that they would be able to remember the transitions which took place clearly. The NCDS cohort covers the whole of Britain, so we selected our interviews by geographical clustering. We carried out full life story interviews with the informants, lasting typically between two and six hours. This was the first time in which they had been interviewed in this way, and the information which they gave us is full and often powerfully moving. To preserve confidentiality we have disguised them and all speak here under pseudonyms.

Our book is an analysis of the experiences conveyed through these interviews from men and women who for at least part of their childhood grew up in stepfamilies. But because most of them earlier experienced living in intact families and often also in single-parent families, it inevitably at the same time provides a much wider perspective on British family life in the last thirty-five years. We have set it in the context of other current research. The key themes around which our interpretation is structured are gender, class, communication within families, discipline, sources of support from the extended family and beyond, the continuing role of the non-custodial parent, and, above all, the factors which help or hinder stepchildren in the long term. We emphasize how change is possible not only in childhood, but also in adulthood. Finally, we consider the implications of our findings for further research and for professional clinical and social work.

We believe that because of its research design *Growing up in Stepfamilies* makes a unique contribution to our understanding of the long-term impact of stepfamily life in Britain. It is also exceptional internationally for its use of life story interviews within the context of a quantitative longitudinal study. And it is founded on a genuinely interdisciplinary fusion of perspectives, drawing together sociological and social historical interpretations through the life story method with clinical experience in child and adolescent psychiatry and the family systems approach used in family therapy.

Of the authors, both Gill Gorell Barnes and Gwyn Daniel are experienced family therapists. Gill Gorell Barnes is Consultant for Training at the Institute of Family Therapy, Senior Lecturer in Clinical Work at the Tavistock Clinic, and author of *Working with Families*. Gwyn Daniel was formerly Director for Training at the Institute of Family Therapy and is founder-director of the Oxford Family Institute. She has written earlier on gender in family therapy. Natasha Burchardt until recently practised as a consultant child and adolescent psychiatrist with the Oxfordshire Health Authority and has written previously on stepchildren. Paul

Thompson is Research Professor at the University of Essex and his books include *The Voice of the Past*, the leading international text on the life story or oral history method; *The Work of William Morris; I Don't Feel Old: The Experience of Ageing*, and *The Edwardians*. He is also founder-editor of the journal *Oral History* and Founder of the National Life Story Collection at the National Sound Archive. Three of the four authors also have had direct experience of stepfamily life themselves.

While in its final form the book is our collective responsibility, the original lead was taken by Gill Gorell Barnes for Chapters 1 and 7, Paul Thompson Chapters 3 and 5, Gwyn Daniel Chapter 6, Natasha Burchardt Chapter 4, Gwyn Daniel and Paul Thompson Chapter 2, and Gill Gorell Barnes and Gwyn Daniel Chapters 8 and 9. We have intentionally written some chapters in a full descriptive style with many quotations, and others in a more abstract manner.

The success of our project has depended on help and advice from many sources. In addition to the interviews which we carried out ourselves, Michele Abendstern, Madeleine Knowles, and Alan Dein also worked with us as interviewers. We should also particularly mention Professor Tony Cox, who helped us with the design of our interview guide; the participation of Mary Newburn in our earlier discussions; and Marion Haberhauer, for her sensitive transcription of the interviews. Kathleen Kiernan very kindly provided us with some additional information about the whole group of stepfamilies as reinterviewed by NCDS at 33. We are especially endebted to the Wates Foundation for financial help with our fieldwork, and for subsequent assistance to the Henry Gorell Barnes Trust. Above all, we thank the fifty former stepchildren who told us the stories of their lives, and the National Child Development Study for allowing us to approach them; for on their generosity our whole book is founded.

CONTENTS

1

What Do We Know about Stepchildren?

IT is incontestable that the number of stepfamilies in Britain has increased dramatically over the last fifty years. The exact figures are surprisingly elusive, partly because until recently the census did not publish statistics either of stepfamilies by remarriage or of unmarried couples living together. But we do know that the rate of divorce is higher than in any previous period, twice as high as in any other European country, and that in 1991 alone 170,000 children under 16 experienced a parental divorce, while the rate of marriage has increased fourfold over the last twenty years. By the early 1990s one child in twelve was already living in a stepfamily in Britain, and in the United States one in six.[1] And the numbers were predicted to climb further.

What stories lie behind the research headlines on divorce and remarriage, and what are the experiences of the children who go through these transitions as they grow up? Certainly there have been plenty of dire predictions, not only from the pulpit, press, and politicians, but also from researchers. Thus the *Family Policies Study Centre Bulletin* recently outlined a series of key potential risks to the children of divorcing parents, ranging from the effects of prolonged conflict between parents, family disorganization, and diminished parental attention, to economic and material deprivation. These dangers are absolutely clear, and the suffering which they can cause to children is equally well known to clinicians. But it is far more difficult to say with confidence how common the more severe consequences are. It will thus be helpful to begin by setting our own project in the context of a brief overview of other recent research on stepfamilies, to outline what is already known about the experience of growing up in stepfamilies.[2]

There is in fact a good deal of disagreement and debate among researchers about the effects of divorce and remarriage on children. This springs from three fundamental difficulties. The first is that the stepfamily itself is not only a very complex but also a very diverse form of family. The second is that researchers have been unnecessarily divided in their methods between statistical surveys and in-depth studies. The third is that time is a crucial dimension to evaluating the experience of stepchildren; but for researchers, it is far easier to study immediate than long-term consequences.

The Idea of the Family

First then, what is a stepfamily? A stepfamily is created when two adults form a household in which one or both brings a child from a previous relationship, and the new partner becomes a significant adult or parental figure to their partner's child.[3] Families get together following single parenthood without marriage; or divorce; or the break-up of former cohabitations; or following a death. This complexity in itself creates serious problems for any systematic research on the consequences of stepfamily experience. Thus the Stepfamily Association has calculated that there are seventy-two pathways into stepfamily life.[4] These multitudinous paths lead to many different forms of stepfamily household. For example, stepchildren may be full-time or part-time members of the new household, and today, as children move between the two households created by each partner, they are likely to accommodate more than one family style. Each stepfamily needs to be thought of as consisting of at least two different but overlapping family groups, one linked to the new step-parent and the other to the displaced but not replaced natural parent. This is an important distinction which is likely to apply in all stepfamilies, and it is one of the additional tensions they have to manage.

As we shall see (Chapter 4), even when the biological or original parent has died before the child was old enough to form a memory of him or her, the idea of this initial parent may be very important in the child's mind. When the remaining parent is subsequently prepared to let that space be filled by a new partner, they may come to replace the role of mother or father in the child's everyday life; but never to obliterate the original parent in the child's mind. Thus while after a death the incoming step-parent obviously does not have to compete with the 'living' role of father or mother, the legacy they inherit and the roles they move into will already entail pre-programmed expectations and inherent loyalty conflicts. What a 'father' or 'mother' should be, may have been laid down in the child's mind long before their arrival.

Because step-parents are additional rather than replacement parents, one of the fundamental stresses which most modern stepfamilies have to manage, and which marks them out from intact nuclear families, is the shared division of one same-sex parenting role between two people that is a consequence of divorce. Children will have at least three and sometimes four 'parent' figures. For some children this may bring pleasures and bonuses, although these get rarely mentioned in research. For the in-house parent, the continued contact with a former partner, now co-parent, is never easy, as a natural parent's rights in relation to the child are legally as well as initially emotionally greater than those of the subsequent partner; but often over time the balance will change. The way in which contact between former partners is managed on behalf of children and the impact of contact on other family relationships is a key feature of stepfamily living. Families develop many different solutions, which range in practice from the complete severance of contact with the out-house parent to two-home childhoods.

Received ideas of how this should be best managed, and hence by implication of the best model for a stepfamily, have also greatly varied in different periods. Until relatively recently the coherence and integration of the new stepfamily was regarded as the top priority, and this may well remain the most common view in popular thinking. Certainly the new legal focus on shared parental responsibility embodied in the Children Act 1989 infringes on newly forming family boundaries, and the attempted privacy of stepfamily life. The ongoing research study led by Jan Walker in Newcastle has shown that many women wish contact with their former spouse to cease, especially in the context of continuing acrimony and violence.[5] Hence to use the new law to enforce contact may have the effect not only of amplifying conflicts continuing from the first marriage, but also of decreasing the role that an incoming step-parent can play in the child's life.

The modern stepchild thus arrives by very diverse paths into a family form which is not merely inherently complicated and diverse in its sub-varieties, but also, at both a public and a popular level, suffers from a disputed model of how it ought to function.

A further important point is that the experience of stepchildren not only normally involves different parental households, but also, to a much greater extent than for most children from intact families today, the wider family, and particularly grandparental homes. By mitigating both economic and emotional deprivation, as we shall see (Chapter 5), the use of the extended family can dramatically shift predictions about how post-divorce life is managed. Thus widening the lens to include the extended family can complicate predictions in a positive way. Family research of any kind on the role of grandparents is rare, because of the almost exclusive focus on marriage and parenthood. We found, however, that grandmothers in particular were used as an alternative base for children or to hold families on course by maintaining daily routines at the time a parent left.

Those few American researchers who have considered the relationship of the wider family to the child's nuclear household after parental separation have reported that where there was increased contact and support from kin, this was beneficial for the child's functioning.[6] From her Californian research, however, Judith Wallerstein reported that less than one-tenth of children had any help from the wider family. This contrasts very sharply with the strongly positive findings of Frank Furstenberg and Graham Spanier in rural Pennsylvania. And in another smaller American study, Colleen Johnson found, like ourselves, that most grandparents played a significant part in easing the strains, and two-thirds of parents depended most of all on them. Separation led, however, to three distinct tendencies in the restructuring of the family. While the parent–grandparent bond was most often strengthened, one-quarter of the divorced parents retreated within the privacy of household and diminished nuclear family unit. At the opposite extreme over one-third, however, not only depended on grandparents, but through them—and particularly often through their ex-mother-in-law—developed more active relationships with a looser family network of friends and relatives, by blood, marriage, and divorce, of which grandparents were only a part.[7]

In our study all but seven of the young people interviewed remembered ongoing and influential support from different family members in the period of adjustment following the loss of a parent either by death or divorce. A second marriage and its early success cannot therefore be disconnected from the existing extended family network of grandparents, uncles, aunts, and other close relations, which will itself have reorganized in relation to the post-divorce nuclear family, and all of whom will have views on a prospective remarriage.

Following a new cohabitation or remarriage the extended family, now incorporating the kinship network of a larger number of parental adults, may also expand in practice for the children. Children may find that the circle of relatives of which they are a part includes not only the kin network of the new step-parent, but also the relatives of any new partnership that their out-house parent has entered into. Thus stepfamilies are intrinsically highly complex social organizations, and this much wider context of intimate relationship within which a second marriage is formed is likely to have a significant impact on the quality and viability of second family life and the initial success of the couple in managing this.

Hence the adults we interviewed often did not remember so much a shift from belonging to a two-parent family to a lone-parent family, as to becoming part of a wider extended family. This was one reason why few of our informants remembered witnessing either a parent going to pieces, or a change from predictable routines into chaotic lifestyles; two features of the post-divorce family which have been reported by research from the USA and which have thus been widely taken as typical of the post-divorce family living in this country.[8] Once again the root of the difficulty is the failure to recognize the variety of family forms which are significant.

It might be argued that our findings differ from others simply because retrospective interpretations will always tend to be more positive, reflecting a tendency to suppress the most painful memories of stressful experiences in the past. But in fact it is difficult to suppress even the most traumatic of memories, as can be shown from other instances, such as men and women who were survivors of the holocaust, or victims of sexual abuse. Our informants showed that they could talk to us very frankly, and their witness is intrinsically credible. We believe that it is more likely that British experience of stepchildhood in the 1960s and 1970s may have been very different from that reported in North American divorce research on the same period, precisely because there the extended family was a much less available resource.

Our study also highlights the significance of different areas of non-family experience for stepchildren which again rarely feature in research. These include the importance of school as a social milieu; and of friends and peer groups in the alternative worlds of sport and play.

Styles of Research

A second basic difficulty in understanding stepfamily experience has been the polarization of methods used by researchers. On the one hand, there are a small number of statistical studies based on structured interviews with reliable random samples from the general population, which give us indices to assess the basic factors in post-divorce and stepfamily living. They can enable us to quantify some of the crude hazards for children. But they are unable to discuss the positive or negative qualities of family living after divorce. Clinical investigators, on the other hand, through using the evidence of families whom they have come to know personally over time, are certainly able to offer an in-depth focus on the individual experience of children. Some clinical studies have been outstanding in their insights, and invaluable in helping families in difficulties.[9] But too often they have moved on from this to make unwarranted generalizations about the experience of children in divorcing families as a whole: for such children are not a unified group, and those whom they see are likely to have suffered more than many of the others.

Because of their differences in method and sample, statistical and clinical researchers have come up with strikingly different results. In general, statistical researchers have concluded that children of divorce (who may or may not become stepchildren) show only small differences from other children in their social and psychological functioning over time.[10] Clinical investigators by contrast emphasize the emotional dimensions, and some give harrowing accounts of how children can show distress and longing over many years.[11]

Attempts to bridge this methodological gap have been very rare. One useful recent project in Britain has been a small local pilot study of schoolchildren in Exeter. Unfortunately apart from not being generalizable to the country as a whole, it is not long term, the reliability of its sample is somewhat doubtful, and its form of analysis is inappropriately statistical.[12]

Our own research is unique in Britain in using in-depth interviews with former stepchildren selected on a reliable sample base from a national survey; and we also represent among ourselves both clinical and non-clinical viewpoints (see Chapter 2).

In this country two major longitudinal studies have provided anchor-points—however often frustrating in the limitations to the information they hold—for any serious research on child development. They have each followed a national cohort of over 10,000 children, the first born in 1946 and the second in 1958. Both have revealed distinct patterns of disruption following divorce. From the 1946 cohort, analysis has been based on only 82 boy stepchildren, so that comparison with the contemporary situation needs to be cautious. However, analysis of them has drawn attention to changes in economic circumstances and in schooling, and to lower attainment and subsequent relationship problems, which suggest that children of divorced parents are more likely themselves to get divorced.[13]

With the second cohort of children born in 1958, from which the young people in this book were drawn, there were many more stepchildren, altogether 444. A first analysis by Elsa Ferri showed that there were some differences in adjustment between stepchildren and children from intact families, but they were not very strong.[14] More recently a re-analysis by Kathleen Kiernan of the young people at 16 contrasted children from intact families, single-parent families, and stepfamilies. She noted that there were tendencies for stepchildren to leave school early and with fewer qualifications; a lower chance of entry to tertiary education, a higher tendency to leave home early and to form sexual relationships at a young age.[15] Her concern in relation to these findings arose from the potential future correlation between marriage and cohabitation at a young age and the likelihood of subsequent early separation and divorce. It is known that as a whole, those who marry early—defined as under 23—are more likely to divorce young. Early divorce in turn carries the potential for prolonged experience of lone parenthood with its attendant economic vulnerabilities. These may increase risks to the emotional well-being of mothers and children. Earlier marriage and child-bearing have also been seen as likely to further reduce later educational opportunities.

Studies re-analysing evidence from earlier longitudinal cohorts have also suggested that divorce, to a much greater degree than death, has adverse consequences which can persist into adulthood. But a Scottish study of a cohort born in 1972 has produced surprising evidence in the opposite direction, showing, for example, that significantly more women who lost a parent through death than through separation were drug-users.[16]

Essential though they are, however, such statistical analyses are intrinsically unable to explore the subtleties of stepfamily relationships. Indeed the 1958 cohort did not even distinguish step and natural parents in its earlier questioning. They thus could not focus on the new ways in which families see themselves and how they develop resources and new solutions to the crises that might be seen as a 'normal' part of going through family dissolution and change. Research studies of this type can tell us more about potential stresses for children than about potential resilience derived from moderating factors in the child's family world. They can primarily help us to predict the risk factors which may lead children to a less secure sense of who they are, and who they could become, as stepchildren.

Transitions and Points in Time

A third and ultimately more intractable difficulty is the prolonged time-track which stepchildhood implies. A stepchild's life is often built on earlier experience, first in its intact parental home, and then a phase in a single-parent family household. Indeed, it is the transitions between these states as much as belonging to a stepfamily in itself which constitute many of the defining moments of such a childhood. And the impact of being a stepchild is likely to be very different in the first initial months, and after settling down: and subsequently, at leaving home, and in turn on marrying and becoming a parent, and so on. As Mavis Hetherington, the most experienced of all systematic stepfamily researchers, put it to a joint conference of the Stepfamily Association and the Institute of Family Therapy in 1994:

Divorce or remarriage is simply one point in a series of transitions, and where a researcher taps into that series of transitions will determine their answer to the question, 'How does divorce or remarriage affect parents or children?'

What preceded a transition will affect the child or the parent's adaptation to that transition, and the adaptation to divorce is going to be influenced by the quality of life in the marriage that preceded it. The adaptation to remarriage is going to be related to the quality of life in the course of the series of transitions that are associated with marital dissolution, and the kinds of resources or protective factors vary across time. So, to tap in at one point in time and say, 'This is how children are adjusting following divorce', gives you a very warped picture of what is going on. You need to look at trajectories.

In our own case, the fact that we interviewed young adults in their early thirties meant that some of the information we gathered throws a different light on the predictions which were made earlier through an analysis of cohort data from the age when they were children of 16.[17] There had then been worrying evidence of a diminished continuation with education by children of divorcing parents. Our interviews also showed that most children did finish school early, often as soon as they could, and left for employment rather than further education. But subsequently many of them nevertheless returned to higher education or higher training in their later teens or twenties. In addition the fear that a high proportion of those who formed early intimate relationships would also experience their early breakdown was not borne out by our informants. The majority of those who had married before 20 were still in the same relationship at 32.

In short, the outcome of the research is likely to depend crucially on the point of time chosen for focus. And researchers interested, as we are, in long-term outcomes from new perspectives, are forced between using retrospective accounts and launching new longitudinal studies whose results will not be known for twenty or thirty years. This is why we decided to attach our retrospective life story interviewing to an existing longitudinal study, thereby gaining some of the strengths of both approaches.

Accepting the centrality of transitions and trajectories does however immediately bring valuable new perspectives for the understanding of stepchildhood. Thus many of the difficulties and problems stepfamilies experience can be seen as resulting from transitions from one state of kinship organization or family system to another. Such transitions incur many losses which create cumulative stress. Even when compensating gains may come later, the breaking up of a marriage or the death of a parent disrupts intimate relationships. Losses will often include the absolute or partial loss of a parent following divorce, and indeed until the late 1990s estimates were that over one-third of all children in divorcing families lost touch with their fathers. The subsequent creation of a single-parent household, with the second parent living out of the home, will be interrupted in turn when the residential parent forms a second intimate relationship with another adult partner. Each transition in relationships requires significant adaptations by the children. In addition children will often change home, school, and neighbourhood.

In the 1990s assumptions about successful child development are still commonly rooted in the need for an ongoing continuity of attachment to one set of biological parents. Children who live in stepfamilies, however, are likely to have experienced more than one change. Some children may have taken part in several household changes in their lives. Their life courses will be different from those of children growing up in intact families, even though certain features will certainly remain similar. We need to be better informed about these common differences resulting from divorce, so that models of family life other than those of intact families inform our thinking about 'normal' family development.

A research approach which focused primarily on transitions could also help us to understand more confidently what promotes the resilience which children need in these circumstances.[18] It may well be that disruption of family ties and changes in family circumstances, frequently linked with acute or continuing adversity, may result in changes in the quality of attachments in both children and adults. How are the attachment needs of children met as families change? What aspects of family life, or the child's own daily social world promote children's emotional growth successfully and create the conditions for the development of competence and self-esteem. What do second family members, who are themselves highly aware of the dilemmas of continuity and change, themselves understand about the stresses associated with divorce and death, and what do they have to say about extended family tensions that remarriage brings?

The Impact of Divorce

The framework for our study is thus the young person growing up in the context of multiple transitions, which follow the loss of a parent. Such transitions contain new starting-points for parents and for children which involve both stresses and opportunities. Reliable studies, mostly from the United States and Australia but a few from Britain, show that in the years following divorce families as a whole typically encounter common stresses. These include lowered family income, the loss of one parent on a daily basis, a possible change of home, and also of school. The American studies also show other important changes, such as the loss of ongoing contact with fathers with 37.5 per cent seeing them less than twice a year.[19]

What happens to fathering in the immediate aftermath of divorce? Frank Furstenberg and his colleagues analysed a nationally representative sample of American children aged 11 to 16 in 1981, and looked at first, the incidence of marital disruption, secondly the subsequent living arrangements for children, and thirdly the amount of contact children maintained with the out-of-house parent. They found the amount of contact children maintained with the out-of-house parent was uniformly low across the entire sample. Only 17 per cent of children saw their non-custodial parent once a week. Lack of contact also coincided with lack of parental maintenance payments. Even so, the level of contact between fathers and children dropped sharply following the fathers' remarriage. Furstenberg coined the idea of 'sociological parenthood', and saw the relationship that children and their stepfathers develop as a form of parenting that took over from the biological fathering role.[20] Other smaller scale work on fathers following divorce has shown that many factors influence the development of the post-divorce fathering role, including men's own ability to develop flexibility in arrangements for looking after children. This is related to their own capacity to take on patterns of caretaking, including aspects of role construed as 'female', or more usually seen culturally within the domain of 'mothering'[21]: a point to which we shall return (Chapters 3 and 6).

We have already encountered Hetherington, whose work has occupied a central place in American research on children and divorce since the late 1970s. She highlighted the fact that children were seen to show continued distress in the aftermath of legal proceedings, and noted significant deterioration in mother–child relations in the short-term period. She has also pointed out the diversity in children's responses. She has set out the distinction between longer term responses and a short-term crisis period following divorce, which is characterized by confusion and apprehension about what will happen next, and identified key behaviours such as non-compliance and aggression as a response to ongoing parental conflict.[22] Another study has found a tendency for many children to show difficulties in social relations in the two years following divorce and to display behaviour that indicated stress more than might be expected in a randomly chosen sample. This concluded however, that many children respond to divorce with transient symptomatic behaviour, which disappears within two years.[23]

The question of what helps children rebalance themselves within the normal range of behaviours and what tips them into longer term disturbance has been identified further by other researchers. The quality of post-divorce parental cooperation plays one part. A British study by Mary Lund, based on a sample of schoolchildren, focused on the question of parental communication following separation. Families broadly fell into three main groups: harmonious co-parent families, conflicted co-parent families, and absent parent families. She found that children whose parents were able to work harmoniously together after separating showed fewer emotional problems, higher self-esteem, and better school performance than children who had either lost touch with the non-caretaking parent or whose parents continued to be in conflict. Children who had lost contact with the departed parent were seen as having the most emotional problems compared with the other children. They retained a sense of the importance of the parent who had gone despite their absence. These children often seemed depressed and showed a tendency to blame themselves for their parents' separation and to withdraw into themselves.[24]

The continuing controversy over the value for the child of maintaining contact with a parent who has left within the ongoing context of an acrimonious relationship between divorced parents, is a key feature of many studies of post-divorce living.[25] Whether a divorce increased or decreased parental disputes seems to be of key importance, for ongoing parental conflict is highlighted by many studies from different sources as one of the key factors in the well-being of children.[26] Indeed children themselves continue to provide one of the ties that give angry former spouses the opportunity to continue unresolved fighting.[27] Walker has recently warned against professionals adopting the model of co-operative parenting as a universal norm, showing on the basis of her Newcastle research that for at least one-quarter of parents who divorce, silent toleration of the fact of the other parent's continuing existence may be the most that can be hoped for.[28] The ways in which children themselves report on this is further discussed in Chapters 4 and 10.

The findings on how women and children fare emotionally following divorce are varied, but there is now universal recognition of its economic impact. Mental health professionals have often neglected to take account of how powerful a factor this economic decline can be, especially for women, following divorce.[29] The Australian 'Children in Families' study found this the major problem for over 70 per cent of divorcees, and most reports from the United States confirm this as a major dimension of stress in family life.[30] Two studies with a different bias, one from Canada and one from Sweden, highlight how diminished post-divorce stress can be where the economic situation remains good enough.[31] The Canadian sample was of parents of college education level, who retained their standard of living through appropriate maintenance from their ex-partners, family support (one-third), and government support (one-third). In spite of the high index of negative reported emotion towards fathers and their ongoing involvement, only 20 per cent of women felt the separation had negative effects on their children, and 20 per cent of women felt they were better off in the calm of post-divorce life. Half the mothers reported an increase in their own tolerance towards children.

On the basis of the Australian study, Ochiltree questions whether the bad effects, so often attributed to fatherlessness in post-divorce families, arise primarily from the absence of a male figure, or from the poverty, exploitation, and prejudice which is frequently experienced by children living in a fatherless home. The combination of less money, poorer housing, and more over-crowding, and more limited play space, creates a powerful socially structured series of connected and impoverishing events. These are likely to have as great an impact as are more intimate inter-personal processes on the well-being of children.[32]

A small number of British studies have also explored the divorce experience from the child's point of view. Ann Mitchell inter-viewed fifty children, one child from each of fifty families drawn from a reliable sample of all social classes in the city of Edinburgh, and discovered that as the children described it, two-thirds of the parents had given them no explanation for what had happened. The children had found this lack of communication distressing. Comparing accounts given by parents and children in the same family, however, she discovered that people had very different perceptions of the same event. Parents often believed that they had given explanations. Emotions were also perceived in different ways by parent and child. For example, distress on the part of the parent was often seen as anger by the child. Such mismatches of perceptions hindered requests for further understanding.[33]

An English study interviewed a hundred volunteers whose parents had separated before they were 18. One-quarter of those interviewed felt that the experience had affected them badly and a further one-third that they had very mixed feelings about the consequences. Like the children in Mitchell's sample, a key feature was the poor communication between parents and children and the lack of explanation to the child. This study also highlighted the importance of people outside the family to whom the children could talk, and the need as the child saw it, for someone in whom to confide.[34]

This however is mild pessimism when compared with the conclusions of the long-term follow-up evaluation of Judith Wallerstein.[35] As a researcher, her determination has been to convey the emotional impact of separation on children as well as the practical, financial, and emotional consequences for their parents. But while admiring the passion and determination with which she has pursued her research project over many years, we believe that her work is seriously misleading as a whole because it is based on a sample of children who came to her clinic precisely because they were suffering and needed help.

The post-divorce adjustment of children in her descriptions include the degree to which the child was able to maintain relationships with both parents, as well as how the separation was managed in terms of the presence or absence of conflict between the parents and how far the children were protected from this over time. Her presentations have grown progressively more pessimistic, and her most recent long-term evaluation—based on the minority of families still in touch with the clinic—portrays children often overburdened by the responsibility of caring for lone parents 'going to pieces'. While she draws attention to the potential significance of people outside the family for young people to turn to in order to counterbalance the stressful experience at home, the impression she gives is that most children were singularly isolated from extended family support. Neither conclusion is suppported by our own evidence.

In an earlier follow-up at ten years after divorce she identified an important gender difference in the process of adjustment. While boys appeared initially to suffer most, girls, after appearing to be better adjusted to parental separation earlier on, experienced a delayed reaction to the trauma of divorce. She argued that typically the 'child of divorce' is subject to a continuum that begins with parental failure to sustain love and commitment, proceeds through the emotional turmoil and dislocation of the divorce process, and continues to overshadow the young person for many years, particularly in relation to adult decisions of love commitment and marriage. But while this certainly rings true for some children, her overall long-term conclusion that most children are irreparably damaged by divorce is not shared by other researchers.

A group of British researchers have criticized Wallerstein's sweeping assertions in three major ways. These are important in distinguishing how our own study was set up. First, the original sample she used was a clinical one, rather than one drawn from the general divorcing population; and moreover, the families studied were also of high rather than average income. In addition, the resulting difficulties were exacerbated by her choosing most of the material for quotation from the half of her sample who did not do well, not from the half who did. Secondly, the extent to which young people relate primarily to the divorce in distinction to any other aspect of their lives is never discussed, or how far such an assumption may have shaped her questioning. Thirdly, her work misleadingly suggests that adverse consequences for children are both more common than other research indicates, and that most people whose parents have divorced continue, as a group, to be dominated by unsettling memories. Divorce, rather than other life factors, therefore becomes the organizing principle for their subsequent lives.[36]

These are pitfalls which we have felt it especially important to avoid in designing our own research. Our study is retrospective and looks at family processes through the eyes of the child grown up. We found that unsettling memories do indeed continue to exist, but that normally many factors moderated the degree to which they dominated other aspects of emotional and social development. We sought to look at the child's life in the wider context of family relations, and to consider what most helps the child to manage stressful life events better. It was clear that a crucial memory for most of those we interviewed was the resilience of their remaining parent and the continuing maintenance of a routine in their everyday lives.

A more convincing account of how children's and young people's competence and self-esteem are affected following divorce, and the processes by which these are enhanced or diminished on parental remarriage, is provided by the Australian study of children in families, which is based on a reliable sample.[37] Whereas in intact families the relationships with both mother and father were associated with children's self-esteem, in one-parent families the influence of the non-residential father was weak. But this did not appear to be correlated with frequency of contact with the father. The significant relationship for the child showed itself to be the relationship between the child and the residential parent. In a further analysis the researchers looked at children's competence in everyday life, distinguishing competence from self-esteem. Although children developed greater social skills in lone-parent families, they did not necessarily develop higher self-esteem. The skills learnt in the lone-parent context continued after their custodial parent remarried, but they did not necessarily gain in self-confidence.[38] Childhood after divorce, in short, normally brought both pains and also new strengths to handle them.

Ochiltree also found that the impact of a parent leaving for these Australian children was affected by the quality of their parents' marital relationship, and also by whether or not the child had lost the parent to whom they felt closest, and with whom they had the most 'protective' relationship. If a child had been closer to a father than to a mother and the father left, the impact of parting was much more stressful.[39] If the remaining parent is then emotionally unavailable to the child, two sources of comfort and support will have been removed. The meaning that the child attaches to the events going on around him or her will also make a difference. The opportunities a child has to make sense of his or her experience with others may moderate the degree of stress involved.

It may also be that the childhood stress which is associated with divorce originates in the unresolved conflict between the child's parents in the intact pre-divorce family. An important early study by Sir Michael Rutter based on a substantial sample of children in the Isle of Wight indicated that it was discord before separation, rather than separation itself, which was most strongly associated with subsequent deviant behaviour in children.[40] More recently Jane Elliott and Martin Richards have shown how children whose parents' relationship shows serious and prolonged discord reflect this in poor educational performance two years before a divorce takes place in the family.[41] Research remains to be done on how such children would have fared if they had stayed in the context of a marital relationship marked by serious discord rather than by divorce. The damaging effects of one family mode in comparison to another cannot in reality be truly compared, although it is exactly the kind of question that parents in considering separation ask themselves all the time, and try to weigh up on behalf of their children. In considering the damaging effect of the absence of a parent the field of research as a whole has ignored the question of how it would have been for the child had they continued living in the midst of bitterly acrimonious relationships.[42]

Growing up in Stepfamilies

Although there have been a number of major American studies of stepfamilies, there have been very few in Britain, and none primarily from the child's perspective. In general too, both in

America and elsewhere there has been much more research on the impact of separation than of remarriage.

Remarriage of course cannot be isolated from the prior family history (as anyone who has experienced it will know). It is thus surprising that in the accounts of stepfamily life covered by current research there has been little that distinguishes between stepfamilies created by death, and stepfamilies created by divorce. It has been suggested that from the child's point of view a step-parent, if entering a family where there has already been a divorce, will face the challenge of hopes that a new marriage will make better a family that has previously gone wrong. However we found that step-parents in families created by death as well as in those created by divorce were also initially viewed with suspiciousness and ambivalence by their stepchildren, even while many of their good qualities were recognized. In our study we have distinguished between the two groups of children where our evidence indicates that it may be important for future thinking about stepfamily life to do so.

We have already suggested how too much of the emphasis in research has been on the stresses and risks for children, and too little on the protective factors which can mitigate them. The earlier sources which may amplify or moderate stress continue into the lives of children growing up in stepfamilies. We know from extensive clinical research that some children enter stepfamilies with existing problems created by earlier marital conflict. These may be exacerbated or amplified by post-divorce living arrangements: quarrelling between parents after divorce, poverty, loss of contact with their out-of-house parent, poor relationships with their residential parent, and after parental remarriage conflict between the new couple.

We know less about the protective factors operating in families during these times, and also following a parental decision to repartner or remarry. Our own aim has therefore been not only to document the children's experience of stress recalled from an adult viewpoint, but also to use these personal accounts to indicate some of the social and relationship factors experienced as moderating stress.

In our study we follow the child's experience through the processes of divorce, and living with only one parent, to the point when the adult appears who was to become their step-parent.

During the period prior to the beginning of stepfamily life, we focused on areas of family relationships, roles, and emotional loyalties which would clearly affect how a step-parent was likely to be received. Was the divorce preceded and accompanied by quarrelling and violence? Did the child maintain a close relationship with one parent, in spite of the loss of the other? Was the child given any adequate explanation of what was going on, or helped to make sense of the loss or separation in subsequent years? What was the quality of communication in the family? We explore these questions in Chapter 3. Equally, we asked about the degree and quality of the contact with the non-residential parent after parental separation; and we also enquired about the effect of the loss of a parent through death. This is recounted in Chapter 4. In Chapter 5 we look at some of the other changes that took place in the child's life; changes for the better such as more close contact with other family members, or changes for the worse because they entailed additional loss, such as moving home to another neighbourhood, or transferring to another school.

Thus throughout we have attempted to examine how a parent's incoming partner relates to the children in the household in the wider context of the family's past and present. A number of studies have indicated that the intimate parent–child bond that is established during the post-divorce lone-parent phase is experienced as being disrupted by the incoming of a new partner. This can cause resentment in children and particularly in girls. New partners can be seen by children more as rivals for parental affection than as parental resources for themselves.[43] We therefore asked in detail about the introduction of step-parents into the children's lives and their early lives together. Other research has reported that there is often a quiet period and then an emergence of anger, jealousy, and behaviour problems but we did not find that one pattern prevailed.[44] Much depended on questions such as the temperament and goodwill of the incoming step-parent; the expectations placed on them; the inclusion or not of stepsiblings, and the degree of overcrowding; and the extent of disruption or maintenance of former routines (Chapters 3 and 5). Like other researchers, we also found that the fact that parent and step-parent were seen by the child to love each other did not

necessarily bring a loving relationship between the children and
their new step-parent.[45]

The relationship between the newly forming family and the
biological parent who lived out of the house could also have an
important influence on how family life developed for the second
time round. Where a parent maintains contact and frequent visiting, this may crucially affect the new family. Furstenberg points
out that if the quality of the relationship between divorced partners is good, it does not diminish that of the new spousal relationship.[46] By contrast Walker, focusing on acrimonious divorced
couples at the other end of the 'good behaviour' spectrum, highlights the distress and anger that continuing visits can create.[47]
Half of our children who entered stepfamilies through divorce did
retain some contact with their biological parent, and their experiences, and the different meanings that parental visitation could
have for them, are further discussed in Chapter 4 and Chapter 7.

An additional important issue, which Ochiltree has also noted,
was how the children perceived the balance of power in the newly
reorganized family. Where structures that had been set up by the
mother following separation were honoured by the incoming
stepfather, then there was less likely to be hostility expressed by
the children.[48] The expectations of stepfathers and the very different expectations of newly married women taking on the role of
'stepmother' are discussed in Chapters 3 and 6. As the courts
during the time of our study more often granted custody to
mothers than to fathers—over 85 per cent—the contexts in which
fathers obtain custody imply that the relationships between children and their mothers were poor or erratic prior to separation. In
our study, fathers usually obtained custody only if the mother had
left the home with another partner, and little contact was maintained with them.[49] An equal number of boys stayed with their
fathers as stayed with their mothers, whereas only one girl
remained with her father. However, a number of girls lived with
both parents at different points in their growing up, thus gaining a
wider experience of a stepmother who was their primary maternal
caregiver.

Various studies have shown how stepfathers become important
to children in terms of social parenting, and have attempted to
establish differences in this between boys and girls.[50] The potential importance of such step-parental relationships was certainly

borne out in our study. The number of ways in which stepfathers, who had often been critically examined for many years, were also remembered for small positive parenting behaviours was extensive (Chapters 3 and 8).[51] Positive memories of stepfathers typically went with those of lack of interference in the mother's way of doing things; whereas accounts of a more autocratic style of 'fathering' were characteristically recalled as disliked or even as provoking active rebellion.[52]

In that our study was based on not only memory of the past but also on subsequent reflection and evaluation over time, the way in which young people viewed their step-parents was richly and complexly described and showed not only the hatred often felt towards incoming intruders, but also the love and respect which developed over time in many families. The question of 'social parenting' or 'child swapping', as following remarriage stepfathers shifted their attention away from their biological to their step-children, was looked at through the eyes of the stepchildren themselves, just as some of them had to make sense of their own fathers at the same time also becoming attached to children in another family. Nevertheless it is also clear that the meaning of original biological parenthood remained strong for most young people, whether or not they continued to see their parents. Many of them attempted to sort out the relationships in adolescence or young adulthood when they had not seen their missing parent for many years.

Every stepfamily has another fundamental dimension in the presence or absence of half-siblings and stepsiblings, but it has evoked surprisingly little attention from most researchers. Hetherington has described the relationship between stepsiblings as more avoidant, aggressive, and rivalrous than full siblings in non-divorced families.[53] The general finding that children in step-families have more difficulties in adjusting where there are larger numbers of children, is replicated in research on intact families where more than four siblings becomes in itself a risk factor for the child's well-being.[54] But the internal dynamics of the step-family depend on much more than the numbers in the household, and we discuss the complex relationships developed between both stepsiblings and half-siblings in our sample in Chapter 5.

In short, many factors may shape how a new relationship between parent and a second partner begins and develops in the eyes of the children and wider family. We have followed the course of stepfamily life through the child's growing years, exploring their relationships with their step-parent in the context of wider family relationships, including those with grandparents, and we have also looked at the effect of the arrival of siblings, stepsiblings, and half-siblings. Beyond the family we discuss the physical home and neighbourhood, the school and the world of play and sport.

Then in Chapters 7 and 8 we turn to topics which have not yet been considered in any other stepfamily study: first, examining the continuing capacity for subsequent development and change in the late teens and early twenties, in relationships with work, with partners, and with children: and secondly, the young adults' own subjective perspectives as they reflect on how childhood experience has affected their adult choices. Finally, in Chapter 10 we end with some of our own thoughts on the implications of our study for services for families, and how they might usefully change and develop in order to respond to the primary health-care needs of families going through the transitions of divorce and remarriage.

Stepfamily research, as we have begun to indicate, has its own peculiar difficulties, and each way of solving them has implications for the character and outcome of the research. Let us therefore now turn to examine in more detail the strategies which we developed for our own project.

2

Researching the Issues

IN setting out on this research we had three fundamental objectives in mind. First, in sharp contrast to the great majority of
existing studies, we wanted to focus, not on the immediate
experiences of difficulties in stepfamily life, but on its long-
term impact: and in particular, on what was distinctive about
the experience of those members of families who in the long run
fared best. It was precisely these relatively more successful
experiences of stepchildhood which were and are least studied,
although understanding them must be crucial to helping stepfamily members in the future. Secondly, with this in mind we
wanted to combine the strengths of quantitative and qualitative
research, through carrying out a set of in-depth interviews with
informants who were chosen from a reliable sample of the
general population, in contrast to a clinical sample. And thirdly,
we wanted to bring together the different skills and insights of
social-science researchers, on the one hand, and therapists and
clinicians, on the other, to produce a study which was both
reliable and useful.

Researching stepfamilies, particularly on a relatively small
budget, inevitably raises complex methodological issues. This
is because stepfamilies are created through a great diversity of
paths, as well as taking a variety of structural forms; and on top
of this, because social stigma makes obtaining random samples
of them unusually difficult. But like all researchers, we had to
find technical solutions to such problems in a wider context.
Before discussing our chosen methodology, we need to refer
briefly to the contemporary political context of research on
stepfamilies; to the changing methodological perspectives of
our disciplines; and to the specific historical context of our
long-term study.

The Politics of Research and its Methodologies

Research into divorce, single parenthood, and stepfamilies has increasingly taken place against the background of a wider political debate in which different family forms are measured against each other in terms, not only of what they offer to the developmental needs of children, but also what they are assumed to contribute to, or detract from, the stability of the social fabric. Discourses about families which depart from the two-parent biological 'norm' are couched in stark evaluative terms: 'The social science evidence is in', proclaims the *Atlantic Monthly*, 'the dissolution of intact two-parent families is harmful to large numbers of children.'[1] British research is often presented in a similar style. A recent report on *Marital Breakdown and the Health of the Nation* by the research agency One plus One is advertised with starred headline findings that men and women who divorce are four times as likely to kill themselves or go into mental hospital, the men are twice as likely to die, and their children are five times as likely to suffer psychiatric illness. Even the normally dry pages of the *ESRC Data Archive Bulletin* have not been immune from passionate debate on this topic, as the exchange of letters between Kiernan, Richards, and Ni Brochlain illustrates.[2]

Emotive issues are at stake; the object of study, is by definition, likely to impinge directly on the lives of most researchers, clinicians, journalists, and politicians. Evidence of the shortcomings of single-parent families is routinely discussed as if they constituted a uniform group of deliberate and selfish deviants, and many derogatory pronouncements also have to be seen as hidden justifications for planned cuts in welfare spending. Criticism of divorcing parents for putting their own needs before those of their children may also be conveying veiled attacks on women for demanding for themselves the opportunities and choices that men have traditionally taken for granted. More generally, lamenting family breakdown frequently masks a larger political debate about the extent to which the state should be taking responsibility for the welfare and development of its youngest citizens.

On the other hand, to respond to such conservative critiques by defending more permissive attitudes towards families and relationships would be equally simplisitic if it implied, either that there can be a painless divorce as far as children are concerned, or that a decision to bring up a child alone or with a series of different partners does not carry with it any disadvantages. In studying stepfamilies, we have therefore wanted to recognize their variety, and that they can indeed successfully nurture children, while avoiding over-optimism or the use of bland euphemisms—such as 'blended families'—which can give rise to unrealistic expectations.

We have also been mindful that research on the family not only takes place within the context of public political debate, but also can directly or indirectly affect individual lives and decisions. It can feed into the innumerable self-help manuals, telephone helplines, newspaper articles, and media programmes concerning the family, on which 'common knowledge' draws. As Giddens has put it, widely publicized researches can

alter the aspects of social life they report on or analyse. . . . Anyone . . . who faces the break up of a marriage or a long term intimate relationship, knows a great deal (not always at the level of discursive awareness) about 'what is going on' in the social arena of marriage and divorce. Such knowledge is not incidental to what is actually going on, but constitutive of it.[3]

A second area of polarization lies within the research field itself, in the difficulty in making connections between large-scale quantitative studies and small-scale qualitative ones. Large-scale studies are essential for gaining a broad picture of trends and correlations between different sets of data. Only they can buttress or challenge convincingly the cherished tenets of policy-makers, or service deliverers. Because they can, by their nature only set out to answer quite simple questions, they are open to the charge of failing to address other questions or that a different analysis of the data would yield a different result. If the results are controversial, the most simplistic conclusion usually gets relayed by the media or taken up by politicians, while other researchers may be more likely to question the research design or statistical method rather than explore the different ways in which these findings could be understood. Qualitative studies, on the other hand, generally attract less publicity because, rather than claiming to prove a case, they tend to focus on drawing out the subjective meanings of lived experiences. In some instances they will take account of the subjectivity of the researcher too, and eschew generalizations in the belief that only individual accounts of experience can be authentically described. The opportunity to connect these accounts to the larger field or to use them to supplement quantitative studies may thus be missed.

In our own research project, we have been influenced by these wider debates and have tried to find ways in which to address them. We share an unease about the pathologizing effect which sweeping conclusions can have when widely and simplistically reported in the media. We are equally aware that constructing less negative new images of stepfamilies could not only raise unrealistic hopes, but also impose new norms which risk constraining the plethora of different stepfamily pathways into a prescriptive developmental framework. Nevertheless we share, from our different professional and academic backgrounds, a common philosophy which can perhaps best be summed up as a commitment to understanding people's lives in terms of their strengths, their survival strategies, and their resources and, above all, how these qualities evolve or are stifled in different social, familial, and ideological contexts.

Our principal aim has thus been to draw out key themes from our fifty individual accounts of growing up in stepfamilies, to relate these to factors that seemed either to promote resilience and coping or to increase stress, and to understand both in the context of intergenerational family patterns and societal and cultural influences. Our interviews are drawn from an exceptionally strong sample basis and in the process of analysing them we have extensively tabulated the patterns of information which they yield. Thus while our interpretation focuses on the subjective experience of our informants, on their understandings and interpretations of events and how these have changed over time, our intention has been to identify recurrent themes from the individual narratives and relate them to the wider context.

We are therefore concerned to draw out the complex interrelationship, not only between those factors that seem, over time, to have promoted resilience and coping, but how these have found a place in the individual's life story. We are also interested in the relationship between the stability or otherwise of informants' lives at the time of interview and the quality of their narrative about their childhood experiences of loss, disruption, and changing family membership.

Thus, as well as the family context, we address what Antony Giddens calls 'the reflexive project of self';[4] to highlight the processes whereby individuals develop a sense of identity, agency, and coherence over time. This project, as Giddens argues, takes place within a world where identity is derived less from the relatively static roles and structures of family and work, but where a coherent narrative has continuously to be negotiated within a multitude of changes, influences, and choices. The ability to reflect and give meaning to seemingly incoherent or uncontrollable life events, the 'capacity to appraise', are core dimensions that we explore in this study.[5]

More importantly though, this context of rapidly changing family structures requires us to develop different ways of understanding the individual's experience within these new structures. We wish to understand what enables some children to cope well and maintain self-esteem despite experiencing multiple transitions, while others remain anxious, depressed, and vulnerable to further loss or disruption well into adult life. This involves understanding which relationships did provide intimacy and continuity for children, and what were important influences and sources of stability outside the family, while at the same time recognizing that looking for different factors can never fully account for the idiosyncratic and unexpected ways in which particular individuals manage to survive.

Life Stories and Family Systems

Our conceptual framework both reflects and influences our wish to explore our topic at two linked levels: the subjective experience of growing up in stepfamilies, of managing transitions, losses, and the complexities of relationships; and the context of intergenerational family patterns, social, familial, and economic resources, and gender relations, as they evolve over time. This led us to our choice of a retrospective study of interviews with former stepchildren now grown up, and to what has proved an extremely fruitful combination of the life story and family systems approaches.

Before commenting on each approach separately, we can usefully summarize some of the main connections between them.[6]
First, both pay attention to an understanding of the complexity of
individual experience in relation to different levels of context,
which include family, culture, and society. Secondly, both stress
the importance of understanding beliefs as they evolve over time
and particularly how they are shaped by intergenerational patterns, and highlighted at life cycle and other transitions. Thirdly, in
using life stories and more recently in the family systems
approach, the focus on narrative is crucial: how the story is told
and the meaning that is attached to life events are as important as
the events themselves. Lastly, both view the interview itself,
whether for clinical or research purposes, as co-constructed, so
that the beliefs and intentionality of the interviewer play a vital
part in shaping what is recounted. This implies accepting that the
clinician or researcher is actively engaged in the creation of a
narrative that is only one of many stories about the past.

The life story method in sociology and oral history method in
social history are slightly variant approaches for exploring the
evolution of the present and recent past through in-depth retrospective interviewing.[7] While the interviewer always comes with
an agenda, the style of the interview is flexible, encouraging a
wide-ranging exploration of past experience. Such interviews are
dynamically interactive in a double sense, accounts of a life and its
meaning drawn out between two people and between past and
present. The outcome, especially when the focus is on private
aspects of life which are rarely otherwise documented, or from
perspectives (such as those of children) which tend to remain
hidden, is a mixture of information allowing us to reconstruct
typical patterns of behaviour, subjective interpretations of experience and accounts of feeling, and unconscious assumptions conveyed by the narrative form. We use all these dimensions here.

Retrospective interviews are inevitably filtered through the
processes of forgetting and remembering, which together shape
memory to make sense of the past. But their reliance on memory
is neither unique, nor is it merely a handicap. Memory and the
interaction between past and present are fundamental to the
human condition, and to what we do and say and who we think
we are at any given moment: 'we are our memories'.[8] Almost all
the documents commonly used by historians were created with

the help of memory, and the craft of professional historians is itself the construction of public memory through selecting from the stories they discover. And in contemporary large-scale survey work short-term memory, and still more the interactive skill of interviewers in drawing out information, are no less vital for being hidden and ignored in analysis.[9] Longer term memory can also bring some special advantages, both in terms of the depth of reflection and interpretation, and also because—as we ourselves found—sometimes family secrets concealed in interviews closer to the time were now no longer hidden.

The fullness and length of in-depth life stories itself limits the number which can be effectively analysed in a project, so that they cannot challenge the numerical scale of survey work. This certainly does not condemn them to being simply anecdotal, individual, and subjective. The constraining assumptions of polar opposites, that which is subjective is by definition not objective, that the individual cannot stand for the larger group, are a trap: they would prevent us from seeing how motives and perceptions are forces shaping events, and that the group acts through individuals, so that the well-chosen case can validly represent wider experience. We have sought to understand subjective accounts of feeling and experience here in relation to structural and material contexts and to information from other interviews and from the findings of other studies.

The relationship of the individual to the collective is a primary focus for both systemic family therapists and life story sociologists. Both approaches explore the diversity of individual experience in relation to collective patterns, beliefs, and themes as they evolve over time. In the case of life story sociology, these themes have typically been social, economic, or political, at the level of a substantial sector or whole society, while family therapists, operating in a clinical domain, have, while being mindful of wider systems, concentrated their attention more on idiosyncratic family patterns and beliefs. Significantly, however, there have been recent signs of a convergence between the two approaches. While sociologists and social historians have come to focus on the family as the key crucible for the transmission of beliefs over the generations,[10] family therapists have moved away from what was a somewhat objectifying view of families.[11] They have become much more interested in understanding how the wider societal contexts in which families are embedded affect their beliefs about themselves and the possibilities for change. Their approach to families becomes less an analysis of structure and roles and more an exploration of socially constructed meaning. Feminist critiques of family therapy and its implicitly functionalist value base have also played a key part in this shift of emphasis.[12]

Thus family systems concepts can help to provide social scientists with tools for understanding family beliefs, patterns, and myths[13] as mediators between individuals and their transactions in the wider society and culture. Conversely the life story researchers' expertise in exploring narrative offers an invaluable research method to family therapists, increasingly concerned with understanding how family patterns, rules, and beliefs are constructed over time and communicated through language.

What then are the characteristics of the family systems approach itself?[14] Family systems theory has developed on the basis of a contextual understanding of individual behaviour and examines psychological development through observing how feedback processes operate within intimate relationships. It therefore focuses primarily on circular patterns of interaction rather than on linear cause and effect. These patterns of interaction can be traced between different system levels: between individuals, families, and the wider society. Family systems theory is thus a much more multi-contextual approach to human relationships than either psychoanalytic on behavioural theories.

Family therapists also look at the relationship between patterns of interaction in the present and intergenerational patterns and beliefs. Transitional phases, whether these are life cycle transitions or the structural changes involved in death, divorce, or stepfamily formation, are times when these patterns and beliefs may be highlighted or challenged as new ways of coping are called for.

Intergenerational patterns are the often invisible guidelines to family life which appear to indicate the way a family regulates its present interactions in response to what has gone before. This may take the form either of constraints which only become visible when some action happens to challenge them, or of patterns which are consciously followed or avoided. The recognition of avoidance or reversal as a form of intergenerational influence is particularly important in this context. Whereas many sociologists would see repeating and non-repeating patterns straightforwardly in terms of transmission or non-transmission from one generation to another, a systemic approach recognizes this as only part of the process. Experiences in the present also feed back to these traditions by either confirming or challenging them. Thus new meanings evolve and change over time.

Thinking about the life cycle has helped family therapists to identify points in family development when change occurs in the ordinary course of events, typically around an entrance such as the birth of children, an exit as when young people leave home or at the death of a parent, or a change in role or position such as the onset of adolescence or the frailty of an elderly family member.[15] The processes of divorce and stepfamily formation can also be seen in life cycle terms, a formulation which connects individual experience to changes occurring in the family system. Many texts on stepfamily thus follow a developmental approach.[16]

However, a life cycle approach to understanding families has serious limitations. It derives too much from individual developmental frameworks to be an adequate way of understanding complex systems. By providing a 'map' to guide stepfamilies and professionals through confusing and often chaotic processes, it may fail to do justice either to the power of repeating patterns or to the propensity of systems to effect discontinuous changes. Understanding families in terms of life cycle stages can also imply that for families as well as individuals, the proper living of a life means following 'stages'. As Keith and Whitaker point out: 'Families are too complicated to simplify with a theory of life cycle development. The strongest determinants for continuity and change are the patterns that emanate from past families, the patterns that look for something to attach to, shadowy fabricated patterns.'[17] It is in the interaction between life cycle and intergenerational patterns and beliefs that the most fruitful understanding of family dynamics and equilibrium can be made.

Clinicians and researchers, in studies of the family, consistently emphasize qualities of cohesion, adaptability, and communication.[18] These seem to be core indicators of the ways in which families manage both developmental and structural changes. In our study we were interested in how a sense of cohesion was maintained in the face of major changes, how families adapted to the losses and gains of a member or members, and how boundaries, which promote family cohesion by defining membership, were able to be flexible enough to include a relationship with the absent parent. We were also particularly interested in the theme of communication, and in exploring the relationship between family communicational patterns, especially around crucial times of change, and the quality of narrative that our respondents subsequently demonstrated.

Unfortunately, too much research in the family systems field has focused on comparisons between individual families while paying scant attention to how experiences in families are mediated by the context of societal and cultural beliefs and norms. Family therapists now pay increasing attention to the qualitatively different experiences which men and women have in families rather than examining the parental and marital bond as if it existed independently of this gendered context. In our research, gender was a central theme which connected to all the other themes we explored.

This increasing focus on gender, as well as cultural and ethnic differences, has been accompanied by a major transition in family systems thinking over the past ten years. Family therapists had originally moved from an individual to an interactional focus through studying the patterns, structures, and rules that were seen to be maintaining symptoms or problems. In terms of therapy the conceptual shift was from one locus of intervention (the individual) to another (the family). Much research into families continues to reflect this basically reductionist view.[19] However, family therapy theory, under the influence of cybernetic, constructivist, and social constructionist theories has moved to a 'second order' position[20] in which those measures of family interaction used by therapists or researchers to evaluate functioning are recognized as themselves constructions of the observer. Certainties about the nature of that which is being observed, including diagnoses of 'family dysfunction', thus give way to the assumption that there can be many different descriptions of problems and relationships, and that the therapist's ideas are only useful in as far as they achieve a good enough fit with the family's view.

In the process of making this shift, gender and culture have come to the fore as key mediators of the therapeutic encounter. Thus 'family' is not always the main system in focus: the different perspectives of men and women, or the external connections of family members, for example with friends or professional helpers, may equally be seen as key elements of the system.

Language and narrative are central to this new focus because problems are seen, not as products of dysfunctional relationships, but as embedded in descriptions which are not fixed but can be challenged or confirmed in the course of the therapeutic conversation.[21] This has obvious parallels with the life story sociologist's understanding of narratives.

Family therapists attempt to elicit narratives in therapy which reflect upon resources and strengths rather than pathology and deficit, and which thus challenge existing beliefs. Inevitably there are many stories which families who present for therapy never bring to the attention of the therapist because they are not 'part of the problem'; just as we must assume aspects of families which do not emerge in research studies because no manageable research project can be sufficiently inclusive. As Edward Bruner reminds us, 'Life experience is richer than discourse. Narrative structures organise and give meaning to experience, but there are always feeling and lived experiences not fully encompassed by the dominant story'.[22] But it has certainly been our aim here to ensure, in contrast to the focus of much family research on problems and failures, that we listen equally for tales of survival and strength.

Common Influences

We can point to four other approaches to research which have influenced our own study. The importance of feminist and gender perspectives can already be inferred. We have also drawn inspiration from interactionist sociological studies of marriage by Penny Mansfield and Jean Collard and parenting by Kathryn Backett which have interpreted interviews in terms of negotiations of ideas between partners.[23] A third influence has been attachment theory. Lastly and more generally, we have been stimulated by the now very substantial literature on social construction.[24]

Social constructionist research emphasizes how through the interview process research data is co-produced rather than simply discovered. The observer or researcher is part of the system being observed and both interviewer and interviewee participate in the creation of a narrative. Taking such a 'reflexive' stance in research

requires us to assume responsibility for choosing the categories
we use and to acknowledge that they will inevitably influence the
results of our research. To cite Edward Bruner again:

We begin with a narrative that already contains a beginning and an
ending, which frames and hence enables us to interpret the present. It is
not that we already have a body of data, the facts, and we then must
construct a story or narrative or theory to account for them. Instead . . .
the narrative structures we construct are not secondary narratives about
data but primary narratives that establish what is to count as data.[25]

Awareness of such inevitable constraints has kept us constantly
mindful of the contradictory and overlapping categories that lie
within this definition of 'stepfamily' as a family form; and equally
of the need to maintain a focus on process rather than structure
and to address the complex and shifting relationship between
family transitions and the individual's subjective experiences of
them.

Much research into the family has avoided encompassing such
complexities by attempting to analyse observable transactional
patterns. However researchers have found these notoriously difficult to analyse and evaluate.[26] Studies which look instead at the
family belief system and construction of reality[27] can be open to
the criticism that they treat the 'belief system' as if it were fixed,
unitary, and measurable, rather than fluid, negotiated over time,
and influenced as much by gender and cultural difference as by
idiosyncratic family values. The social constructionist approach
offers a promising alternative for exploring common themes in the
different narratives of family members. While family therapists
have long been interested in 'the pattern that connects' the different positions and perceptions within a family system, this emphasis on narrative brings subjective experience more clearly to the
fore.

It also offers a way of observing the individual's development of
identity, without losing a contextual focus. The identification of
'trajectories' or pathways rather than life cycle stages is emphasized by both Shotter and Giddens. But while Shotter is concerned
with understanding the 'social conditions for the development of
autonomous personhood',[28] Giddens conceives of personhood
and identity as breaking free of roles in social institutions such
as the family. He focuses instead on the 'pure relationship'

between two equal partners outside a social or legal context, 'no longer anchored in criteria outside the relationship itself—such as kinship, social duty or traditional obligations' in which—

the relationship exists solely for whatever rewards it can deliver. In the context of the pure relationship, trust can only be mobilised by a process of mutual disclosure. . . . Like self-identity, with which it is closely inter-twined, the pure relationship has to be reflexively controlled over the long term, against the backdrop of external transitions and transformations.[29]

Such a formulation has obvious relevance for understanding the aspirations of those embarking on a second marriage, and the idea of negotiation is a crucial and frequently overlooked aspect of stepfamily and indeed all family process. On the other hand, however, Giddens's view of relationships seems to be—especially for a sociologist—surprisingly acontextual, altogether too detached from the socio-economic contexts and intergenerational perspectives which we consider fundamental to the interplay between individual aspirations and systemic constraints.

One other key theoretical perspective, especially relevant in our interpretation of the long-term significance of parent–child relationships and parental loss has been that of attachment theory. While Bowlby's earlier work focused almost exclusively on mothering and thus implicitly linked children's attachment needs to prescribed social roles, he and his colleagues subsequently developed an ethological theory of attachment and loss, according to which the formation of 'internal working models' in infancy lays the foundation for subsequent relationships and affects how loss will be experienced. Whereas in the 1990s concepts of suc-cessful child development still go back to earlier assumptions of continuing attachment to one original set of natural parents, attachment theory can more readily consider a wider range of relationships as salient. Attachment theories can thus have the benefit of pointing to beneficial or adverse processes rather than idealized or pathologized family forms.

In research on attachment the basic concept has been tested empirically by using 'The Strange Situation', an experimental laboratory investigation devised by Ainsworth.[30] This exposed infants, under controlled conditions, to a moderately stressful procedure of brief separations from their mothers, followed by reunion. The purpose was to examine the balance between the infant's motivational system of attachment and exploration. The babies were allocated to two major categories as 'securely' or 'insecurely' attached, with subsequent more detailed analysis leading to finer distinctions. Later work[31] demonstrated the stability of secure attachment to the mother, and, independently, to the father, so long as there were no major changes in life circumstances—a continuity which, of course, our informants did not experience. Among 6-year-olds, characteristic differences in response to stressful situation between those judged to be secure or insecure as infants were observed, including greater verbal fluency in the securely attached and dysfluency in the insecurely attached: a first foreshadowing of differences to be found later in narrative coherence.

Attachment theory presumes internal working models to be always open to modifications, but to become more resistant to change with increasing age. By the time of adolescence and early adulthood, individuals are expected to have integrated their experiences into an overall predisposition towards patterns of attachment.[32] In more recent research on adult memories of early childhood, Main and Goldwyn have developed the 'Adult attachment interview'.[33] This is a structured interview in which adults are asked about their current perspectives on their childhood relationship experiences. They found that the parents of securely attached infants demonstrated a greater readiness of recall, ease of discussing attachment experiences, and most striking of all, coherence in discussing their own attachment history and its influence.

By contrast, the parents of infants classified as 'insecure-avoidant' were frequently unable to recall the period of childhood under discussion in the interview, and their accounts tended to demonstrate contradictions between a generalized picture of an almost ideal parent and specific memories of rejection; whilst the parents of infants classified as 'insecure-disorganized' demonstrated an apparent irrationality and an inability to remain within the topic of the interview. It seems that when a parent's own experiences and feelings are not integrated, restrictions follow on the flow of information about attachment. These restrictions appear in the form of inconsistencies in speech, and insensitive behaviour towards their infants.[34]

There has been little research using these methods to relate earlier childhood attachment experiences to psychological states in

middle adulthood and coherence in recounting life story narratives which might show how earlier losses might have been overcome. We have nevertheless been intrigued by the resonances of
earlier parent–child relationships on the very different degrees to
which informants were able to offer coherent and detailed
accounts of their earlier lives. As we will explore in Chapter 9,
we were especially interested in how people with seemingly very
poor early relationships were apparently able to facilitate secure
attachments for their own children. The role of mediating experiences is thus crucial, especially in relation to attachments to other
significant caregivers in childhood and to the part played by
spouses. Sir Michael Rutter and David Quinton's study of girls
who grew up in care[35] points to the impact of a supportive spouse
on the ability to parent and comments that the effects of such
support are substantially more marked in the presence of other
adversities or stressors.

Whereas attachment research findings can be presented and
used in somewhat deterministic ways, we found that they provided many exciting pointers to understanding the complex and
multifaceted influences on the lives of children who experienced
loss and disruption as they grew up.

The Long-Term, Time, and History

All research inevitably takes place at specific moments in historical
time, but the implications of this take on a greater significance
when the project seeks to understand outcomes over the longer
term, rather than immediate effects. This has been one of our
fundamental objectives.

Most research into the effects of divorce and stepfamily life has
looked at individual and family functioning at particular points in
the life cycle. By capturing and fixing lives at these somewhat
arbitrary times, we can understand the short-term detrimental
effects of changes, but cannot foresee or do justice to subsequent
reparative experiences. While this difficulty is in principle overcome in the small number of longitudinal studies of family break-
up and reconstitution, in practice, because they are normally
based on large samples using structured questionnaire interviews,
and these interviews are carried out with substantial intervals at

separate life stages, it can often be difficult to use them to develop
an understanding of process and the connections between these
life stages.

Our own project takes place within the context of such a longitudinal quantitative study, from which much important data has
already been analysed.[36] The use of retrospective in-depth interviewing with the same sample, and the presence of the earlier as
well as contemporary findings from such a longitudinal project, in
our view offers the most practicable solution available to the
formidable methodological difficulties in studying such complex
and subtle processes over the long term. Even with unlimited
resources no research method can grasp such an unfolding process
very satisfactorily. Continuous observation, besides being impos-
sibly costly and intrusive over such a timespan, would, in itself,
distort the essential nature of the process by making it wholly
public. Interviewing can only take place at intervals, and during
the earlier stages of childhood, the inverview must be with the
parent rather than with the child. The parent's answers will always
be influenced by social expectations of the parental role, and this
pressure is probably increased when the interviewer is seen as
representing a powerful official body, as some of our cases show
the NCDS to have been imagined: with results which include
instances of sustained misinformation by some parents (such as
to a child's paternity).[37] Any narrative account drawn from an
interview will be subject to many possible social pressures, and
these will change with context and time: as indeed do private
accounts. Diane Vaughan has indeed nicely shown in her study of
New York couples separating how the reconstruction of the story
of their relationship is intrinsic to the separation process itself.[38]

Retrospective interviewing has the advantage of lessening such
pressures, and making candour about the past easier. It is also
easier for the child, now become adult, to make sense of the story
as a whole, and give a balanced evaluation. But, on the other hand,
that interpretation in itself brings a selectivity in what is recalled.
And, more fundamentally, the nature of human memory brings
serious limits in itself. No adult can remember the crucial developments of their own infancy and early childhood, and some—
most often men—have only rough recollections of relationships
throughout their childhoods. To these normal limitations are
added, in many of the families here, some of the typical conse-

quences of trauma: the idealization of a lost parent, or a memory
which remains confused and fragmentary because incidents were
never understood at the time, or a blank, a blotting out of a past
which remains, consciously or unconsciously, too painful a suffering to recall: leaving crucial moments of which 'I can't remember
at all. Total block'.

Our own interviews share these qualities. On the one hand,
they convey very powerfully, from the perspective of a child now
become adult, testimonies of how relationships with natural parents and step-parents have evolved, and of how far they are still
marked by past pain. On the other hand, while they certainly take
us back into the past, they can only enable us to reach back
tentatively. In interpreting them for this study, we have tried
throughout to remain sensitive to their limitations as well as to
their strengths.

A final time dimension is also an inevitable consequence of
seeking to trace longer-term outcomes. Any cohort study necessarily follows a particular generation, and by the time that it
reaches adulthood the period of its childhood has already receded
into history. Social historians have shown that while most elements of the life cycle repeat continuously over long periods, in
other respects the moment in historical time when each generation grows up shapes its experience in markedly different ways.[39]
There is no way of solving this limitation. Our informants were all
born in one week in 1958, and it is important to remember that
their experiences cannot be invariably assumed as relevant to the
present or the future. Indeed there are some respects in which our
study could be read as a document of family change during three
momentous decades.

Stepfamilies in the 1950s were an exceptionally rare phenom-
enon. In the past they had been very common: indeed, as common
as today. But they were formed, not after the divorce of parents,
but through the remarriage of a widowed parent who had lost a
spouse through death. From the mid-nineteenth century onwards,
however, adult death rates fell steadily. And while the possibility of
divorce, which in England had only been through a personal Act
of Parliament, was gradually opened, its numerical impact on
marriage remained very small. Hence between the 1920s and
1950s fewer than 20 per cent of marriages were broken by death
or divorce, in contrast to over 30 per cent today. In the 1950s the

proportion of married couples divorcing was a mere fifth of the present rate; and of all those who remarried, under 10 per cent had been divorced, in contrast to over one-third at present. In retrospect, indeed, the 1950s appear as the last decade of a brief and historically unique era of familial stability for childrearing, when the sting of death had eased and that of divorce had yet to make its impact.[40]

More generally, the family structures of the 1950s in Britain had changed remarkably little since the late nineteenth century, and certainly much less than it has since. With thoroughly reliable contraceptive methods not yet available, sexual relationships took place overwhelmingly within marriage. Although most abortion was illegal, less than one in twenty births were outside marriage, compared with more than one-quarter today. Only a minority experienced premarital sexual relationships, usually as a brief preliminary to marriage, and unmarried cohabition was rare. Today two-thirds of couples live together before marriage, and long-term cohabitation without marriage is socially accepted. The decisions to enter into a sexual relationship, live as a couple, marry, and bear children were all closely tied together, while today they have become separated.

All these patterns were to change rapidly from the 1960s onwards. Above all, fuelled both by a falling age of marriage, with the portion of marriages involving teenagers doubling to peak at 28 per cent in the early 1970s (which made break-up more likely) and by legal changes (notably the availability of legal aid for divorce, and the new divorce law in 1969), from the 1960s the divorce rate shot upwards. And the majority of petitioners for divorce under the new laws were wives, not husbands, as had once been the case.

These and other dramatic changes not only provide the context for our informants lives, but also make it difficult, and sometimes irrelevant, to compare their experiences and the choices they have made with those of their parents' generation.

The rarity of divorce in the 1950s was itself one reason for a climate of opinion which was hardly conducive to open discussion about family break-up. Very few of our informants recall other children in the same position, or schoolteachers who were sensitive to or even aware of the changes they were undergoing in their lives. The much greater social stigma attached to divorce in the

1950s and 1960s, coupled with less effective help and support being available from professionals may certainly have contributed to the climate of silence, lack of information, and secrecy which the majority of our informants recalled about parental break-up. The fear of social opprobrium led many stepfamilies, as Burgoyne and Clark still found at a later date,[41] to present themselves as 'just an ordinary family': as indeed some of our own informants' parents did to earlier NCDS interviewers. The particularly strong taboo against the discussion of death in the same period meant that the situation was little better for a child when a parent had died. Thus the lack of public discussion at the time meant that very few of our informants remembered having, at the time when they entered stepfamilies, preconceptions about what this might be like.

Another important aspect of the period was that our informants' parents were marrying a decade before the women's movement developed any momentum, and most organized their families along stereotypical non-egalitarian gender roles. Yet subsequently it was above all women who as the predominant petitioners led the rising divorce rate, and when our informants came to the age of marriage themselves many of them viewed it in quite different ways. The domestic tensions that were soon to explode into wider social consciousness were also apparent in many of their narratives. (We discuss this further in Chapter 6.)

Parallel with these changes in family structure there have been striking changes in parent–child relationships. On the one hand, the 1960s and early 1970s witnessed a continent-wide assault on the authority of parents and the older generation in general over young people, just at the time when our informants were teenagers. On the other hand, with increased affluence the contribution of children's earnings to family income became insignificant for most families. Subsequently, however, because unemployment has affected the young more than those in middle age, in the more recent recession years children have become economically dependent on their parents until a much later age than in the past.[42]

It is widely believed that just as the nuclear family was more stable and clearly bounded in the past, so the extended family was stronger and more effective. This is much more doubtful. Longer life and better health have meant that many more grandparents are alive and well enough to play an active role in their grandchildren's lives, and the spread of the telephone and motor car have counterbalanced geographical mobility. It is still too soon to know how far the increase of divorce in future grandparental generations, combined with increased inequality and poverty and worse public transport, are currently undermining the effectiveness of the extended family.

Perhaps most important of all, the general economic and political context of the 1950s and 1960s contrast sharply with that of the 1980s and 1990s. Our informants were born in the middle of the long post-war economic boom, which brought full employment and steadily rising incomes to families of all social classes. It was only in the mid-1970s—precisely at the moment when our informants began to enter the labour market—that unemployment rose even briefly over 4 per cent. These were also the decades of the post-war consensus on the welfare state. Benefits for the unemployed were much more generous than today, and both Labour and Conservative Governments funded expanding state provision of housing, health, and education. Our informants thus grew up in a period in which there was widespread optimism for rising standards of living, and social mobility through work or education was a real possiblity. And although by the time that they entered their early twenties the economic context had already begun to shift radically and the erosion of the welfare state was beginning, the doors still remained sufficiently open for a significant minority of them to rise occupationally above the level of their parents—a much less likely outcome for stepchildren born a decade later.

Methodology of the Study

Evolving a research methodology sufficiently sensitive to all these issues for stepfamily life has been a long journey in itself, which has occasionally tested to the limit the team's new 'marriage' of life story sociologist and family therapists, evoking loyalty to old patterns in all of us! We had two basic decisions to make: how the evolution of stepfamilies would best be observed, and which stepfamilies to choose.

At an initial stage we decided to carry out an exploratory pilot project with a very small clinical group of four stepfamilies being seen at the Institute of Family Therapy. The insights of the family systems approach have been generated from clinical sessions with families. Since we could not simulate sessions of this type for research purposes, we needed to know whether single interviews could generate as revealing material. With those stepfamilies who were willing to participate in this experiment, transcripts of first family therapy sessions were made and subsequently separate individual life story interviews were carried out with the parent and step-parent. This enabled the individual narrative to be considered alongside observation of family interactions at the clinic session.

It was quickly apparent that a larger project on this model would not only suffer the disadvantages of being based on a clinical sample, but raise severe ethical problems when we wanted to interview two individuals in dispute, and would generate unwieldy material. Nevertheless the pilot was of double value to us. First, it helped us to identify important themes for further exploration which interviews were likely to yield. Secondly and crucially, comparison between the clinical session and the life story interviews made it clear that, while the session was more effective in highlighting immediate tensions, it did not allow space for sustained individual contributions. The life story interview by contrast offered more coherent and fully developed accounts of the long-term developments through which the stepfamily had arisen, and also showed that it was certainly possible, with a sensitive and experienced interview, to ensure that the 'family dimension' was kept salient. We were particularly impressed by the value of the retrospective emphasis of the life story in encouraging the exploration of changes in patterns of family life and perspectives over time.

While in no doubt that a qualitative in-depth approach was essential to our purposes, we also wished to give it a double strength by adopting some aspects of quantitative methodology. Thus our interpretations were developed hand-in-hand with the construction of numerous outcome tables, not because these could pretend to any generalizable reliability from such a small numerical base—which is why we have included very few in this book itself—but in order to discipline our hunches. At the interview itself in addition to the text of the life story we collected a simple quantifiable health questionnaire filled in by our informants, which offered an additional numerical measure for their current state of being. And most important of all, given the special difficulties which research projects on stepfamilies have encountered in seeking a reliable sample base,[43] we were able to choose our stepfamily informants on an exceptionally representative basis.

The fifty adults who were interviewed for this book were selected from the National Child Development Study. This very large-scale national longitudinal project has sought to follow all the 17,000 children born nationally in a single week in 1958 through structured survey questionnaire interviews. Waves of interviewing, at first with parents, later with teachers and with the children themselves, were carried out at irregular intervals of roughly five years. The response rates remain high for a group in a more mobile phase of the life cycle, though they have dipped below the 85 per cent maintained up to the age of 20. Although it was brought home to us by some of the trails which we followed unsuccessfully, for example to a centre for treating drug and alcohol abuse, that some of those who have dropped out of the survey are those with particularly unstable lives, we were also impressed by how interviewees of very different kinds had developed a personal loyalty to the study as if part of their own identity.

At 23 those interviewed included 444 who had become stepchildren by the age of 16. From these we decided to select fifty who had entered stepfamilies between the ages of 7 and 16, in order that they might show good memories of the familial transitions which they had experienced. The cohort is scattered across the entire country, so we narrowed our choices further by a carefully balanced geographical clustering; and where informants had moved, we did not attempt to follow them to new areas.[44]

Once contact was made, although we deliberately avoided pressurizing potential interviewees, and a few hesitated in arranging a definite time for interview, we met with only five direct refusals. By far the most common reason for an interview not taking place was therefore that the potential interviewee had moved since NCDS had last been given an address. We were in fact somewhat more successful in obtaining interviews than was the average for the whole NCDS re-study at age 33. Our stories do represent outcomes which range from marked success to delinquency and catastrophe, and very many of them are full of suffering and some also of anger, so that we are certain that they represent the whole range of stepfamily experience. At the same time we strongly suspect that our sample reflects to a heightened degree the tendency in the NCDS study as a whole to underrepresent those in the cohort who saw themselves as social failures or who lived an unstable life.[45]

In preparation for interviewing we developed an elaborate interview guide which in its final form was over fifty pages long. It was, however, always intended to be—and indeed was—used very flexibly, so that informants were given plenty of space to raise issues and shape the dialogue with the interviewer as well as fully expressing their own views in response to questions. The format was based on earlier life story interviews designed by Paul Thompson and Daniel Bertaux for a transgenerational project on families and social mobility,[46] and then elaborated for research on stepfamilies through joint discussions primarily with Gill Gorell Barnes, but at a later stage also with Antony Cox. He shared with us his own experience of psychiatric research on a series of projects, some jointly with Sir Michael Rutter, helped us to clarify what could most usefully be quantified, and provided us with an abbreviated, self-administered questionnaire as a measure of current psychic ill-health or well-being.

The interview guide has a number of distinctive features worth noting. It does not confine itself to immediate family relationships, but also explores the extended family and relationships with neighbours, schools, and work, and the physical environment of the house and its surroundings, and the effects of moving from one place to another. The sequence followed is essentially chronological, beginning with family background and grandparents, but varied greatly depending on whether the informant could remember an intact family in earlier childhood, or had experienced a single-parent phase. The sections covered in adulthood similarly varied depending on whether the informant had remained single, was married, or divorced. At each stage however, in order to understand both the continuities and discontinuities which stepchildren experienced, the guide seeks to alternate narrative accounts of major transition points, often laden with conflict and drama, with more humdrum descriptive detail of patterns of everyday living, such as who carried out which of the household chores, illustrating how family relationships worked in practice. At each point too, we encouraged informants not only to narrate and describe, but to reflect on how they had been told about events, and their own feelings about the relationships and experiences which they thought most significant.

The guide seeks to draw out the informant's perception of family ideals, traditions, and boundaries, and also configurations of alliances between family members. It emphasizes the need to focus on the key individuals picked out by the informant, who might be peripheral or outside the family itself, and explore the quality of relationships with them in terms of availability, activities, and responsibilities. It encourages particular attention, in exploring both marital and adult–child relationships, to the quality of communication, the expression of affection, the character of discipline and to the presence or absence of violence.

The interviews were carried out by a team of five women and two men, of whom four were clinicians and three researchers. Each interview was tape-recorded and the transcript used as the basis for analysis, but the interviewers also added comments about the interview process and what can best be described as the 'emotional atmosphere'. At most interviews, a family tree was drawn as a guide to information about the extended family. The interviews typically varied in length between two and six hours, some interviews in a single session as long as three or four hours and others with a second visit.

All the interviews took place in informants' homes. Despite the various constraints which this setting imposed, such as interruptions from neighbours or from noisy or demanding children, there were also many advantages. It could enable informants to convey a sense of achievement and pride about their homes and how far the home itself represented a major source of stability. One man, who had lived in the same village all his life, treated the interviewer to a lively and detailed description of its history and conveyed a powerful impression of how important a sense of place had been in his emotional development. When there were interruptions, sometimes their nature was revealing in itself. One woman became very alarmed when her mother called by unexpectedly. She thought her mother would be upset if she knew that she was being interviewed as a member of a stepfamily, because she had brought her up to believe that her stepfather was her real father.

We noted important differences in the fullness of the interviews which are to a considerable extent, as we explore in Chapter 6, related to gender. Whilst a few informants, mainly men, gave the minimum responses to questions and were clearly reluctant to review this period of their lives, for others the opportunity was eagerly seized upon. Some life stories were so vivid in their descriptive detail, extraordinary in their drama, humour, or pathos or awe-inspiring as an example of strength and survival that they ran the risk of dominating our team discussions at the expense of less gripping stories.

In at least ten interviews, spouses—generally wives—were present and contributed in varying degrees, from the odd sardonic interjection to supplying full and insightful commentary on family relationships. Although this was not part of our original design, having the opportunity to observe the couple's interaction and relate it to the personal story gave us added valuable information.

It also reminded us how the story which we collected from the informant was never the only possible perspective. We can assume that many of our informants' accounts of events would have been contradicted by other family members had they been present at the interview. For example our informants rarely recounted being given adequate preparation or even explanation for the step-parent's entry to their family, and many said they were told nothing at all. If their parents had been interviewed, probably some of them would have assured us that of course they told the child what was going to happen. This does not mean that either memory is false. The contradictory accounts could reflect the difference between a parent giving information once, and a child taking it in and making sense of it when feeling emotionally unprepared and unready for the entry of a new family member. In the longer perspective, both memories could be accepted as valid.

We were also made acutely aware of the assumptions behind the language we use. Thus for the interview guide we had designed questions eliciting the informant's memories of how 'your stepfather' joined the family. It very quickly became apparent to us that by naming the relationship we were defining it in a particular way before we had checked how the informant saw it. We then replaced it with a more open question, and learnt more by questioning our own categories than by sticking rigidly to them.

For several informants the interview itself raised basic questions as to how they conceived the story of their lives, especially when the significance of being a 'stepfamily' had been underplayed or denied in their upbringing. For them, the interview could bring out unexpected memories and change their perceptions of their own past. Thus while memory is certainly constructed from the present, so that the core of a life narrative can be described as consisting of a cluster of memories which we highlight because they either 'fit' in some way with the on-going story of our lives or because they throw it into relief by contradicting it, we must also assume that the perspective of the present is not necessarily rigid.

Just as in a therapeutic session, in a research interview 'dominant' stories may be challenged and, sometimes to the expressed surprise of the informant, alternative memories and new perspectives may emerge. This can often happen when the interviewer queries inconsistencies, or frames new contexts which have hitherto been submerged in the narrative. For example, one man, who had stayed with his father after his mother left home suddenly, found it difficult to describe how he and his father had managed their relationship afterwards and how they had handled daily tasks. Following questions about the part played by his older sister, he gradually began to talk about how important she had been and how she had taken over many of the emotional tasks previously handled by his mother. He was so struck by his new understanding of what he owed his sister that he asked the interviewer if she could supply him with another copy of the interview guide so that he could question his sister directly about her own experience.

For some informants, the interview brought to light meaningful connections, for example of a recurring pattern. One man who had lost touch with his own daughter after his first marriage ended, discussed his belief that one day she might just turn up unannounced on his doorstep. He suddenly remarked on how similar this would be to his own experience when his parents split up, in that he did not see his mother for several years until he made a decision to turn up unexpectedly on her doorstep. Another man, who had refused to answer several factual questions, and warned the interviewer that she would be unleashing uncontrollable emotions if she opened up certain areas, nevertheless proved to be virtually unstoppable in his self-revelation and clearly had the need for the interviewer to bear witness to his experiences. The process is thus one in which the boundaries between research and therapy may at times be thin.

The interviewers therefore had to take great care in handling painful memories and especially in how to manage the ending of the interview. Many of the informants manifested their need to have their life experience validated by the interviewer, and indeed we saw this as intrinsic to the interviewer's responsibility for all interviews, given that most contained stories of loss, fracture, disruption, and sometimes a continuing sense of betrayal. In the research interview as in the therapeutic session, stories of failure and deficit can be elicited and predominate or, without minimizing the extent of painful or difficult life events, a sense of agency and resource can be highlighted.

This brings us back to our choice of themes, which are indicated by the chapter titles which follow. They emerged partly from parallel clinical experience and findings from other research studies, and partly from our initial discussions of the themes emerging from the pilot study, but they crystallized above all through confronting ourselves with the fifty narrative interviews which we had collected. We aim to contextualize as well as to convey the experience of growing up in stepfamilies, rather than isolating this experience within the stepfamily form, and to explore the wider influences of gender assumptions, the continuing or changing patterns of communication and discipline through successive transitions, the relevance of the relationship to the other parent, and the often crucial roles of extended family, community, school and economic factors. Above all, our interest in stress and protective factors, and in the relevance of research for action, connects tightly with our fundamental aim: to hear, and to understand, how some life stories, despite their pain, could have emerged as narratives of resistance, strength, and survival.

3

Communication, Roles, Order and Disorder: From First Family to Stepfamily

COMMUNICATION, roles, and the maintenance of order within families evolve through a lengthy and subtle cumulative process which comes into play with the child's birth and continues to evolve into adulthood. It is an interactive process between individual personalities, yet always also moulded by powerful wider social expectations, as well as by particular family cultures and traditions; a set of relationships built slowly, through mutual experience, yet always with the potential of sharp turning points, and even particular incidents which may retain, in retrospect, a powerful symbolic meaning.

We have discussed earlier (Chapter 2) the strengths and weaknesses of retrospective memories for grasping such an unfolding narrative process. We need to bear this caution especially in mind as we begin by considering the recollections of these families while they were still intact before parents were parted by separation or death.

Communication and Discipline in the Intact Family

The thirty-six parents who can be remembered when together present an encouragingly ordinary range, from the garrulous to the laconic, and from the gentle reasoner to the harsh disciplinarian: and in patterns which fit those which have been found from other research on parent–child relationships in Britain.[1] Thus in wholly working-class families there were more instances of severe or harsh discipline, and none of control through reasoning and discussion; and there was also more likely to be little or no intimate communication between either parent and the children.

In terms of gender, fathers were almost always non-communicators, but mothers more varied, almost half 'easy to talk to'. There was no such division of gender roles in terms of discipline: the leading disciplinary role was as often taken by a father or a mother. Lastly, the patterns remembered vary between those families which were to be divided by a death and by a separation, not in terms of harshness, but in that those who were later to split include none of those who used verbal reasoning, and many more of the families with no intimate parent–child communication. This difference is particularly interesting, for it ties in with other research suggesting how conflictual 'rowing' between parents was also a source of problems in these families which preceded rather than followed parental separation.[2]

At one end of the spectrum are two classic middle-class 'verbal' families. The Rogers were proud of their continuing family traditions of emotional expressiveness—'we are a touchy lovey family'—and of confiding over mealtimes: 'mealtimes are so important . . . it was all talked about at the table'; and in the same spirit, if there were problems, 'you would have to sit round a table and sort it out'. The Herberts shared similarly high standards of behaviour, and they also had a strong sense of a family story, although in their case both parents had suffered separation and loss in their own childhoods; they were moreover, one of only two families who entirely eschewed even the mildest physical punishment. Instead, the father would impose, and enforce, stringent restrictions—'I would go to my room, or I wasn't allowed out to play for a week: and that would stick.' But in an instance of apparently severe misconduct, when a complaining neighbour came 'storming round to my father . . . I wasn't shouted at: they asked for my side of the story, and I explained what had happened, and I had to go and apologise to this woman, and I was told I couldn't ride my bike for the rest of the week.'

As a whole, in nearly one-third of the families the child remembered being able to talk easily to at least one parent, and in all of these, discipline was enforced mildly with resort only to 'the odd slap'. But in the majority, by contrast, there is no memory of verbal intimacy. Sometimes it was by default, such as where both parents were almost always out working, but in many other families, formality was seen as a virtue: good manners would include not talking at all, or only very restrictedly, at mealtimes.

In yet others, there were family secrets—of children's paternity or of mental illness—to be kept hidden; or a mother already suffering from a 'pig' of a violent husband might 'bottle it up' rather than confide in a child. Discipline in some of these families was also mild. Nevertheless, they also include a group of ten families at the opposite end of the spectrum from, and also more numerous than the 'verbal' families, in which punishment was harsh to the point of violence: as with a mother who belted 'with the dog strap', or a father, 'a right whacker', who at 'any trivial thing, he'd go bananas'.

All the difficulties of these harsh families are exemplifed in the Gordons. Here an ex-policeman was struggling to maintain 'military standards' of housekeeping with a mentally sick wife. 'Me dad was the sergeant sort and he liked to put people straight. So he wouldn't stand any nonsense . . .: he used to hit us all. . . . If you done wrong you got hit and that was it.' If the boy was not 'belted' he was sent to bed for the day. There was no discussion of any kind in this home; no family stories, or even bare information about grandparents; no family photos. Mention of the mother's illness was absolutely 'taboo', although it shaped the family life. 'It was like being the headmaster and the headmistress, you daren't say anything.'

It was not that the father here was uncaring. On the contrary, he was making strenuous efforts to cope in an extremely difficult situation. When his wife was at home, she 'just sat in the chair all day long', oblivious that the house was 'a tip'; but at increasingly frequent intervals she was in hospital after overdoses, where visits involved long and complicated bus journeys to find her, often 'so bloated' with drugs that 'you wouldn't recognize her'—a nightmare for the boy, worse than anything else he was to suffer later. And his father did succeed in keeping the home running, cooking, looking after the children. Even while their mother was alive, 'my dad did more for us than anybody'. And he did more than basic caring. He also tried to help the children by entertaining them in his own way. He was a fanatical modelmaker and 'the house was littered with models everywhere . . . suitcases full' of models of ships and planes. The chef d'oeuvre was the boys' bedroom. Here he painted all the walls blue with clouds, and a village, and he built a huge train set, over three-feet high. 'It was fantastic. . . .

That was great because you could bring all your friends back to see all this big layout.'

Such a combination of physical toughness with showing caring through doing recurs in several of these family stories. It needs to be understood as an expression of an alternative male model of intimacy. Thus while harshness, above all from men, was probably at this initial stage the most serious risk faced by the child, it is also important to emphasize that even brutally tough fathers could be pivotal sources of self-identity for their sons. Such men were admired in working-class communities in which toughness, physical strength, and even limited violence were closely linked to ideals of masculinity. As one son put it of an ex-boxer father, 'Dad was a giant of a man . . . a wild man. . . . In his younger days, I don't think there were many people, that could touch my father. . . . People say, "You're the bloody spit of your father."' Physical roughness was in itself a form of non-verbal intimacy. And because men were expected to be doers rather than talkers, to call a father 'a pretty quiet bloke' could be a compliment, while men could make their children presents, or provide examples in manual skill, with few words spoken.

Among those whose memories go back to when both parents were together the Bolsovers are a striking instance of this. Here again the father was both taciturn and harsh. He 'could be bloody ruthless. If we were, like, being idle as young'uns. . . . If you'd been a bad little bugger, you got it. . . . You got the belt off him, like. . . . If I did anything wrong, my dad never believed in sparing the rod. He would clout us if I'd been bad, as simple as that. But at the same time, he'd be fair as well.' Young Bolsover could have readily talked to his mother, but he found her feminine talkativeness and demonstrative affection too threatening: 'brawling', 'over-protective', 'overpowering'—and he still does: 'It smothers you.' He remains distant from his mother, taking his father as a model, following the same job based on a knack in dealing with machinery and with the same ambitions, pursuing the same interest in dogs and shooting, visiting his grave still: 'I would have liked to have been like my dad.' They may not have talked much, but they felt an intimacy in doing, moving together. 'When I was a young'un, I mean we'd go all over. It was always like me dad, our Jim [his brother], me, would go for a walk round the wood.' And when he is confronted with a crisis, rather than talk, he still goes to the wood.

Thus for a working-class boy sometimes, if rarely, identification with such a model of tough and taciturn masculinity through a father could provide a source of strength in facing subsequent difficulties. Middle-class verbal skills cannot be assumed as the sole path to survival. Equally, it would be mistaken to interpret all the problems of these families before break-up in terms of a failure to live up to social expectations: on the contrary, they could be rooted precisely in the gender models of the community.

Secrecy, Confusion, and Reaching an
Understanding of Separation and Loss

Every one of our families underwent a crisis of loss and realignment—often turbulent—following a death or separation. How did they manage it?

The children first needed to understand what was happening. The failure of the parents to meet this need has been observed in other research.[3] Here it was very striking, for fewer than one-quarter of the children felt their situation had been adequately explained to them. The remainder either say they were not told at all, or that the news was conveyed in a way which did not allow them to take it in and understand it. Thus one mother disappeared simply leaving 'a letter on the mantelpiece'. Another, the mother of an illegitimate child, 'never really . . . wanted to tell me. . . . From what I've learnt over t'years, it were a one-night stand. I don't think it was a very pleasant experience for her. And I was the result.' Twice when in the street, 'my mum's said, "That was your father." But it didn't mean anything to me, just seeing this person, and being told that's who it was. I didn't know him.'

For a young child especially, moreover, unexpected news might at first be impossible to grasp. When Eileen Moriarty's mother suddenly left home, she had been wholly unaware of her parents' quarrelling: 'they made every effort to conceal it from us.' Her mother had said goodnight to the children quite normally. They only sensed something was wrong when—

we came down, and my father was crying in the chair. . . . I just remember him saying something about she'd 'gone'—and that was it. I think when you're 7, you probably don't know how to take things like that. You don't believe people 'go', you can't: people don't 'go', do they? I mean, you're 7.

I think we had a few tears then. And I suppose it was probably about a week before we actually realized she wasn't coming back . . .

Her father never explained, 'Not at all, never. She'd "gone". That was it.' So Eileen and her brother were 'petrified about what would happen. I remember thinking we'd be put in a home.'

Parents therefore needed both the wish and the skills to tell a child, and to be prepared to go on telling and answering questions. In general, while an earlier openness more often led to a better handling of the crisis, there are several families in which communication patterns were transformed by the shock, some negatively and some positively. Mothers—and grandmothers—were more likely to attempt to explain than fathers; but again there were marked shifts by some of each. More surprisingly, explanations of death were as badly handled as those of separation.

In half of the families the death or separation had taken place before the age of 7, and it was these children who were most likely to remain confused. Most had been so young that without subsequent contact the child could have had no direct memory of the lost parent: 'I don't know anything about him'; 'I can't remember at all'. Not one of these children's curiosity was fully met. Sometimes a survivor talked; others kept photographs; yet there seemed to be a failure even with the well-intentioned. 'I never really knew my own father, and only from what my mother told me, which was quite distorted,' recalled one orphaned girl: 'she wouldn't let me have my father's picture in the house.' She later found a much better source of information in her paternal grandmother. Another, whose mother talked openly, had succeeded in getting a photograph through a recently discovered stepsister.

As often, however, the remaining parent was deliberately silent, even to the point of intentional deception. For Martine Brabourne her stepfather 'is the person who I have taken to be my father . . . I was led to believe was my father.' She 'linked up' with her father and his family later on, as a teenager, but she had unknowingly met her father earlier: 'I had seen him when quite young, because he did come to the house . . . And I remember him giving me a big doll, and perhaps I was told he was some special kind of uncle.' Mandy Pope grew up believing that her (first) stepfather was her real father until the age of 16, when he explained that he was not; her father was then contacted through a newspaper advertisement and she met him twice. Yet she had always been puzzled why her half-sister not only looked so different, but was more fussed over. She was a child of a brief liaison between the two chief men in her mother's life, and one must presume that social embarrassment explains her mother's secrecy, not only to her children, but also to outsiders.

Linda Clarke was similarly the child of a brief encounter between two main relationships, and again both she and outsiders did not know her real paternity until much later. The deception was easier to maintain because there were, in any case, two other sets of half-siblings in the home. 'I've grown up—because we are a split family—and it's been sort of like all hidden. . . . You were just a family, and that was it.' In this case, however, the older half-siblings did understand, and tried to explain: 'as I was getting older, my brother used to say to me, "Oh, your dad's not your dad", you know: "Oh, thank you John", you know! "Dad's not really your dad, it's someone else." So then I used to think, "Oh well, I must be like Linda and Robert", because I was like, in the middle.' She only discovered the truth of her paternity when, at 17, she asked her mother for her birth certificate for a passport.

For children who experienced the separation of their parents at a later age, memory of the loss of a parent was confused in another way when separation led directly to entry into a stepfamily.[4] Again, in not a single instance was a satisfying explanation given. In one family in which both parents had had other relationships, the child at first stayed with the father, who concealed the fact the he 'had been carrying on behind my mother's back since I was 3, and it was her best friend', cut off contact with her, 'vetted all the mail that came in' to prevent her letters arriving, and 'just said that she'd run away for another man, and she didn't love us any more. . . . And for a while I didn't want anything to do with my mother.' Another mother narrowly missed losing her daughter through failing to explain the separation. The child was simply told, 'Daddy's gone off to work', and so was quite unprepared when her father appeared in the afternoon at home: 'he was there on the doorstep, and he wanted to take me, just me, none of the boys, and live with him'.

Such deliberately confusing jockeying for the child's loyalties was, however, exceptional in this context. Most children were simply thrown into an utterly unexpected new reality with little or no explanation whatever. Thus a girl describes how—

we were sat down, and mum more or less announced to us that [my father] . . . he'd gone, and that he wasn't coming back this time, and that we'd be moving into this big house in Maldon, and living with Wesley . . .

I was very bitter about that. In one day, my safe secure little world went to pieces, because that weekend, we packed our cases, and we went, and I never saw that house again. . . . I left a lot of stuff behind. . . . It was a very abrupt, very quick upheaval. And it didn't give you time to think anything through.

An equally startled boy found himself split from not only his mother but also his sisters: 'I didn't know why, but I was taken to another house. . . . I was asked to move my bags, because we were going to another house. It's as simple as that! My father just told me we were moving. . . . I couldn't understand why my mother had left me. . . . I just thought my mother didn't love me any more! That was as simple as that. I didn't see her for two years.' Even today, his father has never explained 'why he left my mother . . . and I've never asked him'.

Among the remaining families who separated, but with an interval before the child entered a stepfamily, as also those struck by death when the child was older, there was much greater variety in communication, ranging from secrecy and denial to open confiding.

Talking about death itself when the other parent had died was especially difficult for most surviving parents.[5] One father whose wife was run over and killed was direct enough: 'he come to the school straightaway, as soon as he heard'. Some others tried to explain, but especially with younger children, the message was not understood: 'it didn't really sink in'; 'to me it was downstairs, and it didn't mean anything to me. . . . In that day and age, cancer was a thing that couldn't be cured, they didn't talk about it.' Only one child recollected going to the funeral itself. More typically, neither the illness nor the death was explained, and there was no adult willing to share their grief. Indeed, in several cases any discussion was explicitly prohibited. One girl was sent to a boarding school where she was forbidden to talk about her mother, and the toys which she had made for her were taken away. Four families allowed no discussion of the parent's illness, and in one case where they had 'hidden it', continued the pretence when the child 'walked in' to the room in which her father lay dead.

Even the Rogers family, despite their belief in 'talking', could not talk about death. In crisis, their openness capsized:

You see, it was all hidden from me, I wasn't told. The day of his funeral, which I don't know about, I was at Auntie Tessie's. She took me to town to be measured for some new shoes. I don't know how long after, I just—'Where is me dad?' You know, sometimes he did go away to conferences and things: 'oh, he's at a conference.' And it was just—I was in Auntie Tessie's and I said, 'Why does me mum keep crying?' and 'Why isn't she at work now, what's wrong with her?' And I always remember my Auntie Tessie said, 'Go in the parlour and I'll go and see your mum', and she went to me mum's and she said, 'You're gonna have to tell her.'

But her mother would not. So it was left to the neighbour: 'Me mum couldn't tell me. So Auntie Tessie told me.' Her mother still cannot talk about her father's death to her child; nor can most of these widowed parents. Some, indeed, have sought to survive through totally expunging all reminders of their former spouse. Celia Newton's mother, for example, destroyed all her father's possessions:

I can remember her breaking all his records . . . that was obviously her way of dealing with things. But there was very little for me to touch, or to hold, or to have, that belonged to my father. I found one photograph of myself with my father, but I am literally just a baby in arms, and there was only one. And my mother would never talk about him. Nanny told me more about my father than I've ever been able to get out of my mum.

Although talking about separation seemed to be less difficult for the adults than talking about death, in a similar way all traces of the absent parent might be destroyed. In three families it was denied that they had ever existed; in seven others, all contact was severed and the absent parent never mentioned. In another family the mother's departure was a 'mystery' which the father refused to discuss, and when after a year an aunt put them in touch, the children kept their visits to her secret: 'we didn't want to upset him, by knowing that we were seeing her'.

Most remarkable of all are the Moriartys, who acted as if magnetized by a peculiar family destiny. Eileen's father's mother had 'left when he was very young as well, and it was an exact repetition of the situation that I had.' Only after she died did they discover, through a gas meter reader, that she had returned to live close by, 'and he'd never known, all his life.' Yet when Mr Moriarty's wife disappeared in turn, he pushed her out of his life just as his father had his own mother: 'It was something that was never talked about, once she was gone. Everything was banished from the house one night; and that was it. . . . It went straight to him. Just that day. Dad just—everything, like, little photos, he cut in half; he cut her picture up and everything; it was just gone. Amazing.' Eileen is still haunted by the fear that her father will be the next to disappear. When she goes away for any length of time she phones daily not to talk, but to be sure he is still there. 'It's very strange, the same happened to him, as what happened to us. It's really awful to think that—I hope it will never happen again. Oh yeh, I often do [wonder], yeh; but to think that someone was so near . . .'

It may be significant that these are instances of mothers who left; and there is another in which the father's attitude was similarly hostile to her contact with the children. Albert Black's father also became 'very, very, very bitter' after the split, and tried to cut off the children from their mother: 'dad tried to turn us against her. . . . Mention my mother's name in front of him and he'll throw a wobbly. . . . He was really wild.' But here, although there was a long gap in which the children did not see her, the link was never broken: 'he was very bitter towards me, Steve, because we kept in contact with our mother'—and when their sister finally went to live with her, 'that was the straw that broke the camel's back', a period of 'hell' in which his father had a 'nervous breakdown'.

With absent fathers, on the other hand, as we shall see in Chapter 4 with the exception of those eight who had left infants of up to 2 years old, all but one of whom did disappear completely, only six of the remaining twenty-one did not keep some contact. Through such contacts some children came gradually to recognize that their parents could not live together and also, in close connection, how there is more than one side to every family story. It was not easy for a child to reach an explanation of what had happened, especially when these parents were themselves unable to confront it. In this situation, contact with the absent parent could help a child's gradual development of their own independent understanding.

The nature of this long process is especially well conveyed by Caroline Herbert. 'It was a combination of what my father told me, what my mother told me, and what my grandmother told me. And little bits of what I can remember.' Even before her mother had left her father, taking her with her, there had been odd incidents which later were to make sense. When she was 6, they had gone on holiday with another couple, and they were in the hotel room, 'and my mother locked my father out, and I didn't understand why. And I can remember saying, "Please let daddy in".' And now I can remember, I realized that he obviously had gone somewhere with this woman, Gwen, who is now my stepmother. I sort of pieced it together in later years.' Another time she was puzzled to find her mother crying at night: 'she said that she'd burnt herself on the washing machine. I knew that wasn't the case. I'm sure I'd heard them arguing before I'd come down, but she would never tell me what was going on. She always protected me.' After the split Caroline was happy to go on seeing her father, whom she was given no reason to blame: it was another four years before she understood that he was living with another woman through actually meeting her. 'I never talked to him at all, actually, about it. It was as though . . . I knew that I shouldn't talk to him about it.' And her mother continued to protect her from the whole truth. 'She did start to mention things, of my father . . . [but] I never blamed my father at that stage for anything, because my mother never really explained. I didn't know anything, I hadn't clicked anything together at all about my stepmother, Gwen. I didn't know what was going on.' But when, at 12, at her mother's suggestion she decided to go to live with her father, her mother 'said to my father that I must be told, and my dad just couldn't bring himself to tell me. I can remember going to the home where they lived. . . . I was surprised. I had no idea. But I accepted it. . . . My mother explained everything to me then, I was told.' The significance of her mother's boyfriend was also made clear. And perhaps crucially, she was able to talk to a neutral, understanding adult about the whole story: her father's mother, to whom she had already been close in earlier childhood. 'I always relied, I always felt me grandmother told me the truth. Because she used to tell me how difficult my father was . . . how difficult she found it to cope with him, from a very young age. . . . I can remember her saying, "I can understand why your parents split up."'

Living in a Single-Parent Family

We have so far focused on the child's understanding in the deeper sense of the crisis after a death or separation which had disrupted each of these families. But beyond that, everyday communication between parent and child, and also order and discipline, needed to be re-established in the new context. For the great majority of these children the break was followed by at least briefly living with a lone parent before entering a stepfamily; and for 29, this was a significant phase of over two years, an important experience of another form of family life. What do the memories of these latter children convey of everyday relationships with the caretaking parent at this stage? Typically an important double shift in patterns now took place, each highlighting important different facets of an alternative model of adult-child relationships: first, a shift towards closer communication, and second, away from harsh discipline.

It did not always move towards a more confiding, gentler relationship. In half of the families the caretaking parent was unable to encourage a child to confide, 'not so outgoing' in nature, and sometimes also physically undemonstrative: 'I've never kissed me mother. No.' Two fathers, never open, were driven by the crisis to become still less accessible, violently bitter. Another previously affectionate father took to drink, leaving his daughter 'to fend for myself'. In three other families, which had been open, death or division resulted in a quite new suppression of intimate communication; or a parent who now withdrew into a shell of depression—'she was vacant, when she was there, she was like, cloud nine somewhere'. A child in this situation could well feel more aware of the parent's misery than their own, and a responsibility not to make things worse by demands to meet their own needs. One boy remembers how 'I used to say to her, "Why aren't you eating?" . . . I suppose that was me trying to look after her'.[6]

Yet paradoxically, it was precisely an acceptance of the mutuality of needs which probably accounted for the special closeness between parent and child which is remembered in some of those families where communication was open. Thus one daughter describes a father as more like 'a friend . . . I could say anything to him and he'll take it', and a son his mother as 'my best friend'. Similarly, another son describes his father as 'a brother—oh, very easy-going and likeable chap', and a daughter her collapsed, suicidal mother becoming more like a friend than a parent; and another comments, 'she's not like a mother, she's like a sister'.

A second factor in half of these families was the introduction of new carers. Those few children who were sent away to boarding schools all have negative memories, and this could also happen when, much more typically, the new carers were relatives. One boy explained how immediately after the break, his father 'managed very well: he's got nine sisters, and a brother, the majority of which live very close to where he was—and they helped out. . . . We were palmed off onto various relations for a week here and a week there. . . . That wasn't a very pleasant time.' Much more often, however, the intervention of relatives seemed strongly positive. They were mostly grandmothers but sometimes aunts or grandfathers too. One boy and his father moved in with his grandfather, whom he remembers with special intensity as 'a very loveable man . . . very strict, very honest. A very, very hard man. . . . He was my conscience . . . my grandfather was the rock. He was a rock in the whirlpool. Everything was rushing around, and he was there, and he was solid.' Another grandson said of a grandmother, 'she guided me; she looked after me the most'; while a granddaughter of another grandmother, that she 'worshipped her'.

It is the same combination which explains why there was a marked mitigation of severity in discipline during this single-parent phase.[7] There were now only two families in which the discipline was harsh: in both an embittered lone father became violent when drunk, and in one of them, his belting was encouraged by the uncle in whose home they now lived. But in all other families the tendency was in the opposite direction. Parents who were absorbed by their own problems, or closer to their children, were unable or unwilling to enforce strict standards. In this spirit a father would let his daughter 'have a lot of my own way, and never ever smacked me. But if I was really naughty, he used to say he would join the Navy and I'd be left on my own, and that cured it straightaway.' And a daughter remembers her mother as 'firm; but then it was only over a few things that she was firm about. I mean . . . she almost didn't have any standards. She didn't really care if we roller-skated in the hall, damaged the furniture, oh no.' Even ex-sergeant Gordon spent his much briefer time as a lone parent self-absorbed and 'sighing', so abandoning his normal military standards that there were now 'no real manners in the house whatsoever. . . . Come in grabbed a loaf, and went out street.'

Where, on the other hand, responsibility was partly or wholly taken over by a grandparent, there were invariably higher standards, but never harshly enforced. These older people were experienced parents who could afford to carry their authority lightly, because the child usually did not care to challenge it. A grandmother is remembered as 'the kindest, most gentlest person'; a great-grandmother as a 'powerful woman' who 'spoilt me', but never needed to smack because 'you did what she said, simple as that'.

Even a grandmother who still believed in severity was hardly likely to have the sheer strength to be harsh. Harry Bolsover remembers his grandmother as a 'loving' woman with a 'forceful personality. . . . She was forceful. She didn't have to crack you to make you think. She could speak to you, and you knew.' Even so, he and his brother became hard to control as teenagers. When they truanted from school 'she used to play hell about us not going'. 'I was bloody naive at the time, but—you always know better, and that. I wish me grandmother had flogged us with a bit of ninetail—it might have knocked a bit of sense into us earlier!' She was indeed provoked sometimes 'to beat us: . . . when you were like 14, 15 and that, and you start fighting on the bloody lawn, she used to think nowt about just getting a bucket of water and throwing it over you, you know. It was a sharp shock! It used to save all the hassle at the time!' Almost always, however, her strategies were subtler. She wanted them home by nine at night; and if they were late, she would simply not open the door for another hour. 'She used to be sitting in the back kitchen, on the chair, just sitting there, saying "I'll teach you, you bugger"'—and then, in the end, 'she'd always open the door.' The point had been made; but without confrontation.

Entering Stepfamilies in Early Childhood: Family Secrets and Myths

We have now reached the crux of the story: the child's entry into a stepfamily. What can these life stories tell us about the handling of this second turning-point in family life? Because with our cases the factors and long-term outcomes both differ according to the age at which the child entered the stepfamily, they are best divided into groups according to age of entry.

We thus begin with the relatively small group of ten who became stepchildren before the age of 7. They are an anomaly, because we had deliberately only sampled from those recorded by NCDS as entering stepfamilies after this age, to give a better chance for the transition to be clearly remembered. In other words, they are there because the parents did not make the presence of a step-parent clear to the NCDS interviewer when the child was 7. In some the child was equally misled and a fiction maintained that the stepfather was a natural father. Hence they cannot be taken as typical of early entrants to stepfamilies in general.

As a group, despite the relative security of their childhoods, several of them suffered from serious psychological and relationship difficulties. It seems most likely, however, that this was a later consequence of the confusion which they had experienced as children, rather than of early entry into a stepfamily. Indeed, on the other hand, they also seemed to gain some advantages from their longer years within a stable stepfamily. They did reasonably well occupationally, and nearly all also bonded closely enough to the stepfather for this relationship to survive the emotional problems which most faced in later years.[8] Their stories provide a first indication of the surprising tolerance with which stepfathers were evaluated. They also suggest an important general caution: that a heavy price could be paid much later for a too smooth entry bought at the expense of family secrets.

Nine of these children lived with stepfathers, and eight of them were girls. Typically—although we shall see that there were two striking exceptions—discipline was never problematic for them. Most were relatively compliant children, some brought up more strictly than others, but without much recourse to physical punishment. The difficulties which most of them were—sooner or later—to face were more often concerned with communication.

Clearly the most secretive mothers were those who concealed their daughters' true paternity. The most surprising instance was that of Mary Birch. She had been conceived extramaritally while her mother was married to the man Mary knew as her 'father'. When he died, her mother then quickly remarried the 'stepfather', Mary's natural father. But her mother 'never finds it easy to discuss anything': a brother who died is also 'just not mentioned'. So she never told her the truth about her father. In fact Mary suspected it: 'Oh—well, yes. It was silly little things. When we used to sit on his knee, when I was obviously older and Ben was there, he'd often say to me, "Ben's your real brother and Fred's your stepbrother"—and being 11 or 12, these things click around in your brain, and you'll come to realize. But my mum denied it every time.' It was only just before her own marriage, at 20, her 'stepfather' finally told her outright himself:

He actually gave me a letter, which he had sent to my mum saying how pleased he was that he now had a daughter and wanted my mother to leave her present husband, but she wouldn't. So—and that's how I found out. He gave me the letter to read.

And I had an almighty row with my mother. Yes, because I had asked her loads of times and she denied it every time. . . . She said that 'you were too young to know'.

With the other secretive mothers, the child grew up with a 'father' who was really a stepfather. Two of these mothers were also unavailable for more everyday confiding. But their silence made it much simpler for their daughters to relate to their stepfathers in early childhood; and the bonding is indeed such that each remains even now 'my real dad'. Linda Clarke recalls 'my dad' as an 'easy sort', 'good as gold with all of us'; Mandy Pope says, 'I call him my father because to me, he's my dad . . . He's just always been there. . . . We get on great.' Neither father was a strong authority figure. Mandy's childhood was complicated by the fact that she grew up in a split household. She and her elder half-sister lived with her great-grandmother, a loving and caring old woman to whom she became much closer than to her mother: for Mandy, 'she were mum'. However, it was only at 16 or 17 that both Linda and Mandy discovered the deception which had underlain their entire family lives. Significantly, neither turned their anger against their colluding stepfathers. Subsequently too, both of these two young women have continued to be haunted by difficulties from deceptions in personal relationships.

Martine Brabourne was also 'led to believe' by her mother that her stepfather was her father, but her story was otherwise very different, for she came from a 'complicated network' of a family shaped by particular cultural influences. Her mother was a West Indian who had already conceived Martine by another man when she set out as a teenager for London, where she quickly married Delano Brabourne. Delano remains 'the most significant person' for Martine, even though he broke up with her mother after eight years, and subsequently Martine re-contacted her real father 'out of curiosity'. After Delano left, he and Martine remained in regular weekly contact—more actively, indeed, than most natural fathers. This was no doubt partly because although Delano had only played a modest paternal role, and at the last stage had even pulled out a knife on her mother, he compared very favourably with his successor Gladwyn, who combined effusive affection with both fighting her mother from the start and sexually abusing Martine. Her relationship with her mother was still more confusing. On the one hand, they were unusually close: 'she talked to me about all kinds of intimate secrets. . . . I was really like her companion, rather than her daughter.' But she kept some of the key secrets to herself, nor did Martine find it so easy to confide her own problems; she often sought out a sympathetic aunt instead. And at the same time her mother was a violent disciplinarian: 'she never knew how to discipline us really, without going over the top. . . . I can remember getting a black eye, from just being boxed with a basket, for repeatedly buying the wrong vegetables.' Martine left home as a teenager, soon after she had finished school. It was to be a long struggle for her before she found her sense of direction.

Yasmin Hassan also comes from a complex family with its roots in another culture. This makes it much less easy to evaluate the significance of the patterns of secrecy and communication in her family. Certainly she has 'never been close' to a mother who was very secretive about Yasmin's dead father, and also so absorbed in running her shop that 'I don't think she gave us much time, she was too busy'. On the other hand, Yasmin's mother could not have succeeded in expunging her father's memory, for Yasmin remained in touch with the network of members of her father's large Pakistani family: most notably a next-door uncle, who later found her work, and became 'absolutely like a father, he's taken over the role, completely', and a grandmother who has been—

very important to me all my life. . . . She helped me through a lot, made me understand a lot of things which I valued, and then realized which way I'm going—which I didn't get from my own mother. . . . I didn't know where I was going, confused, very complicated—and she sort of ironed all those things out made me understand things to me, especially a lot to do with my own father who I didn't know.

On the other hand, recourse to them was impeded by the tensions between her mother and her father's family, who presumably disapproved of the remarriage: anger over money, and at least at times, prohibitions of contact.

The resulting tug of loyalties was further exacerbated by the manner in which the stepfather's arrival was handled in terms both of communication with both parents and his disciplinary role. He appeared when she was 3, but when five years later they married, 'it was a complete shock to me. In fact, she didn't even allow us to come to the wedding because she was too embarrassed.' It was originally 'a love marriage', but it became stormy with 'fighting, screaming and shouting' after the birth of her half-siblings. In retrospect she can see him—

looking back, he is a nice man: but when I was young I hated him. . . . Now I can understand his good points, but I couldn't when I was young. . . . He wanted life to be rosy: he wanted to be our father, and provide for us—he wanted us to be a family. . . . He wanted us to take [his] name . . .

The biggest mistake they made, is that they wanted it to be like a family: for instance, that he was the father. And he forced me to call him 'dad', which was the biggest mistake. I *hated* that. . . . And the trouble was that he had a temper, and . . . he screamed and shouted, and punished me, and I was forced to call him 'daddy'. . . . And I was forced when he was away to write him letters which I didn't want to write . . .

And I always wanted them to face the fact that he wasn't my father, and we didn't have a family.

Matters were made worse by the birth of a half-sister whom she 'resented'. By the time she was 11, both she and her brother 'were going through a lot of psychological problems'.

Nevertheless, despite her mother's hostility, at this point she succeeded in re-establishing contact with her father's relatives in Pakistan. Her brother now moved back to live with them in Pakistan, and she tried a school there herself, but could not settle. She returned to her mother, and was sent to an unsympathetic boarding school, returning for the holidays to a home which was now 'just tension, just tension'. Finally, at 16, she escaped, first to live with her uncle, then with her grandmother, and finally to an unsuccessful arranged marriage.

With the two boys who became stepchildren at this early age, it is less clear, mainly because of the vagueness of their memories, why they knew nothing about their fathers, although one had remained in touch with the boy's mother. Certainly one seems to have been an uncommunicative widow, and her son has suffered severe problems in forming relationships as an adult. Both boys, however, accepted their stepfathers as full replacements, even though neither was close to them. One 'dad' was 'totally uninvolved'; the other took some occasional interest, and Jack Finlay describes him as 'my old man', 'just a dad'; 'yeh, it was always "dad"'. This stepfather would also punish the children from time to time, which led to some violent conflict in later years: 'I got to the stage of hitting him back, as I grew older.'

There was no initial communication problem for two of the other girls. Each remembers the actual parting 'as clear as a day'— and the reason for it was clear too: arguing, and in one case violence. Both mothers were open, 'lovely': 'I was always talking to her.' Contact with the violent father was not wanted by either mother or child; while with the other father it was a part of daily life, since he lived next door. Nor were there initially problems with either stepfather. One was an easy-going, sensitive younger man who announced on moving in, 'he said, "You've always got a dad: you can call me 'dad' if you want to", he said, "but you've got a dad and I don't want to stand on his toes"; and we've always called him "Jack"'. The other was 'Okay to start with . . . I can always remember him taking care and making us a pair of wooden stilts.' There were thus no special difficulties in the transition itself.

The problems came later. As we have already seen with Yasmin Hassan, it was as crucial for the child as for the mother that the second marriage succeeded. But in Maureen O'Nally's family too it turned out almost as bad as the first. Indeed, the new family soon reached a point when difficulties were as likely to be fought out as talked through. The apparently 'very patient' stepfather proved also 'moody' and 'very violent towards my mother. . . . I think if my mother crossed him in any way, he didn't seem to be able to talk. It was always fists.' Maureen would try to stop them by screaming and shouting, but was too small to 'interfere physically. . . . It was a nightmare and my sister still has nightmares. . . . She wakes up screaming.' And she herself is haunted by anxieties that she may suffer a similar fate, by what seems almost a transgenerational family destiny. 'My mother had a very violent father . . . but then you see, she married two men who were also violent. . . . I don't know whether this theory of women being attracted to men because of their childhood. . . . It doesn't bode very well for me, does it, really?'

For Wendy Johnson, by contrast, there were never problems within the stepfamily itself: indeed she did not regard herself as part of a stepfamily because of her closeness, not only to her stepfather, but also to her two half-brothers. The difficulties were (unusually) with her maternal grandmother, who was always stirring trouble by falsely blaming her: 'we just didn't like each other. . . . No, hated each other.' But the grandmother was equally at war with the stepfather, especially after the whole family decided to move deep into the countryside to get out of 'the rat race'. An old Londoner, she never 'got used' to country life, and put the blame on the stepfather: 'they really hated each other.' It was partly to escape her that as a teenager Wendy herself left home for London to rejoin her father, briefly and unsuccessfully. 'Mind you, she could be an awful woman . . . —evil.'

Lastly, just one of these children entered a stepmother family. Ann Highfield's father proved singularly inept, both in communicating with his children and in judging relationships. When her mother died, he felt that remarrying would save a wage. He assumed that—'he couldn't look after three children, and go to work. So, initially he advertised for a housekeeper to come and live in. And within six months, they got married. So I think it was a matter of convenience, more than anything else. That's why he got married.' When this housekeeper-stepmother first arrived, bringing with her two children of her own, 'we all thought she was really nice'. But as soon as she was married, 'she realized that she didn't have to be nice to us any more. . . . She was more secure in the house; he couldn't just sack her.' She emerged as an alcoholic, violent to the children, discriminating between them—such as only washing her own children's clothes, refusing to look after one of the sisters when she was paralysed in an accident, and eventually seeking money for her drink through sex with other men. Ann sums her up as 'like the wicked stepmother, straight out of the books'.

The children had been too frightened to tell their father, and he was 'amazed' when he finally stumbled on the truth of what was happening. By then they were in their teens, and Ann had run away from home five times. Yet astonishingly, he was to fall into the same trap again. He advertised for a housekeeper-nurse who could help with his paralysed daughter. This time the children insisted on taking part in the choice, aiming to 'get the ugliest one that's the nicest one'. But he went on to marry her too; and she proved a second disaster.

What can we draw from these ten first stories? In some ways they anticipate transitions at later ages. They suggest how relatively easy it was for a man to be accepted by a child; indeed, how it was a stepfather who insisted most on imposing himself in a strong role who was most disliked.

We can also see how for some children the frame in which relationships came to be understood was partly drawn in terms of family or social myth. We have encountered earlier a haunting transgenerational family script with the Moriartys: here the

O'Nally's provide a second instance. Two other stories here are centred on an 'evil' woman: one, our first 'wicked stepmother'.

Above all, however, and in this they are unique, they illustrate the lasting dangers of misleading or confusing young stepchildren through family secrecies about relationships.

Entering Stepfamilies in Middle and Later Childhood

Let us now consider our forty remaining stepfamilies. They divide almost equally into two groups: 21 who came together in middle childhood, between the ages of 7 and 12, and 19 who entered stepfamilies as teenagers. Both groups are also mixed in terms both of background—class and gender—and of whether they arrived in stepfamilies through deaths or divorce.

A closer look also soon reveals a crucial distinction which they share: it was far easier for a stepfather to be accepted than for a stepmother. Two-thirds of the stepmothers were actively disliked, as often by girls as by boys; but only one-third of the stepfathers— and in those instances, by only one boy, and otherwise entirely by girls.

Before exploring the reasons for this, we need to note a few points which do distinguish entry in the teenage years. Not only are the teenage years in general more problematic in the majority of families of all types, but also this cohort entered them in 1970 just at the moment when adult authority was being fiercely challenged in the wider society.

There were also some potentially negative influences which were more likely to affect children entering stepfamilies in this phase. First, many younger children had been stabilized through the influence of supportive grandparents; but by this time they were less likely to be alive and fit enough to be available. Secondly, the stepfamilies they entered were likely to be more complicated, with older stepsiblings—sometimes on each side— as well as the possibility of younger half-siblings.[9] Thirdly, children who entered stepfamilies after the age of 13 had less time ahead in which to settle down to the new situation. Quite soon they could seriously consider leaving home through early independence, starting work, entering a sexual relationship, marrying, or getting pregnant.

Teenage entry into stepfamilies is also distinctive in two ways which are essentially different sides of the same coin. Because they were older and bigger, they could argue and fight much more powerfully, both between each other and with adults. As a result, it was more difficult for parents to ignore their wishes, and for the transition to take place without any warning or discussion. On the other hand, teenagers, if more troublesome, were seen by the parents in most of these families as more open to reason than younger children.[10]

Stepfathers: Marginality and the Continuity of Order

The easier acceptance by children of entry into a stepfather family depended partly on typical differences in parents' communication skills, and partly on differences between the roles expected of stepfathers and stepmothers in contributing to the everyday order and discipline of the household.

In the first place, mothers seem to have been more skilled, or at least less inept, in handling the arrival of a new partner. Most often, the stepfather was introduced in a way which helped to win over the child. In three-quarters of the families, there had been an interval of at least three years since the father had left. In several, the future stepfather had already been known for some time, sometimes as 'Uncle Bill' or 'Uncle Pat', and in one he had originally been the lodger. A daughter remarked of a future stepfather who had been around for over a year, 'He became part of the family quite quickly. To be told she was getting married, it wasn't drastic.' Typically, the new partner at first appeared as a friend—for example, going out on a picnic: 'I think they did it gradually.' One son indeed felt almost courted: 'they'd obviously been planning what they were going to do, I should think, because he was always pretty good to me, and gave me a good time.'

It also was often evident to the child that there would be practical gains. Four of the men who arrived looked to be immediate improvements on the violent fathers who had left. Another five children were conscious of being financially better off: 'it were a lot easier, more than anything else, because they had more money coming into the house'; 'a man to look after her and the children

made her sigh with relief'; 'financially. . . life was a lot better. . . .
Clothes weren't a problem any more.' For one of them, whose
working-class mother married a middle-class man 20 years older,
'we went quite up-market in a way, cos we lived in a quite posh
area.'

Several children also quickly noticed the positive change in their
mother: 'I thought, "This is going to be good for my mother"';
'he made my mother happy'; 'she had a life to lead again'; or, she
was 'happier with him than she's ever been'. Others were quite
simply pleased 'to have a man in the house again'; 'I realized, "Oh,
he's a man about the house. . . . He can put a plug on"'; 'I
desperately wanted a daddy'; 'I was just happy to have a father.
I remember being excited about that.'

Equally importantly, more than half of the mothers clearly
explained to the child that they were intending to remarry, and
most succeeded in conveying that they cared about the child's
feelings. One daughter who was anxious for her mother's new
friend to become her father asked, 'Is Philip going to marry you?';
and her mother replied reassuringly that he had not asked her yet,
'but don't worry, I'll tell him to'. Another daughter recalls how at
a bedtime, 'I must have sensed perhaps that things were happening, obviously this was before Joshua moved in with us: but I said,
"Are you going to marry him?" And she said, "Would you like
that?" And I said, "Yes". And then she said, "Yes, I am." I always
remember that conversation.'

Teenagers were more likely to be told in a formal way of the
forthcoming change, for example with the children all together,
and sometimes there was an attempt to allow some discussion: as
with the future stepfather who 'actually said to me—he asked me
and said, "What would you think if I married your mother?"'
Teenagers were also more often invited to the wedding itself, or,
more rarely, involved in the preparations; although this did not
always go down well. Harry Bolsover's mother invited him to the
wedding and introduced his future stepfather, but he was furious
at the idea. 'Total offence, you know—"How the hell can me
mother, if she did love me father, marry someone else?" That
really got me going. I just walked out, took the dog down the
wood, and spent about eight hours down the wood.' But his
brother did agree to act as best man, and before long Harry

himself came to like his stepfather, because 'he looked after me mother'.

In eight families, on the other hand—all with girls—the relationship with a stepfather started less well, and five of them never accepted the incomer. This was only partly because their mothers failed to help them.

In two families, the child was unable to settle because of parental disputes. One girl felt that the new marriage—which did not, in fact, last—was flawed from the outset. The stepfather was 'self-centred and arrogant. . . . I never saw any love between them. . . . They even argued over the way flowers were in a vase. . . . We just didn't get on, and we never have.' Lorna Maclean had the especially traumatic experience of being systematically deceived by her father, who briefly kept her, and was later so difficult that Lorna and her mother had to travel to 'literally spy on my father. And I had to tag along, and I had to sit outside his house at night. I wanted to tell him, but there was no way I could. It was crazy—he was adamant.' Torn between these warring parents, she understandably 'felt very guilty', and was never able to relate well to her stepfather. He was, in any case, never interested in children, 'difficult to live with, because he had very set ways', and eventually became violent towards her mother. Both of these daughters were fortunate in being able to find refuge in their grandmothers' homes.

Two other stepfathers were also disliked from the start for a double reason. Both were imposed rapidly because their mothers were pregnant, and with one there was also a sudden move into his larger but unwelcoming house. Much worse still, both proved violent. Jenny Dale suffered especially seriously from this combination of a badly handled entry of an intrinsically intolerable stepparent. She felt 'pushed out' by her pretty new half-sister, 'Miss Curls', who she had to help look after: '"Get this, get that"—I just felt that I was the skivvy then.' Worse still, the stepfather turned out to be a moody and 'very violent person. He would beat my mum up, he would hit me. . . . I just remember being petrified of him the whole time.' Worst of all, when her mother was out at work, he would interfere with her sexually. 'It went on for several years. . . . He abused me: I just can't, can't forgive him.' Eventually at 14, after he had attacked her with a horsewhip, she fled to her grandmother's.

It is a jealousy for lost intimacy with the parent rather than stepsibling jealousy which appears to have been a commoner initial problem. In one family an elder brother is remembered who 'threw a mental! . . . and hysterics: "You promised you'd never marry again"—which she hadn't'. One man himself vividly conveys his feelings as a 9-year-old watching the open sexual relationship between his mother and stepfather: 'Yeah, embarrassing really. It was probably young love really, but it didn't seem to me—it didn't seem right in a way. If I was, say, like in their shoes, I wouldn't do it. It's all right if you are a proper mum and dad, but being sort of an outsider—I don't agree with it . . . It didn't make me feel jealous: maybe angry. Because it got embarrassing sometimes.'[11]

It seemed much easier, however, for girls to talk about jealousy. Perhaps they were quicker to recognize it; also they were sexually mature earlier, and the younger girls had often become very close and intimate with their mothers in single parenthood.[12] Three of those who entered stepfamilies in middle childhood eventually came to terms with the stepfather. For Caroline Herbert, hostility was quickly overcome through mutual understanding on both sides.

I can remember being jealous because he was taking some of my mum's attention. I don't think I disliked him for that; but there again, my mother was happy . . . I'm sure my nose must have been out of joint . . . but my mother did work hard to make sure that she wouldn't leave me out of anything. . . . I never had the feeling that I couldn't go along as well. They made me welcome.

The other mothers failed to take such care to reassure their daughters. Tracy Sims's stepfather had first arrived as a lodger: 'My mum gave me all the time, until he came along, and the love and affection. . . . I slept with her in a bed, and then he came along, and I didn't sleep with her in a bed. I did very much resent him in that way, because he took my mum. . . . It upset me because my mum and him were kissing and cuddling.' Tracy also resented him because he proved a very strict disciplinarian, although he 'never once laid a finger on me'. On the other hand, she too could see that 'he was the best thing that ever happened to my mum. . . . Without each other, it's like their left arms have been cut off.' And eventually she came to feel that he had been 'good to me, even though I hated him then'. She sums him up as 'a right bastard' but 'a brilliant father'. 'My stepfather was my father, and always will be. . . . He will be the one to walk me down the aisle.' Celia Newton was also clumsily confronted with the change. She had known her new stepfather from infancy, but 'to start with, I didn't like it at all. I didn't like him living there before he was married, and I didn't want them to get married.' And she was not helped when, immediately after the marriage, she was abruptly told, 'He is your father and you're to call him "dad"', and forced to change her name on her schoolbooks: 'that was something I really resented.' Nevertheless, time has healed her wounds too: he is now 'the only "dad" I speak of.'

Doreen Gower, however, stood firm. Although she can see her stepfather in retrospect as basically 'a nice person', she refused ever to accept this 'obnoxious . . . fuddy-duddy', continually running away to her grandmother. Her jealousy was explicitly sexual. 'I felt that we were all close together and I felt that a man was intruding on us and I didn't like the fact that me mum slept with him. That bothered me.' She was only 8 at the time, but interestingly, had felt this kind of fear for years: 'he used to take her out, but I never liked it. I thought he was spoiling things in a way. . . . I've been like that with me mum. I mean, we used to get on buses and all the conductors used to be after her because she was very good-looking, she was lovely. And I didn't like it. A man always had to spoil things in a way, I always felt.'

With older children there was also a danger of a hostile reaction from a sense of displacement, but in a different way. On the one hand, one of the attractions of the advent of a stepfather might be the lessening of the sense of responsibility brought by living with a lone parent: 'I didn't feel as responsible for me mum then.' But this shift could be a delicate matter. For Tom Rice it was handled with notable sensitivity: having a stepfather in the home 'gave me more time for myself, I didn't have to look after my mum so much. But I still had a lot of authority over my sister. . . . He didn't interrupt, no, he was good. . . . No, my nose weren't put out of joint.' When his mother was ill, morever, his stepfather helped by taking him on hospital visits. He sums him up as 'ever such a friendly bloke—like we took to him straight away, and I think he wanted the good for us'.

In some other families, by contrast, the transition was unhappy precisely because of this aspect. Joanna Austin, who had become much closer to her mother as a single parent than ever before, now found this intimate friendship lost: 'having taken us out of the "kids in their place" role . . . she almost tried to put us back into it. She's got an adult in her life now. That was part of the reason why I resented it. . . . But that was temporary. Things evened out after a bit.' Another difficult entry was due to the violently hostile reaction of an elder brother, who had taken over control of both discipline and finances in the family. This brother had already left home and married, but had kept his former role. The news of the change burst one evening when he called to see his mother, found her new friend and attacked him; 'I could hear our Bill saying, "I'll kill him" . . . There was a lot of noise downstairs and commotion. I was in bed.' This type of bad start is peculiar to the teenage entries, and it evidently left sore memories.

The second fundamental reason for the relatively easy acceptance of stepfathers lies in the gender differences of expectations which we explore in Chapter 6. Less was demanded of stepfathers than of stepmothers, and they were therefore less likely to impose on the child. Stepfathers seem to have been, and expected to be, marginal figures in the new stepfamily household. 'He was more there for workwise, and that was it, really. Never, never become close.' Although almost half were called 'dad', they were rarely expected to fulfil the role of a father except in the most limited ways. It was reasonable to be 'more like an uncle'; 'we never called him "dad" and he never expected that.' In some families, he was not even seen as a stepfather—and this again could be positive: 'I never thought really, "Oh, he's me stepfather". He was more of a friend.' They did not get emotionally close enough for the child to confide, but conveyed support in lesser ways: practical advice with school or work; a small loan or gift; 'making us bikes', or taking a child shopping, or 'showing an interest' by taking her out in his van, where he specially 'rigged up a seat'; or just being able to 'enjoy a laugh' together. Later on, they might help a teenager to find work. A man did not have to do much to be remembered as an 'extremely nice' stepfather. Indeed a complimentary description will often include words or phrases like 'quiet', 'very easy-going' or 'laid back', or 'a friendly bloke'.

In almost every case, the household routine was maintained in the mother's old style. No stepfather who came into the mother's house brought any sharp changes in daily routine: even where some adaptation was needed, there were 'just minor arguments over differing tastes'. But most seemed to have impinged remarkably little. The extreme instance was of one who would not only 'bend over backwards' to avoid everyday frictions, but even changed his own name to match that of the mother.

Significantly, in both instances where the stepfather insisted on imposing some of his own rules, he had remained in his own house—and he was disliked by the child. In one instance the issue was apparently trivial, a strict new bedtime: 'it was always for nine o'clock because the nine o'clock news used to be on and he waited—that was his time. He had to watch the nine o'clock news and we all had to be in bed—quiet.' Another was detested as not only rigid, but violent: 'As far as he was concerned, he was master in his own house, and that was it. It was *his* house . . . "In my house, you behave as I would have you behave."'

More often, particularly in teenage families when there were disagreements over the rules in the newly expanded household, the child's view was almost always taken seriously. Joanna Austin, for example, was able to put her stepfather in his place with apparent impunity: 'Although I liked him—not when he first moved in, but after a while when he was definitely permanent—I got so that, if he told me what to do, or asked me to do something, I didn't want him to speak to me, it used to make my flesh creep. "You—this is not your place." "I know", he used to say. I never argued with him, I used to argue with mum.' More rarely, there would be explicit negotiations. Two children, for example, found themselves in much larger households with step-siblings. One recalled 'the transition from being the four family unit, to the ten family unit, did all smooth over, within the space of about twelve months. . . . With there being eight of us children . . . we used to do the dishes once every eight weeks.' Another put it: 'There was a lot of give and take on both sides just to plan together, and I think the major thing said was, "Right, now we're a family."'

Equally crucially, all but two of these stepfathers initially avoided any role in disciplining the child. Typical comments are: 'he wasn't forceful'; 'he never really told us off'. In a few families the stepfather later on 'gradually' began to tell the child off for misbehaviour. In one exception when this went on to physical discipline, which even then 'was very infrequent', significantly the boy, who was already in trouble, was able to win outside sympathy through complaining of his stepfather: 'a bit of a *Sun* reporting job on it, I think. Something like that. Bit fabricated there.' It seems clear, in fact, that there was a widespread social expectation that stepfathers should not take on a disciplinary role.[13]

The extent to which in extreme instances such abstinence could be taken is illustrated by the Armstrong family. Here the daughter Becky found it 'one of the problems' that she was treated more leniently by her mother than her younger half-brother, on whom stricter table manners were imposed. 'I remember Sunday afternoons, he'd be made to sit with a cold Sunday dinner in front of him, and made to finish it; which, at the time, I used to feel was very unfair. I don't really think they got their act together. . . . I think they should have agreed a set of rules for the children, which they both adhered to, for all the children.' Both sets of families still remained as a family unit within the double family: 'There'd be rules for us. . . . It seemed like we were two families. If we went out on a Sunday, we had two cars; and there'd be myself, my two brothers and mum in one car, and [her stepfather and half-brother] in the other. . . . There wasn't much blending.'

The restriction of the stepfather's disciplinary role could sometimes be a source of tension in itself when he was of an authoritarian disposition. Alan Downs had an ex-naval stepfather:

He wanted the house to be run like a ship. . . . I was at the age where I wasn't just going to say 'Yes sir', 'No sir', and obviously, him being disciplined from the Navy, he expected there was to be a certain amount of discipline. I think there was a bit of clash between him and my mother, initially. . . . He didn't agree with a lot of things, but my mother would always tell him that I wasn't his responsibility. . . . I used to enjoy to wind him up.

Nevertheless, much more typical comments were in straightforward approval of stepfathers who assumed no disciplinary role: 'He never instilled any authority: I think basically he would leave that to me mother'; 'I think he was always careful because he wasn't our real father'; that was 'my mother's patch'; 'me mum always stresses that [her stepfathers] they've got nothing to do with us and they can't tell us what to do.' One son recalls a stepfather who 'has never told me off in 20 years of being married to my mum. My mum would say, "They're not your kids."'

In short, paradoxically, the stepfathers who were accepted and liked were those who remained at the margins of the household, bringing in additional income and companionship for the mother, doing small things for the child, but rarely becoming intimate, and leaving control of household order and discipline to the mother. Conversely, those who were disliked were almost always those who intruded most on the child's world.

It is no doubt this marginality which explains why feeling about stepfathers, positive or negative, rarely ran high. The worst of these were the three who were violent to the child. Yet even of them, only the abuser was not merely disliked, but hated, and is still today unforgiven. In this he is unique among all of our stepfathers, including the first group who came in early childhood. 'I absolutely hated him. . . . I just can't, can't forgive him.'

Stepmothers: Involvement, Demonization, and Disorder

Stepmothers, by contrast, with whom these children lived, almost all evoke strong feelings. They came into the heart of the household. In stepmother families we certainly find more of an attempt at 'blending', but more often than not it proved a painful process.

Stepmothers were almost all highly involved substitute parents, and there are, indeed, three families in which no difficulties are remembered. In each the stepmother is described as child-centred and affectionate: 'outgoing' and relatively 'easy-going'; 'very friendly, very outgoing, very conscientious'. Equally important, the advent of each was handled sensitively, and changes introduced gradually: 'nothing that you'd notice, subtle changes'.

More typically, the problems started at the beginning, to a considerable extent due to the incompetence of the fathers. Half of them proved either unable to explain what was happening, or gave misleading explanations. In one instance, the child was not even warned that the wedding was taking place: 'I came home from school one day, and suddenly saw a load of family out, the household, and was told there and then on the spot, "Oh, we just got married today."' It did not feel much better for a girl who, instead of being invited to the wedding, was 'left at home to clean up, and get everything ready'. Some fathers took more trouble, but even so, one deputed the explaining role to the future stepmother, while others handled it very crudely. One daughter was told by her father, '"If you don't like it, well she's going to be my wife, so you could go and live with grandma, it's up to you." And I thought, "I don't want to lose my dad as well, so I might as well get on with it."'

There were, on the other hand, as with the stepfathers, other factors to help entry into a stepfamily. Some of the future stepmothers were already familiar, for example as a housekeeper already living with them, or as a long-standing 'friend of the family'—'we were two families that were very close, and she was part of the other family. We all went to chapel together.' Some children could see that the remarriage was good for the father: he had recovered his sense of humour, and was 'a happier person'; 'I was quite pleased, because it cheered him up.' At least one daughter was relieved to have less responsibility for the housework—'it was easier for me in that way'—although in another family a teenage sister, who had become her lone father's housewife, was 'very bitter' precisely at this displacement. One boy was delighted to find his father much more at home: 'we were a family then'; while another puts it, 'different food . . . I started to play games again. . . . I thought it was great to be able to get back to a normal family again. You can—say you've got a full set of parents.'

Most crucially, much more was expected of a stepmother than of a stepfather.[14] She was not recognized as a real mother—few were called 'mum' by the child's choice—but she was evaluated as a mother, in some cases in direct comparison. 'She could never replace my mother.' Typically they are critically remembered as insufficiently affectionate, not inviting confiding: 'a hard person, cut and dried'; 'I never thought of her as a mother at all'—that is to say, as 'a mother' as distinct from 'my mother'. Stepmothers were expected to be emotional carers for already pained children. It was a challenging task in which less than one-third succeeded. At the same time, they had to be practical carers: for all of them took over responsibility for the domestic routine of the household. And most of them were also, again in contrast to the stepfathers, expected to play at least some disciplinary role.

There was only one of these families in which the father retained primary control of daily routine and order after his remarriage. He was another man who married his housekeeper; but he kept her in a subordinate role, with her few suggestions 'stamped on'. More typically these fathers left responsibility to the new wife, retaining at the most a back-up role in discipline.

As a result, normally with the arrival of the stepmother domestic routine changed markedly. 'It sort of went back. Very tidy. Had to make sure you washed properly. Table manners. Use a serviette. For just about all areas . . . once Jill was in the fold, discipline returned.' This often led to intense resentment by the child and dislike of the stepmother: especially those who were 'heavy-handed' in day-to-day discipline. For Nigel Griffiths this proved intolerable, partly because the discipline imposed was tough. To protect the newly tidy house, none of his friends were allowed to cross the threshold for fear they would 'mess it up'. 'It was very difficult really, because my stepmother was very strict, and unfortunately my father always took her side regardless.'

There was, moreover, never among these stepmother families a sense that the new rules and discipline could be disputed or even explicitly negotiated, such as we have seen in some of the stepfather families. It seems likely that this was because, while a mother could use her continuing authority to negotiate between a stepfather and the child, a father's aim was to transfer this authority, and he was thus likely to see his primary duty as support for the new authority of the stepmother. Children were thus not party to disagreements between the father and stepmother, and some couples deliberately chose to put on a united front:

My father and stepmother decided any decisions are going to be joint decisions. . . . I didn't like my stepmother. I didn't like somebody else telling me what to do . . . (but) and as I stayed there longer, Gwen would discipline me, which I hated. I hated being told off by someone else who wasn't actually my mother. I can remember saying to her, 'You're not my mother' . . . She would be hurt and my dad would be furious, he would be absolutely furious.

Gwen was, in fact, eventually one of the few successful step-mothers, and a positive life influence, particularly in her step-daughter's career.

At the worst, these stepmothers take on, at least in retrospect, a truly mythical malevolence. One girl was bitter at the way in which she had lost any chance of closeness to her father: 'she turned him against me. . . . He just used to say, "I can't be nice to you because she doesn't like it."' She still feels hatred for this stepmother, who 'had two kids of her own. They got everything, we got nowt. It was one of them cases. She was wicked. . . . She was horrible. Evil.' One boy used similar metaphors in portraying a 'wicked stepmother' who imposed new rules—'This is the time you'll go to bed'—which stopped him going out in the evenings, and had his beloved dog put down. Another portrayed his step-mother as a witch.

Most striking of all is Joy Carmichael's story of the stepmother whom she 'absolutely hated'. She again was 'very heavyhanded'. 'She used to really hit us, and if they were having an argument, he used to have to lock us in our bedroom so she couldn't get at us. . . . She really used to whack us, mainly round the head. . . . They were normally arguing about something I'd said.' The stepmother tried to avoid these arguments by keeping her 'at arms length from my dad. . . . My stepmum would never let us really have anything to do with him. Because we'd have eaten by the time he came home and we weren't allowed to sit at the table. The only time we ever ate together was Sundays.' Nevertheless she insisted that the father should buy the girl's clothes, even sanitary towels, 'because she wouldn't do it'. She would buy no new clothes; all came from jumble sales. 'We had to do all our own washing by hand.' And she treated the stepdaughters 'like unpaid servants. . . . We used to have to clean the house from top to bottom, and she'd go round and check everything.' Eventually when the girl was 'going through a very honest patch', she decided to try to put their relationship on a straight footing.

We were sitting at the tea table and she was between me and the door. And I said to her this is etched on my brain—I said, 'Mum, I hope you don't mind me saying this'—because we had to call her 'mum', which was something else that I hated. . . . I said, 'Mum, I hope you don't mind my saying this, but I don't like you very much.' And she stood up and threw a chair at me—it just missed me . . . as I legged it out of the kitchen . . . and locked myself in our playroom . . . But I really did think she ought to know.

No doubt she did know that her stepdaughter hated her; and was only too glad when finally, after five years, the girl went to live with her mother and stepfather.

It is not only troublesome stepmothers who appear in these recollections. There is also a difficult stepgrandmother and an 'evil' grandmother. It is clear that not only was there a far higher level of parenting demanded of women, but there was also a far more devastating condemnation of those who fell short of it. There are much less caring, much more violent men in these recollections, but they are not mythologized in an equivalent style: indeed, as we have seen they might even be to an extent admired. Perhaps it required the more recent unearthing of sexual abuse to create an equally powerful image of the truly evil male parent, whether father, grandfather, or stepfather. For this generation, it seems that the ultimate offence by a parent, the unnatural betrayal, the primeval sin, was a woman's failure in the caring that for her should have been natural.

The myth of the wicked stepmother certainly did not impose itself on every stepmother family experience. On the contrary, there were many memories of a completely different character. But the myth did offer a cultural stereotype which made the task of a woman in mothering stepchildren potentially more difficult. It must have made the task in itself more daunting to some women. And for children already vulnerable to pain and resentment, the stepmother also offered a ready frame for hostile interpretation, which smothered subtler attempts to understand what was going wrong by offering an easy target for all the blame.[15]

The intensity of hostility in the most unsuccessful stepmother families could lead not only to demonization but also to disintegration in disorder. Especially when there were teenage boys in the household, it could prove impossible for a hated stepmother at its hub to hold down the explosive anger which she generated. Albert Black found his stepmother 'domineering, catty'. Because 'her two kids could do no wrong', she was always 'walloping' him and his brother. His father would sometimes 'try to be the peacemaker', sometimes 'ignore [the dispute] as a fly on the wall;

callous. Sometimes pull his hair out. Or he'd go on a binge.' So this allowed the two brothers to fight back 'hammer and tongs'. Albert has 'very sordid memories of violence' between himself and this woman whom he regards as 'a bastard witch'.

Such violence with teenage boys could be an expression not so much of dislike for the stepmother, but more of their pain and shock at both the degree and the sheer suddenness with which their world was once again convulsed. For Brian Carter and his two brothers, for example, within a year life had been transformed in rapid succession by the sudden and unexpected death of their mother, the emotional collapse of their father and the responsibility that this brought to Brian as the eldest boy, and now the announcement that their father was to remarry. The new wife was 'all right', a 'sensible down-to-earth' woman, and although she took over the house did not attempt to impose discipline on her stepsons. However, she brought with her two stepsiblings whom she 'favoured'. All the children now had to squeeze into a three-bedroomed house, and the three brothers were forced back into a single room. All three quickly went wild; there were triangular arguments and fighting in which the incomers 'started getting a bit violent towards my dad'; and within months all three boys left—two to become seriously delinquent—leaving the step-mother and her two children in peace in the old home.

We can end with another well-intentioned stepmother who also failed against the odds to create a new order in her stepfamily: the Gordons. It is a family which broke into fragments in the face of a convergence of characteristically painful difficulties in entering a stepfamily: deep-rooted problems in communication, at a time of double difficulty, when unexpected and unwelcome changes in everyday order were being introduced, just at the moment when disciplinary responsibilities between the new parental couple were not yet clear.

Jim Gordon's ex-policeman father had slumped on becoming a widower, and the positive impact for him of finding a new wife was obvious to the children. Suddenly it was 'magic'; 'everything was, as you can imagine, lots of smiles, and fun and laughter.' Again, the fundamental difficulty was not so much the nature of the new wife, who was both a better carer—she could cook 'fantastic meals'—and easier to talk to than his own mother, and is remembered as 'my other mum'. Without doubt the children's real problems went back much further, to the experience of their mother's mental illness and suicide, and their father's subsequent suffering, none of which they were able to talk about. And to all this was now added, again without any chance for discussion, a complete change in their style of life.

Nor could the introduction of the new mother have taken them more by surprise. They knew she was coming, but they did not know who she was. Consequently they did not realize that they had already met her as a stern tram supervisor, who would quell their larking about on the tram after school with the other 'lads', where when she was not there they would be fighting at the tram stop, and once in, scribble on the tram with felt-tip pens, damage the seats, and abuse the Pakistani driver. The wedding itself was 'a very quiet set-up' without the children: so the shock came afterwards. 'And then, lo and behold, there she rolled up, and then she's our new mother from then on. . . . Luckily she didn't recognize me, which was absolutely brilliant news.' But in any case, 'we had no choice. Me dad always said, "I want you to call her 'mum', because to make her feel welcome in the house. Because she's your mother, as from now on she is."'

It is now easier to see the good things in her coming. 'Looking back, I can see a great benefit.' The meals improved 'like luxury' and Jim now feels he learnt 'a hell of a lot' from her: 'she was trying to teach us how to behave properly, and how to speak properly, and have manners, etc., etc. But we couldn't see what benefit.' But very soon she was also trying to impose her new rules. This was when the real trouble began:

Then she started getting strict with us then. She started doing things that we all had never, never done. Things like, sitting at table to eat meals—and we'd never done that. . . . So we thought, 'This is not on', and then she'd say, 'don't put your knife in your mouth', and 'Don't talk', and 'Close your mouth when you're eating'. And this was causing a real lot of hassle. And the telly had to be off, completely, we couldn't watch the telly. . . . And then she used to say, 'I want you in the house by ten o'clock' or nine o'clock which we'd never had before, oh it was crazy . . .

So we started rebelling, because we were telling her where to go, saying, 'You're not our mother, you're not telling us what to do', etc., etc., so she used to say, 'Well, go up to bed,' and we used to say, 'We're not going. . . . You're not our mother and that's it.'

So she used to then wait for me dad to come home and then she'd play hell with me dad, 'They're not my kids and why should I look after your kids, why should I give up what I've given up? They're your kids.' And then me dad used to play hell with us. And then on many occasions me mum used to walk out of the house. Just say, 'Right, I'm leaving.' And she used to leave. . . . It were a case of me mum giving him an ultimatum, saying, 'Either he goes, or I go!' And unfortunately on a lot of occasions we had to go.

The changes were made more disturbing because the step-mother, believing—mistakenly, it turned out—that because of his age, the youngest boy would be the easiest to mould to her attitudes, tried to prevent the three brothers from playing together. 'She wouldn't have him associating with us, she used to tell him to keep away from us. She'd say, "The damage is done with them, I can't do aught with them, but I can do something with you. So keep out of their way."' And lastly, she turned both their official moral system and the house upside down. In the past, they had been regular church-attending Catholics. 'There were no two ways about it, we could not miss Sunday church. . . . Me dad always made sure we wore spotless suits, we had our suits on, and always had to have a bath before we went to church, and best clothes on, and all troop down to church.' Churchgoing was now suddenly discouraged. She gave them 'a lecture on Jesus, and how he doesn't exist'. And she turned the house out in the same cause. 'She was completely against religion. She hated religion. So all the crucifixes had to come down, and all the stuff were thrown out.'

All these momentous changes happened within a year of the boy's mother dying. He even moved schools in the same year. And all this was imposed on top of the earlier unexpressed grief, without discussion. 'It was like a different life. Before, when me real mum was alive, and I was at junior school, that was like one life, to me, and when me mum died, and we moved, and we got to. . . . We got to a new mum and a different school: then life was completely different. Like a different life, all over again.' And cumulatively, it was too much for the children: within three years the boy, now sixteen, had left home, along with his two brothers, and his sister was pregnant. 'It was a nightmare, it was: because me mum—I mean, there were this different woman. And as far as we were concerned, we didn't ask me dad to marry her!'

4

Absent Parents?
Parents Who Lived Apart or Died

WE have so far focused on the child's immediate everyday world as it was reshaped into single-parent and then stepfamily life. But over each of those everyday worlds there remained, whether accepted, or felt as an acute pain, or ignored, a shadow. For every one of these fifty adults who had grown up in stepfamilies shared the experience of the loss or absence of one of their two biological parents through some, or all of their childhood. The breaking of a parental partnership whether by death, separation, or divorce inevitably leads to the partial loss of a potential parental resource, and a threat to the acquisition of a secure identity for the developing child. What were the factors that either mitigated or maximized the effects of such a critical loss?

First, let us briefly challenge the notion of the 'absent' parent in families created by divorce—hence the question mark in the title of this chapter. The term 'absent' parent has increasingly come into use in recent years, and has been encapsulated in legislation in the Child Support Act (1991). The complex reality experienced by our twenty-nine children, of whom twenty-five had parents who had separated, and four others parents who had never lived together, is distorted by describing all of these parents as 'absent'. In fact, among the twenty-nine there were only thirteen of whom one parent might accurately be described as 'absent'. The remaining sixteen had varying degrees of contact with the out-of-house parent at different stages, from earlier childhood into their teenage years, and subsequently in their own adult lives, including three girls who lived first with one parent and then with the other during childhood.

Psychological Importance of the 'Absent' Parent in the 'Death' and 'Separated' Groups

For those twenty-one children who suffered the loss of a parent through death, on the other hand, the pattern of the psychological impact, both immediately and subsequently, was quite different than for those who lost contact through separation. No dead parent was remembered negatively. However, among those who were aged 6 or under at the time of the parental death, five fathers and one mother were not remembered at all.

Only Doreen Gower, the second of three daughters, expressed some ambivalence about her dead parent: her mother had told her that her father had wanted a boy rather than three girls. All the other dead parents (including the parents of seven children in the youngest age group) are spoken of positively. For Chloe Pargeter, an adopted child, whose father had died when she was only 6, he was 'a strong influence'. Among those who became stepchildren between 7 and 11, Sid Western, whose mother had died when he was 11, reflects, 'she gave me a very good, a very good start in life bringing me up properly. . . . She always insisted that I went to church, Sunday school, fairness, honesty, all that sort of thing.' Rosa Daniels, 10 when her mother died, continued to identify with her mother, describing her as 'just like me . . . just a double, double of me, yeh'. As we shall see, she became deeply depressed when she reached the same age as her mother had been when she had died. Among those who were oldest when becoming stepchildren, Jamsie Noble, whose mother had died after a long illness, thought that it was his mother's attitude to life, expressed through her commitment to 'charity work', that had influenced him to become the helpful sort of person which he considered himself to be. For Harry Bolsover, his father's sudden death when he was 12 came as a terrible shock, and his powerful reaction to this dominated his teenage years. He went to live with his paternal grandmother, rejecting his own mother; and his oppositional behaviour at school and truanting led inevitably to a lack of educational progress. Subsequently, through marriage as a young man he found another crucial emotional support, but Harry still consciously continues both to model himself on his father, and to idealize him.

Let us now look at the twenty-nine children whose parents had separated. Among the thirteen who had no further contact, or virtually no further contact, with the separated parent, there were only four whose life stories reflected no discernible influence of the absence of one parent on their life course or self-perception. Of these four, all were infants at the time of separation: two girls who had known themselves to be illegitimate[1] from an early age, but who nevertheless continued to regard their stepfathers as fathers; a boy whose father had won custody of him when he was 3, and whose mother was never spoken of during his child-hood; and another boy whose father had left soon after his birth, and whose mother and her family were the dominating influence in his life. He says, 'I wouldn't even know what he looks like, or obviously his parents', and he is emphatic that he has never had any urge to find out more about his father.

Of the remaining nine in the separated group who had no further contact with the 'absent' parent, in their life stories five expressed a strongly negative psychological influence of the absent parent, and three ambivalence; while a positive attitude was expressed by only one, who as a girl had been encouraged by her mother to think well of her father from as early as she could remember.

The psychological importance of the sixteen separated parents in our study who did remain in contact with their children shows a mixed pattern, with no simple relationship to the developmental stage of the child at the time of separation, or gender of child and parent. It may be that the opportunities for forming attachments to either, or both parents, were crucial in this regard, but the limitations of our material, and the lack of reliable measures of attachment status for older children,[2] let alone retrospectively, means that this must remain speculative. Overall, there were nine cases, three in each of the age groups (entry to stepfamilies at 6 and under, 7 to 11, and 12 to 16) where the psychological importance of the 'absent' parent appears to have been in some sense strong.

These nine include the three women, one from each age group, who lived first with one parent, and then the other, and who continued to have deep, but split, loyalties towards each of their parents. Of the others, in the youngest age group there are also two other cases where the psychological influence of the absent father did not reveal itself until early adulthood, when it was remembered as beginning to assume more importance. Bee Potter perceived her father as having humiliated her (and also her mother) early in life and was determined to get her own back on him; and—as we shall see—David Evans gradually came to a more negative view of his often drunken father. In the 7 to 11 age group two men were ambivalent, in one case towards a frightening father, and in the other towards a mother who had left home; whereas Tracy Sims's memories of violence resulted in a negative image of her absent father. In the 12 to 16 group there were only two other cases, one man and one woman. For both, their fathers remained of great psychological significance, as they had been in earlier childhood.

Memories from Childhood

How far did these childhood memories reflect age and sex at the time of loss in relation to separation, or death of a parent?

In thinking about the information we can glean from the life stories, we need to bear in mind that it is rare for connected memories to remain from before the age of 7. Remembering is dependent on a child's age and stage of development.[3] Jack Finlay, whose father died when he was 2, seems to be trying to understand this, when he says, apologetically, that he can't remember anything before the age of 4. He reflects, 'I suppose you've got to know somebody a bit, anyway, before you can really think about them.' However, there is also considerable variation between individuals in respect of how far memory stretches back, and in detail of recall.

Among those who did retain early memories of a lost parent, for some, diffuse, impressionistic images remained associated with either negative or positive emotion. Tracy Sims, just 7 when her parents split up, recalls her father's violence towards her mother and her brothers; Chloe Pargeter, whose father was ill for three years before he died when she was 6, tells of the enjoyment she and her siblings had in bouncing on his bed during those years. For just a few, even some who had been very young infants at the time, there are vivid, fragmentary memories of traumatic events.[4] Details of violence might remain etched on the memory—Richard

Hammond, only 1 year old at the time, had two such flashes of recollection: the first of watching his father in the mirror while he shaved before drunkenly falling down the stairs; and the second of his father attempting 'to strangle me mum. . . . Me mum was on the settee and he was on top of me mum strangling her, trying to kill her, and then loads of police came.' He goes on to say of his father, 'If he had come back in the past ten years, I would have beat him up really, for all the times he beat my mum up.'

Some of those in the 7 to 11 age group, and a few of the young teenagers, speak of their memory as 'blocked'. These men and women have the sense that they ought to be able to remember but they cannot. They attribute their lack of memory to the failure of the adults around them to explain what was happening at the time, or subsequently, and the painfulness of their own emotions which may have caused them to suppress any memory they had. Sometimes the active hostility of a caretaking parent to the separated partner seems to have been responsible for the other parent not being talked about, and for no explanation being given to the child; while for those whose parents died, the distress of the adults around might be so great that the child was warned off the subject, sensing that it would be 'dangerous' to ask questions. As time passed, and new partners joined the family, children often avoided mentioning the lost parent for fear of giving offence to the incomer. This was so for Gary Butler, 7 at the time of his mother's death, who conjures up a picture of a secure and happy early childhood, surrounded by female members of his father's family, and later a happy family life with his young stepmother, who he immediately called 'mum' when she joined the family. Following his mother's death, she was not spoken of again. When his mother's family moved soon after her death to another part of the country, his father's family lost touch with them. It was not until many years later, at the time of his sister's marriage, when his sister's wedding bouquet was sent to the Garden of Remembrance, that Gary realized that his mother had been cremated. The experience of being interviewed drew his attention to how little he knew about his own mother, and made him determined to find out more. He realized that not only had he 'blocked' the memories of his mother's death but that he had always avoided referring to her for fear of 'upsetting' his father or 'offending' his stepmother.

Quite commonly, there were no direct memories at all to draw on. The image of the lost parent might be constructed from repeatedly looking at old photographs, talking to the surviving parent and those relatives who were willing to do so, and occasionally viewing and reviewing old holiday videos. For Carol Stevenson, 7 when her mother died, her mother's memory was 'kept alive' by talking to her maternal grandmother, looking at old photographs, and much later on, to her father, when he became able, and willing, to do so. For her, and for some others, the reconstructed memory merged with what was remembered, and became indistinguishable from it.

Some gender differences in the interviewees expectations of the likelihood of remembering were apparent. Thus Tony Dickson, whose father had died when he was 9, is emphatic that he could not be expected to have had a view about his father's death at that age. By contrast, Eileen Moriarty seems to blame herself for her lack of memory of her mother, who left the family home suddenly when Eileen was only 7, and was never spoken of there again. Crying with the surviving parent, or crying alone, was mentioned no less frequently by men than by women, although the accounts of crying by women tend to be more specific, referring to the duration, or the particular circumstances. For example, Jean Wheeler, whose father left home when she was 13, describes crying herself to sleep for two weeks after he had gone; and Joy Carmichael describes how her continued and prolonged crying at night at the age of 12 eventually persuaded her father, who had been granted custody after a court battle many years previously, to allow her to go with her younger sister to live with her mother and stepfather which was what the two girls had 'always' wanted.

When Parents Died

At the time of the early childhoods of these twenty-one step-children, death had become a subject not to be spoken of,[5] and from which children in particular needed to be protected. There was during that period no popular conception of the need to mourn,[6] much less the need of children to reach an understanding, and to come to terms with their grief in accordance with their developmental age. We find that the children in our study were almost all deliberately excluded at the time of parental death, and were often sent away till after the funeral. Some surviving parents went to considerable lengths to ensure that their children knew nothing of the funeral. One mother was careful to arrange that the funeral procession would not pass the school playground at a time when she knew that her sons, aged 9 and 7, would be out playing.

The word 'taboo' echoes through the interviews, not only in relation to parental death itself, but also to its aftermath. As one woman, the youngest of three children, 6 at the time of her father's death says, 'Nothing was left of him, really, in the house'—there were no photographs at all: it was 'a taboo subject, really, yes!' A man, 12 at the time of his mother's death after a chronic illness which took her 'in and out of hospital all the time I knew her', said, 'It's always been a great taboo, like.' He thinks that his father subsequently idealized his mother, doubting that he had ever been able to come to a realistic understanding of what sort of person she had been, mainly as a result of his father's attitude. Commonly, dead parents were not spoken of to children again. Fathers, especially, tended to try to keep their grief to themselves, never broaching the subject of a mother's death with the children: 'just scattered the ashes', says Jamsie Noble, 13 years old when his mother died, going on to describe his childhood as seeming 'to kind of been blocked out'.

Children who were left without a coping adult in the aftermath of parental death were especially vulnerable. Brian Carter, whose previously caring and affectionate father 'didn't cope at all well, and was upset all the time', found himself at the age of 14 with the responsibility of caring for himself, and two younger brothers. He remembers taking charge of 'getting them [his brothers] off to school'. Brian's own reaction to his mother's death was profound—he had been able to confide in her 'about anything', but now found that he 'bottled up' his emotions. He 'lost all interest in school', and turned for comfort to numerous sexual relationships, as well as continuing his sporting activities—a link with his mother who had been 'a great sportswoman'. During his later teens, Brian started to drink heavily, and to take drugs. He was 'in and out of prison' until he was 25, but two years later he found a supportive relationship, married and 'settled down'. Brian also refers to the 'delayed effects' of their mother's death on his younger brother, 11 at the time that she died: 'he found it difficult when he got to the age of 20 . . . that's when it started affecting him'. This brother also turned to drugs, and 'tried killing himself once, but now he's all right'.

Rosa Daniels, 10 when her chronically ill mother died unexpectedly from a heart attack, also found herself left to fend not only for herself, but also for a younger brother, by a father who could not cope, and who turned to drink. Things were made even worse for her when her father remarried a woman who ill-treated both her and her brother, and who tried to turn her father against her. 'He [her father] just used to say, I can't be nice to you because she doesn't like it.' Rosa remembers her unhappiness at school, where she kept fainting. She thought constantly of her mother, and continued to do so, even after she herself was happily married. When she reached the same age as her mother had been at the time of her death, she became deeply depressed, preoccupied with the certainty that she, too, was going to die prematurely, and so to abandon her own young child, as her mother had abandoned her. She could not bring herself to share her fears with her generally supportive husband, nor even to tell her doctor, though she went to see him because she felt so ill: 'I was in a right state for twelve months, you know, and I couldn't come to terms with it . . . once I got to 29, I felt relieved, you know—Oh I've done it! I've lived.'

Loss of interest in school is mentioned by both men and women as a consequence of parental death: a reflection of their childhood shock and grief, sometimes exacerbated by the lack of understanding they suffered from the adults around them. Harry Bolsover, who at the age of 12 was deeply shocked by the sudden death of the father to whom he was devoted, remembers losing interest in school, constantly getting into fights, and truanting, so that he only just avoided being formally expelled. For three young children, their suffering was compounded by being sent to boarding schools, where they were treated harshly. Sandra Carstairs, only 5 at the time, was sent to boarding school 'immediately' after her mother's death, giving her no opportunity to reach an understanding of what had happened, and depriving her of the help of her sympathetic father, or other relatives. She remembers that a doll with clothes made for her by her mother was taken away. Camilla Jefferson, also 5 when she was sent away to boarding school by her educationally ambitious newly-widowed mother, thought that this had prevented her from reaching an understanding of her father's death from leukaemia. Celia Newton, whose father had died in her infancy, describes a boarding school where no personal possessions were allowed at all, and where she was made to change the name on all her books to that of her stepfather, adding to her sense of loss of identity, and fuelling the resentment she felt against her stepfather for 'replacing' her own father.

The pervasive secrecy surrounding the death of a parent could especially lead to bewilderment among the younger children. Thus Carol Stevenson, 7 at the time of her mother's death at home, says 'I didn't understand what was going on. To me, it was downstairs, and it didn't mean anything to me.' She was one of those sent away until after the funeral. Stephanie Rogers, 8 at the time of her much-loved father's death from tuberculosis, says, 'It was all hidden from me. I wasn't told.' Stephanie's mother was herself so upset that she could not bring herself to tell her daughter that her father had died, even later, so that Stephanie was eventually told by a neighbour, 'Your daddy's gone to heaven.' Whereupon Stephanie asked, 'When will he be back?'—only to be told, 'Oh, you'll see him on Monday.'

The consequence of this elaborate evasion for Stephanie seems to have been long-standing. She says: 'And I—well, at 8, you don't understand; I didn't, and I just said, 'Oh, all right'—end of that . . . I think it was later on in me teens, I wanted an answer then, 'Why?' . . . You don't get an answer. Even now, to this day, I'm very bitter about my father dying. Very bitter. No one can answer you why, but I want to know why, you know. It's I want to know why.'

Chloe Pargeter, an adopted child who was 6 when her father died, had known that he was ill, and that he would die, for as long as she could remember. Nevertheless his death was not discussed before or after, and she and her 9-year-old brother were sent away until after the funeral. She remembers that her reaction at the time was to be 'quite nasty', so that she was given medicine 'to calm me down'. As she talked about her father's death in the interview, Chloe became increasingly distressed, and had to leave the room. When asked towards the end of her story what she remembered as the 'worst thing' in her life, Chloe Pargeter unhesitatingly refers to her father's death, which she links with the death of her husband's mother, soon after her marriage.

For some of the youngest children, life went on much as before when a father, rather than a mother, died. For others there were changes in their living arrangements which affected them greatly, and for some—such as Stephanie Rogers—an acute consciousness of the absence of especially loved fathers. The death of mothers for children of any age was always likely to bring profound changes in their children's lives, because the central, nurturing role of mothers, even those who had been chronically ill for some time, was inevitably crucial.

Overall, the often deliberate lack of communication with children who suffered the death of a parent left its mark, in that few were able to mourn their dead parent effectively, and some were left with a sense of incompleteness. A yearning wistfulness pervades many of the interviews, particularly interviews with women speaking about their dead mothers. Carol Stevenson, whose mother died when she was 7, was conscious of continuing to miss her. She says she felt this especially keenly after her marriage, wishing that her mother had been there to teach her 'things like how to hang the washing on the line. . . . I'd never had anybody to show me how to do things'; but most of all as a young mother herself, when she had her first baby. Avoidance of explanations to children at the time of death, and subsequently, meant that there was little chance for them to successfully internalize their dead parent, a circumstance which may have left some of them especially vulnerable to future losses in their lives.

While the loss of a parent in childhood is, of course, always a devastating event for the family, it does seem likely that it was handled in an unusually unfortunate way in this period, which while intended to shield vulnerable children in fact exacerbated their distress. Our present evidence can be contrasted with an earlier study made by one of us, based on life story interviews with a nationally representative sample of adult children who had grown up in stepfamilies at the turn of the century,[7] which demonstrates both continuities and differences in reactions to parental death in childhood for stepchildren. Parental death was then, as now, an event of profound significance which, depending partly on the child's age at the time, altered their consciousness and experience of the world. The effects could be buffered by the strengths of the surviving parent and other available adults, but almost always parental death was a grave misfortune which, however well compensated by subsequent life events, led to an enduring sense of loss. But, in contrast to the situation in the early 1960s and 1970s, at the turn of the century death of people of all ages was still so common that a much more matter-of-fact attitude to it prevailed. Children were still then, as in Victorian times, encouraged to think about death, and even to be ready for it to strike at any time. Such attitudes are well expressed in the earlier interviews, together with a greater tendency to idealize a dead parent, especially mothers. Looking back at the death of their mothers in childhood, these adults born at the turn of the twentieth century express the prevailing ideology of motherhood through the imagery which they use: for example mothers are remembered as scrubbing everything 'as white as snow', with 'gleaming hair', and 'always baking'. Fathers, too, tended to be idealized more frequently than in our present sample, though the imagery was on the whole less extravagant than for the mothers. With our present stepchildren, on the other hand, their continued sense of loss, rather than idealization, is most striking, and almost certainly connected with the newly developed lack of opportunity for children to mourn a parent at the time of death, in contrast to the experience of earlier generations—and also, but less markedly, to the practices of the present day.

Today the comparative rarity of parental death in childhood may lead to an embarrassed, or insensitive response towards children by adults. Death is still too often a subject thought to be best avoided for fear of upsetting anyone. As contemporary studies have shown, the result for children of such attitudes may be an increase and prolongation of suffering, which may be manifested in childhood depression, or other symptomatic behaviour.[8]

Contact Following Separation

We know that nationally during the period under consideration, a majority of non-custodial fathers lost contact with their children within two years of divorce,[9] so that far more fathers lost contact at that time than now. How far this loss of contact resulted from the prevailing social and legal ethos, and how much might be attributed to financial and/or emotional constraints, is no longer possible to determine. At that time in the overwhelming majority of cases (over 90 per cent) arrangements between couples concerning children and finances were settled between them before going to court (a step in the divorce process which was then still compulsory). Courts favoured both 'care and control' (residence and on-going care), and 'custody' (responsibility for all major decisions in a child's life, especially in relation to education, religion, and financial matters) going to one parent; and in the case of younger children, this was almost always the mother. 'Reasonable access' was normally granted to the father. Courts were generally reluctant to define access more closely, except when very unusual circumstances were thought to warrant it. The result of these arrangements, given that the small minority of parents who were already in serious dispute were those who applied to the court for a decision, was that fathers tended to be pushed out of their children's lives by mothers who wished to have nothing more to do with their ex-partner. The notion of the 'clean break' was expounded by Lord Scarman in his interpretation of section 23(1) of the Matrimonial Causes Act 1973: 'An object of the modern law was to encourage each [spouse] to put the past behind them and begin a new life which was not overshadowed by the relationship which had broken down.'[10] The 'clean break' became a widely accepted cliché. Arthur Fisher, the younger of two boys, whose father left home when he was 9—and had no further contact with his children—uses the concept of the 'clean break' in his account. He says: 'he obviously didn't want to know us, otherwise he'd have tried to keep in touch a bit more—even sent a birthday card—but he, he never bothered. I suppose he wanted a clean break. I don't know.'

In our group of twenty-nine, as already mentioned, thirteen had no further contact with the separated parent; only two of the remaining sixteen had regular weekly contact with fathers who had left, both girls. One father continued to come for Sunday dinner for several years, until he married for a second time when his daughter was in her teens. After this there was much less contact, but he still remained close to her—his favourite and eldest child. Finally all contact was lost when he married for a third time, and emigrated. Another father who had left home soon after his daughter's birth, visited weekly with maintenance money from

when she was 4 years old. But for the remaining fourteen, contact
was irregular, and varied both over time, and in its significance for
the children concerned.

Taking the whole group of 'absent' parents in contact, most
were seen very irregularly, but six fathers—and also two non-
custodial mothers—were all seen at least monthly. For all these
children the absent parent therefore remained a real person,
neither idealized (like some of those who had died) nor demon-
ized (like a few of those who had left): a three-dimensional figure
who could be re-evaluated. Paradoxically, given how reluctant
some of the mothers must have felt in allowing the continuation
of contact, in most cases the fathers lost estimation with this
process. Perhaps this was partly because they were less able to
provide the intimacy which the child of a single parent had come
to expect. Certainly they are typically portrayed as difficult to talk
to, at best, 'avuncular', offering 'treats', but irresponsible, at worst
deceitful, 'flashy', and violent when drunk. One boy remembers
how his previously violent father would now give him big presents: 'he used to try to out-buy her—to make her present look
small compared to his big present. But there was never any real
feeling in it. . . . For probably a couple of years, I was fooled by
that. But, as you get older, you grow wiser to that.'

For those divorcing in the 1960s and 1970s, there was little
guidance either popular, professional, or judicial on how to do it
'successfully', in terms of the likely emotional impact on those
involved, the most desirable arrangements for children at different
ages, or even what financial arrangements might be appropriate.
Divorce was still largely a private and rather shameful matter, not
to be spoken about more than absolutely necessary. The idea that
arguing in front of the children was to be avoided as far as
possible, was widely acknowledged, but tended to be extended
to withholding essential information from the children, and to
being unaware of the possibility of children's anxieties and concerns. As far as 'absent' parents were concerned, there were no
models of how best to keep a continued relationship with their
children, though certainly some fathers, acting on the 'clean
break' principle, believed that their children would be better off
without them, especially when a substitute (stepfather) had moved
in. There were thus some fathers who were perceived as relin-
quishing the struggle to keep contact with their children, believing

this to be in their children's interests—though often greatly at their own emotional expense: while others were perceived as opting out because they could not themselves tolerate repeated experience of renewed loss, and intense emotional pain, which brief access visits with their children brought.

Less information is available about the pattern of post-divorce contact with separated mothers than with fathers, but it seems that the rupture was even more likely to be complete in the immediate aftermath of separation for mothers than for fathers, though the likelihood of re-establishing contact in later years may have been greater than for separated fathers. Among our subjects, three out of six children who had lost contact with their mothers at the time of separation, eventually had regular contact as adults. By contrast the pattern of no contact with fathers, once established, did not change; moreover contact with fathers generally tended to diminish over time, especially, in our group, after remarriage of either parent.

The younger the age of children at the time of separation, the less likely was contact to be maintained, though there were some notable exceptions. Lily Beck, the younger of two children, a boy and a girl, whose father left home soon after her birth, remembers her father coming with a doll on her fourth birthday, and subsequently his visiting weekly after school, bringing maintenance money to be given to her mother, and ten pence for herself, an arrangement promoted by her maternal grandmother with whom she lived with her mother and brother. Her relationship with her father proved to be some compensation for her poor relationships with her mother and stepfather. She takes on herself the 'blame' for the breakdown of her parent's marriage, simply because she was born a girl rather than a boy. She says, 'I've always blamed myself, because my father left fairly soon after I was born . . . I'm very proud of my dad. . . . As far as I'm concerned, he's up on a pedestal.'

Other Factors Influencing Contact with the 'Absent' Parent

We can identify six other key factors which strongly influenced the nature and degree of contact with separated parents, and the changing pattern over time. These are, first, continuing hostility between parents; secondly, the remarriage of either partner, which could occasionally help to resolve remaining conflict, but was more likely to lead to distancing of ex-partners, and a waning of contact; thirdly, the degree of commitment of the separated parent to the child or children, and whether a particular child was favoured by that parent; fourthly, the motivation of a child to seek or renew contact, or to maintain it if it was already established, a factor which became of increasing importance as the child grew older; fifthly, geographical proximity or otherwise, which might itself reflect the nature of the relationship between ex-partners; and last, but perhaps most crucial of all, the attitude and reactions of the caretaking parent, both at the time of the break, and subsequently.

Continuing hostility between parents most often led to an absence of contact, or a rapid diminishing over time. It is not clear from our material how many children were consciously protected by their parents from being drawn into the marital conflict. It seems that mothers quite often kept silent about the marriage, and the reasons for its breakdown, perhaps hoping to avoid the potential harm to children of speaking against their fathers. But this is not always remembered in retrospect as a positive feature of a child's upbringing. It was sometimes many years before children in this situation could reach a more balanced understanding of how events had unfolded, in the meantime attributing 'blame' to the mother, which they later came to regret. David Evans, whose parents separated when he was 3, and whose mother never criticized his father, regarded his father as 'good fun' in his early childhood, only gradually coming to realize that his father 'had a drink problem'. After his father's first remarriage, David no longer wanted to see him so much, especially after he started to turn up, sometimes at night 'to cause trouble', threatening to fight his stepfather. But David goes on to explain that once his father had met his third wife, he and his brother, by then teenagers, were quite pleased to be taken out by their father now and again. However, when asked at the time of interview who he considered to be part of his family now, he no longer included his father.

All three women who had lived first with one parent, and then with the other, continued to be caught up in the ongoing conflict between the parents. Lorna Maclean, an only child, whose parents first parted when she was 11, then briefly reunited when she was

12, only to split up again, remembers each of them trying to 'draw me in' on their side. She continued to feel 'torn' between them. When she left her father, with his permission, to go and live with her mother, he cried, which made her feel guilty. He refused to divorce her mother, who wanted to remarry. Her mother insisted that she went on long journeys with her 'to literally spy on my father, and I had to tag along; I had to literally sit outside his house at night'. Later in her childhood, after both parents had remarried, she resumed contact with her father, but wished she could have seen more of him. As an adult, she remains emotionally preoccupied with her father, despite her own happy marriage, and her close involvement with her husband, and her own two children. She is burdened by the thought that her stepmother's grandchildren from her first marriage know her father as 'granddad' whilst her children, 'his own natural grandchildren' don't even know where he lives. She tells of her delight when her children show that they know something of her father's relationship to her, when they come running to her when they answer the phone saying, 'It's your dad'. The distress which the relationship continues to provoke for her has prompted her husband to ask her, 'Why don't you finish with it?', but she tells him she cannot.

Joy Carmichael, another woman who had lived with both parents during the course of her childhood, was only 3 at the time of the original separation. Her parents remained hostile to each other but she has continued to feel deeply for them both. She recalls memories of monthly weekend access visits to her mother that were full of emotional pain. 'It used to be awful because dad would never come to me mum's house . . . to drop us off. He used to pick us up from a lay-by. We used to drive off, and just leave mum standing there on the lay-by. It was dreadful.' As an adult, she still finds it difficult to leave her mother on a Sunday evening, describing her feelings in words which echo those of her description of access occasions, 'it evokes such dreadful feelings'.

Where by contrast the relationship between parents remained low-key, a child who lived nearby was sometimes able to have informal contact, or rarely, even regular contact. In such cases, the other parent remained a familiar part of the child's social world. Joanna Austin, the eldest of five children, one of the two children in the whole group of twenty-nine who had regular weekly visits from her father, tells how she considered that after he left home

her father's 'more avuncular role suited him better than if he had
to live in a house full of kids'. In two cases, fathers who had been
well known but not close to their children during childhood,
played a crucial role at a time of crisis in the child's young
adulthood. Jack Tiverton often caught a glimpse of his father in
the neighbourhood, but had little sustained contact with him from
the age of 4, when his parents separated. When Jack found himself
as a young adult unable to get work, after he had been in trouble
with the law through drinking and drugs, at this stage he turned
to his father for help. His father took him on as an apprentice, and
gave him the support he needed then. At the time of interview,
Jack was once more hoping that he would be able to get to know
his father better—he had been struggling to work out a relationship with the two young sons of his partner, and thought that a
closer understanding of his own relationship with his father might
help him in this.

For Wendy Johnson, whose parents had also separated when
she was 4, but whose father continued to live next door for eight
years so that she saw him frequently, there had been very little
contact in her early teens. Then, at 18, as a homeless young adult
with an infant daughter of her own, she turned to her father for
help, and moved in with him and his second wife. But after about
two years she left again, having found that the rivalry with her
stepmother for her father was unbearable. There was then a
further estrangement for ten more years. However, she was able
to make contact with her father once more not long before the
interview; she phoned him impulsively when she was feeling low
after her mother's death, and was delighted to find herself wel-
comed by him, as if the long absence had never happened.

Clearly in this instance Wendy's own initiatives as a young adult
were crucial in restoring contact. This also could occur, albeit
infrequently, with teenage children. One instance is Nigel Griffiths. The oldest of three children, he had remained with his father
when his parents separated when he was 9 years old, as part of a
parental agreement—which had not been explained to him at the
time—that if he did so, his mother, the two younger siblings and
her new partner could remain in the parental home. Whilst
Nigel's father made no attempt to promote contact between
Nigel, his mother and the rest of her family, neither did he oppose
it. Nigel took matters into his own hand, at first by cycling the

relatively short distance to his maternal grandmother's house, where he would occasionally meet his mother; and later, in his teens, tackling the longer journey to his old home, where he sometimes slept overnight on the sofa. At the age of 18, he fell out with his father and stepmother (who disliked Nigel inviting his friends round, especially when the adults were not there). Nigel then moved in with his mother and stepfather for a short time, before striking out on his own. It was perhaps because, as he saw it, his mother continued to 'quite like' his father, even following their separation, that he had the courage to seek continued contact with her, without experiencing a conflict of loyalty.

It is no accident that for all these children the separated parent had continued for at least a period to live relatively close by. For others, on the other hand, sheer geographical distance inevitably resulted in little contact. Rachel Colman's mother had returned to England from Africa with her two young daughters, aged 7 and 4, escaping from an unhappy, and possibly sometimes violent, marriage. Rachel graphically remembers the story of the attenuation of the parental bond. At the separation, her father had apparently intended that—

either he would come and see us, or we'd go and see him every two to three years. He sent a few birthday cards, and he sent me a climbing frame for a birthday when I was about 10 or 11. And that was it. He remarried, and he never really . . . kept up the contact . . .

I remember my mother making us, my sister and I, write birthday and Christmas cards, and up until I was 16, she rigorously made us write to him. And then I put my foot down, and said, 'Well, if he hasn't bothered to send me a birthday or Christmas card for five years, why should I bother?' . . . I remember being very put out—here was I writing cards—and I thought, 'Why should I?' We'd heard absolutely nothing from him . . .

I assumed that he'd got his own family, and wasn't interested in us anymore.

Nevertheless Rachel was upset when her mother 'threw a wobbly' when her younger sister wanted to let her father know when she was getting married, 'and it was the same when I got married a couple of years after my sister. . . . I just wanted to let him know.' Now that she has her own children she thinks 'I'm not that interested in their meeting him as their grandfather, because he was never interested in my sister or I, so why should he be interested in our offspring?' She knew that her aunt, her father's sister, 'looked exactly like me' from photographs, and was curious about what her half-sisters might look like, but her interest was limited to that.

Geographical distance, and remarriage, also played a part in the lack of contact between Tom Rice and his father, through his teenage years. Tom was 12 at the time of his parent's separation. In spite of his father's commitment to his two children, Tom became increasingly resistant to going for weekend access visits to his father, preferring to spend his time with his friends, as might be expected for a young teenager. It was only when his father emigrated, only a year or so later, that Tom began to regret his lost opportunities to spend time with his father. Yet despite distance and a long gap in time, Tom's father's interest in his children remained strong. At the time of our interview with Tom his father, following his second wife's death, was spending several months every year in England with Tom and his family, where he was a welcome guest. Thus, given sufficient financial means, geographical distance was not always an insuperable barrier to continuing meaningful contact.

Nevertheless, it was above all the reactions, attitudes, and behaviour of the caretaking parent, both at the time of separation and subsequently, which most often was to prove crucial for the child's relationship to the other parent. This was especially so in the case of younger children, whose caretaking parent acted as a filter for the child's experience, the most powerful influence in the child's developing world, helping to shape it both socially and psychologically.

Thirteen of our children were 6 or under when their parents separated. Among them five girls were illegitimate—but this was acknowledged to the child by only one mother, and even then parenthetically, when she once pointed out the father to her daughter in the street. Another girl, whose first stepfather, present soon after her birth, was considered by the family to be her dad, was introduced to her biological father as an uncle when she was a young child—but though she knew the 'truth' from quite early on, this did not in itself have much impact on her. Perhaps the most striking example of concealment in the sample was by a mother who conceived her child out of wedlock. Her daughter was brought up to believe that it was her own father who had died in an accident when she was 2 years old, and that the man who was, in fact, her own father, was her stepfather. When, as an adult, she finally confirmed what she had long suspected because of the hints that her real father continued to drop throughout her childhood, she challenged her mother, and was very angry about the misleading information which her mother had insisted on for so long.

Often an extremely close relationship developed between the caretaking parent, and the young child of either sex. Certain children were especially favoured. One specially loved child was Alex Plumber. A youngest child whose father left home soon after his birth, and was not seen again, Alex insisted that his mother, the dominating influence in his childhood, treated all four of her children, including a younger half-brother, equally. Her life revolved around her children, and also her work as a taxi driver, which seems to have given her a special kind of independence— even after she had remarried, she continued to take all the children out on trips, and for holidays, by herself. Alex's maternal grandfather was also an important influence on Alex until his death when the boy was 16. But neither Alex's father nor his stepfather played any significant part in his life, either socially or psychologically. It seems that his mother's attitude as the caretaker could not accommodate any father in her children's lives. Alex refers to his childhood at the beginning of the interview as 'a normal childhood really–but without a father'.

Another caretaking parent, Maureen O'Nally's mother, made no attempt to promote a relationship between her two girls and their father, whom she had left when Maureen, the older of the two, was 6. Her attitude seemed decisive. The girls did not see their father again. Maureen became especially close and protective of her mother (whose second marriage contracted soon after the divorce, though a love match, proved stormy and quite often violent). It was her father whom Maureen blamed for not keeping in touch; she was determined that her own marriage would not follow the same pattern as her parents' marriage, or her mother's second marriage had done, but her loyalty remained exclusively to her mother, and seems to have been determined in her early childhood by her mother's attitude.

Important differences emerge overall in this respect between the form of influence of fathers and mothers as the caretaking parent. A child was much more likely to be encouraged to see an absent father than an absent mother. Fathers who became the caretaker were likely to remain critical, and hostile towards their ex-partners. Mothers, on the other hand, were much more likely at least to remain silent, and some actively encouraged contact between the children and their father. Most of the children retaining contact lived with their mothers. By contrast, of those seven children in our sample living with a father, only one was able to keep contact with a mother during childhood, although one other man, and also the only woman in the sample living with her father, regretted that more contact with their mothers had not been possible. Although some mothers certainly did so, it looks as if caretaking fathers were more likely to override a child's wishes with their own.

The difference in attitudes between a father and a mother are contrasted graphically in Caroline Herbert's story. Her father had left home when she was 8, and she had lived first with her mother and stepfather until she was 11, and then with her father. She remembers that whenever she saw her father, he would 'have something rotten to say about her [mother] all the time', whereas her mother never spoke against her father. It was only at the age of 11, when Caroline, with her mother's encouragement, went to live with her father, that she found out about the long-standing relationship between her father, and her mother's best friend, the woman who was to become her stepmother.

In some cases a caretaking parent set the agenda for a child by deliberately excluding a parent who had deserted from further consideration by the child. Even in such unpromising circumstances, some re-evaluation of the absent parent by the child in later life might prove possible. Albert Black, the eldest of four, was between 7 and 8 years old when his parents separated. His father's bitterness against his mother prevented the children from having anything but a minimum of contact with their mother—'her overtures were rebuffed', he says. In spite of this lack of contact in childhood, after he married (for the first time) when he was 18, Albert sought his mother out, and went to live with her and his stepfather—'a man in a million'—for two years.

In a few instances, mothers were critical of absent fathers to their children. Joanna Austin's mother would sometimes obliquely criticize him by accusing her daughter of being 'just like your father' when she was angry with her, though the parental relationship had remained relatively friendly, even after several subsequent divorces on both sides. Just occasionally, a mother presented a more consistently negative image of a father: Tracy Sims relates that 'if she was ever to say something about him now, it would only be bad things. Such as, he was a gambler, he used to knock her about, he went with women . . . in her eyes, we're the only things that were good that came out of the marriage.' Nevertheless, after her own marriage, Tracy, whose father had left home when she was 7, was curious enough about him to find out where he lived through the Salvation Army. She went with her husband to visit her father, anticipating a 'wonderful meeting'. But she was to be disappointed. Her father 'refused to acknowledge things about himself' which she remembered, such as his eccentric table manners. Worst of all, 'he practically called me mum a shit, and that really got to me'. She says bitterly, 'my father done nothing for me'—her mother's view of her father had been confirmed for her by the meeting. Subsequently she had nothing more to do with him.

Other mothers, by contrast, promoted positive views of absent fathers even when in reality they must have been just as impossible. Richard Hammond's mother, who had brought up five children on her own after fleeing with them from a violent, drunken husband, would talk about him during her youngest son's childhood as 'very nice'. But Richard had his own independent recollections of episodes of violence by his father towards his mother in his infancy. These memories proved more influential than his mother's words. He describes how he 'blocked out' all thought of his father, and never really wanted to know anything about him. When his mother told him that she thought his father had died, he 'just carried on watching television'.

Perhaps the most remarkable case of a mother promoting a positive image of a father for her child, was that of Gill Deighton's mother. She had been already pregnant when she had married Gill's father, and had left him when Gill was only 6 months old, because he was 'seeing another woman all the time'. Nevertheless, Gill's mother 'always talked about him, and said she loved him'. Gill says, 'I wanted to find him all the time.' But it was not until her mother, and stepfather had separated, when she was in her late teens, that she finally sought her father out, sadly only to discover that he had died when she was 14. Even so, finding the rest of her father's family, including several half-sisters, one of whom looked exactly like the only photograph she had of him, was enough to help her to come to terms with her father's absence through her childhood. She 'kept in touch a bit at first, [with her father's family] but now we just send Xmas and birthday cards'. For Gill, discovering her half-sisters 'was like finding part of myself'.

Losing Parents through Death or Separation: Similarities and Differences

Lack of communication with children at the time of parental separation is readily understandable in terms of the turmoil that parents were likely to be experiencing, and possible recrimination between them immediately before and after separation. The deliberate exclusion of children when a parent died is, from our present perspective, perhaps more surprising. For both those who lost a parent by death and by separation with no further contact, the consequences of parental behaviour towards children at the time of crisis, and subsequently, often created difficulties for them which were long-standing. Those parents in the separated group who did stay in contact were usually able to contribute usefully to their children's lives, though sometimes not until the children were grown up, but almost all faced difficulties which could prove insuperable, and required patient persistence, and sometimes a high tolerance of emotional pain, if they were to succeed in doing so.

Sometimes the reaction of a surviving parent to a spouse's death was similar to that of a deserted spouse, wishing to remove all reminders of the lost partner. In both groups there were a few 'absent' parents who were never mentioned again. And in most cases, in a less extreme way, surviving or caretaking parents were reluctant to speak about a 'lost' father or mother.

Only a small minority showed the opposite attitude. In the group who separated with no contact, the mother of Gill Deighton, 'always' spoke at length and positively to her daughter about the father who had deserted her as a baby; and in the death group, one mother of a very young child 'frequently' talked of his father, and had 'loads of photographs'. In the case of Carol Stevenson, an only child, 7 when her mother died, it was many years before her father was able to begin to tell her about her mother—not till after Carol's own marriage when he started to talk about his much-loved, dead wife 'a lot', especially to Carol's husband. Carol took special comfort in the fact that her father spoke of her mother with strong emotion, more so than when he spoke of her stepmother: 'when he talks about my mum, he talks about her in a different way than when he talks about Joan to me—my mum was his first, main love, and Joan came along after that.' Carol's father's discretion in front of his second wife seems the wiser by contrast with the exceptional instance of Jamsie Noble's father. He was unusual in that after the initial shock, he 'always' talked about Jamsie's mother, and repeatedly showed old videos of family holidays with her. Each of his two subsequent marriages failed.

Confusion and anxiety were common in both the separated and death groups following loss of a parent for which no adult explanation or reassurance was forthcoming. In younger children, anxiety might be manifested by clinging behaviour to the caretaking parent. For example, Jack Finlay, 2 when his father died, can remember repeatedly questioning his mother whenever she was going out about when she would be coming back. Eileen Moriarty and her brother were 'petrified' by the sudden unexplained disappearance of their mother when Eileen was 7, and would cling hysterically to their father, literally physically attached to him: 'and after that time, whenever he left, we used to just hang on to his legs, screaming: we wouldn't let him go.' For some children, the insecurity engendered by the loss was exacerbated by subsequent events, leaving them vulnerable to chronic anxiety. Richard Hammond, a youngest child who was very close to his mother, recalled with feeling his mother being late in picking him up from nursery school on the day she had been obliged to attend court for her divorce. Later, when he was 7, his mother was knocked down by a bus, resulting in his being sent away from home to stay with relatives. He describes how he found himself unable to cope with the start of secondary school—he developed a 'school phobia', associated with the severe anxiety which leaving his mother had by then produced in him.

In both groups some children experienced the lack of one parent as humiliating, or shameful. Mandy Pope, illegitimate, and with no knowledge of her father, blurted out her grandfather's name when she was summoned by a headteacher who wished to know who her father was. Doreen Gower, 4 when her father died, similarly felt ashamed because she had no father: 'I always felt a stigma of having no father. . . . I'd make up somebody who was me dad. . . . I just made him up, 'cos I wanted to be like everbody else.'

There were children in both groups who saw themselves as the favourite child of the departed parent, and felt their loss especially keenly. Jean Wheeler, the second girl in the family, was the only one of four children whom her seafaring father had known from the time of birth—he had been away from home when the others were born. A special bond grew between them: Jean remembers herself as his 'favourite'. He was always 'someone who turns up periodically for a few months, and then goes away again'. Later she realized that this 'was *the* contributing factor to my parents' break-up'. But for a child, life was festive when he was around, 'and then, once he went away, it all stopped'. And she and her father maintained a 'very special, very close' relationship through letters. 'All the while he wasn't there, I would write to him, and he'd write back, and I would write to him all the things that I couldn't talk to mum about . . . I can remember at 11, writing off to him with the first boyfriend troubles. . . . And the answer always came back.' When her father set out to sea, she would cry herself to sleep for a fortnight—'but once you'd written your first letter, and had your first reply, then everything settled down again'. Jean was devastated when her father finally left home for good when she was in her early teens, without even saying goodbye. Now her father, even when ashore, scarcely made contact, and the exchange of letters ceased. 'It hurt. And the big thing that hurt . . . was the fact that dad didn't want to see us.'

Stephanie Rogers also thought of herself as her father's favourite. He died when she was 8. He was ever-indulgent towards her. She recalls sitting on his knee, and being cuddled by him. She says 'there was always love', though she goes on to contrast her mother's harsher, disciplinarian style, including hitting her often—'but it does no harm, like, you know'—with her father's, who she remembers as never even telling her off.

The popular conception of the nature of cross-gender attach-ments in families—some girls having an especially close relation-ship with their fathers, and some boys with their mothers—is borne out in these life story interviews. In relation to 'absent' fathers, women tended to focus on the loss of the emotional bond, whereas men sometimes mentioned their consciousness as a child of the absence of their father to encourage them in sporting activities, or other traditionally male pursuits. But the special emotional closeness of some of the boys to their mothers—'I was always her blue-eyed boy'—was not a feature of 'absent' mother relationships. 'Absent' mothers were either rejected or viewed with intense ambivalence by male children.

As we have already seen, negative or ambivalent images of separated parents were common in comparison with the generally positive images of dead parents. Only one father in the separated group was 'idolized'—significantly by a woman who had a very unsatisfactory relationship with her caretaking mother, and a difficult home life; whereas identification with, and idealization of parents who had died, especially by some older children in the sample, was relatively common. The children of parents who had died usually had memories of family harmony before the parental death, or, if they were too young to remember, assumed it, whereas the opposite was likely to be true of children of separated parents. This probably accounts for the more favourable long-term outcome generally reported in the literature for children who suffered parental death rather than parental separation, and also in some respects of our own informants;[11] although, as we have seen in some of the examples detailed, where surviving parents were unable to cope with the care of their children following the death of a spouse, the children could suffer badly, and sometimes enduringly.

The 'Absent' Parent and the New Stepfamily

How did absence, whether partial or complete, of one natural parent from the household impinge on the experience of these children growing up in stepfamilies? How did the relationship with the 'absent' parent affect the child's ability to form a relation-ship with a step-parent and to participate in stepfamily life?

At one extreme, the image of the dead parent or a parent who had disappeared might become 'frozen', a situation which arose almost inevitably when the caretaking parent was unable or unwilling to acknowledge the lost partner (although occasionally a close relative was able to provide another perspective for a child). In such cases a parent who had died might, unlike one who had disappeared, be idealized, and the incoming step-parent regarded as an unwanted intruder. Thus the relationship of Rosa Daniels and her stepmother remained mutually antagonistic. Looking back, Rosa identifies with her idealized mother. She blames her stepmother for the miseries of her homelife in her later teenage years, following her mother's death; and while not exonerating her father completely, regards his failure to protect her and her brother from the worst excesses of her stepmother's treatment of them as attributable to the machinations of her stepmother, rather than to her father's own weakness. Harry Bolsover idealized his dead father, and appears to have rejected both his mother and his stepfather, and had little to do with either of them during the remaining years of his childhood, choosing to live with his grandmother instead.

In more favourable circumstances, the image of the dead or 'absent' parent was not static, but was actively constructed in conjunction with the evolving relationship with the caretaking parent, and subsequently with the step-parent. Here a positive image of a dead or 'absent' parent could be helpful in encouraging the ready acceptance of a step-parent. This was so for Sid Western, whose mother died after a long illness when he was 11, and father remarried one year later. Sid says of his stepmother, 'I just saw her as my mother . . . —as I say, they're of the same age, the same generation, so I think they were probably—much of a muchness.' Sid, the elder of two sons, was his father's favourite, and his younger brother had been sent to live with his grandparents after his mother died. Sid immediately integrated into the newly formed stepfamily. As an adult he remains single, living with his 'parents'—his father and stepmother—and regards his step-mother's relatives as part of his own family, as his aunts and uncles. In a rather similar way Tony Dickson, who was very close to his mother and had positive images of his father who died when he was 9, almost fuses the memories of his father and stepfather as two men with the same occupation and same outlook on life.

Conversely, it would seem that the lack of a strong positive memory or relationship with a dead or separated parent, perhaps, especially for girls, could make it more difficult for them to accept an incoming stepparent, who was felt as an uncomfortable threat to the daughter's closeness to her mother or father.

In other instances the problem was excessive loyalty to the lost parent and the daily ways of living which thus represented a continuing form of memory. Sometimes this loyalty to an absent parent was held by one sibling, thus allowing the other sibling or siblings to attach to the stepparent and the new family. Such was the case for Stephanie Rogers, whose teenage brother, the eldest in the family, was so affronted by his mother's betrayal of their dead father that he picked a fight with the stepfather before walking out of the house, not to return for many years. Meanwhile Stephanie herself was able to settle in harmoniously with the new stepfamily.

In principle the 'absent' parent could provide regular support, both materially and emotionally. But for this generation of step-children, there is strikingly little evidence of either from the interviews. It is possible that some separated parents did provide financial backing without the child knowing, but it is very rarely mentioned that they did so, while it is occasionally of other kin such as grandparents.

There are too few cases of sustained frequent contact, in fact only five, including two children who lived first with one parent and then with the other, for us to draw any lessons from them. Joanna Austin's father did pay regular maintenance, and came most Sundays for a meal and to be with his children and ex-wife; sometimes he too would cook for them in his own new house. Joanna was at first very hostile to her stepfather, and although she got through this phase, never close to him. As an adult, she has not chosen to follow a conventional family pattern. Joy Carmichael and Caroline Herbert both continued in contact with their other parent, Joy with her mother and Caroline with her father, and after a few years moved to live with them. Joy hated her stepmother and scorned her stepfather. Caroline, who felt a strong affection for her stepfather, initially disliked her stepmother, but gained more from her as she grew older. In both cases the original strong contact with the 'absent' parent meant that the child failed to settle in the first stepfamily and moved across to the other. Since neither was as close to their fathers, even though both always remained in contact with them, this move had different implications for them. While Caroline was ambivalent about moving to live with her father, and took time to adjust, Joy, once with her mother, not only had less negative relationships with her resident stepparent, but also less of a tug from outside. Lastly, Wendy Johnson lived for her first eight years with her mother and stepfather in a house next door to her father, seeing him very regularly. She seems to have had no problem in sustaining loving relationships with all three parental figures, although later on, when as a young adult she went to live with her father, she found the rivalry with her stepmother intolerable.

Thus patterns of interaction between children, their 'absent' biological parents, and their stepparents were complex, varying, and variable. Stepparents might, on the one hand, complement or virtually replace a biological parent in a child's emotional world, as well as in everyday life; or on the other, could provoke a conflict of loyalty within the child, which might persist, or be slowly modified over time; and, at the worst, a stepparent might become part of an unhappy system of mutual rejection.

Conclusion

For the majority of our fifty stepchildren, the immediate and longer term impacts of the loss of a parent were profound. For many of those interviewed, the loss was remembered as the 'worst thing' experienced in their lives, and for some the trauma of the event continued to reverberate in the present. Nevertheless, for a small minority who retained vivid memories of violence towards a mother, siblings, or self, the removal of this element from their lives was counted as positive. Thus Tracy Sims, 7 when her father left, says, 'It was mainly the violent side of him that I remember. . . . I remember one day, he was lashing out at her, and I was just watching him punch her as she was sitting on the chair. He pushed her on the chair, and he was lashing out. And that's the only thing I ever remember.' For her, as for some other young children in our sample, her strict but caring stepfather became the male focus of life, compensating for, and almost obliterating the harsh memory of the violent, biological father. 'If I look back, my father done nothing for me. My stepfather was my father, and always will be.'

As we have seen, thirteen of our twenty-nine subjects whose parents separated had no further contact with that parent subsequently. The most likely consequence in the short term—as for those children who lost a parent through death—was the forging of an especially close link with the caretaking parent. In late teenage years, or in early adulthood, there might be an urge to seek more information about the missing parent, or in the case of separated or divorced parents, to seek them out, with variable consequences for child and parent alike.

Parents who lived apart lacked a model of how to promote a continued relationship with their child or children which could be regarded as successful. Of the sixteen out of the twenty-nine in our sample who did retain contact, this was frequent in only five cases. Nevertheless, even irregular or casual contact might confer benefits. In those cases where continued contact proved possible without legal intervention, certain conditions were likely to prevail, including a positive or neutral attitude towards access by the caretaking parent, together with a low level of hostility between ex-partners, and geographical proximity. Occasionally it was the child or children themselves (or in one case a relative who acted as a 'go between' for the children and their mother) who initiated contact, but success depended on the caretaking parent being either indifferent to that contact, or (in the case of relative as go-between) ignorant of the contact, at least until it was well established.

What were the benefits for these children of retained contact with the parent who lived apart? Attributes of the non-caretaking parent's personality might be especially valued by the child, particularly where they contrasted with those of the caretaking parent. Joanna Austin, close to her mother, with whom she lived from the age of 9 when her father left, repeatedly refers to her father's 'calm' as an important influence in her life, contrasting this with her mother's more 'volatile' and 'passionate' nature. For others, even irregular or casual contact during childhood allowed for 'knowing' a real rather than a fantisized person, in some cases resulting in the parent being more readily re-evaluated, whether positively or negatively, as the child matured; but in either case facilitating understanding. One man, who had occasional contact with his father during childhood, had more contact with him in adulthood. He says that it had taken him till the last few years to realize that he had always been frightened of his father because of vivid memories from the age of 10, when his parents separated, of his father's violence towards his mother. In retrospect, he was able to recognize that his parents had 'goaded' each other, a recognition which had allowed him, as an adult now meeting his father 'on equal terms', to appreciate some of his father's more positive qualities.

In at least four cases a parent living apart was able to offer material help in terms of work, or a home for their young adult child. Three young men and one young woman were able to turn to their 'absent' parent for support when they found themselves in need in early adulthood. For example, an 18-year-old, by then married, went to live with his mother and stepfather with whom he had had relatively little contact in childhood; another 18-year-old, a woman with a young baby, moved in with the father, with whom she had had only casual contact in childhood, when she found herself homeless. Dick Pembridge was rescued from delinquency to become his father's apprentice, and thereby set on the path to successful craftsmanship. And for Lily Beck, working in the same office as the father with whom she had lived only briefly, in early infancy, brought special benefits: 'if there was any problem at work I could just nip upstairs and ask my dad'. But, more than that, it gave her the opportunity to get to know him and her stepmother better. Today she contrasts her own mother, whom she describes as 'an empty shell', with her adored father, and her stepmother whom she thought of as 'just like a big sister to me, but more my mother than my mother'.

Sometimes it was not until adulthood that a child was able to make links with a parent who had left during their childhood. But when a relationship was re-established, the child now adult might still experience the original desertion by the parent as a betrayal. Emrys Hughes now sees his mother quite frequently and regularly, but he says he cannot forgive her for deserting him when he was 9 years old: he says that he sees her now 'more out of loyalty than out of love'.

More extremely, a few of our subjects who lost contact in childhood continued to express anger, or even contempt, for a deserting parent, or one who failed to keep in touch. This was true of both sexes speaking of either a mother or a father, but deserting mothers were likely to be more consciously and specifically condemned than deserting fathers, perhaps especially when the child had been closely attached to the mother. Ben Carlisle, for example, whose mother left home when he was 11, remembers the shock of her departure, and that at first he cried a lot. But soon after he resolved to cut all thought of his mother out of his life, a resolve to which he has kept.

Perhaps if any degree of contact had been maintained in childhood, the anger and disappointment for the children with 'absent' parents, might have dissipated over time, allowing them as adults the possibility and potential benefits of relating to a real rather than a fantasy parent. Absence of contact tended to lead to an image of the parent frozen in time. Against this, when asked by the interviewer who they thought of as part of their family now, most named both living biological parents: the consciousness of a non-custodial parent was likely to endure whatever the circumstances in childhood.

For those whose loss was through death, as we have seen, their grief had often not been fully assuaged by the passage of time, and some continued to long for the dead parent. They sometimes found themselves in difficulty in trying to cope with subsequent major losses in their lives, and sometimes reacted irrationally to perceived threats of loss.

Loss of a parent in childhood inevitably remained an event which both in the short and in the longer term was a potent factor in the shaping of each individual life. The emotional pain was inescapable, varying in degree according to the age and sex of the child, the gender of the 'lost' parent in relation to the child, and the strengths of the caretaking parent. But even with the odds stacked against the 'absent' parent, as they were for the children in this study, on account of the prevailing social attitudes, social policy, and the legal framework at that time, when a dead parent could be effectively mourned, or meaningful contact with a separated or divorced parent could be negotiated, the lives of many of those concerned were enriched, bringing both obvious and more hidden benefits.

5

The Widening Circle

WHEN a child loses a parent, where can he or she hope to find compensating support? What are the resources on which a child can draw, both in the household and beyond it?

Parental Figures

The questions seem simple enough: but the loss that needs making up is not always so clear. As we have seen (Chapter 4), it was rare for any parent who died or left to be totally lost. The way in which they disappeared shapes the child's sense of the parent who has gone. And there are some whose detachment from a child's daily life could be as much gain as loss.

Twenty-one of our stepchildren had lost a parent through death, and of these, ten had scarcely any memory at all of the absent father or mother. This was the most absolute loss, for it was indefinable. It was difficult for the child to imagine the parent who had gone. We have seen (Chapters 3 and 4) how some children, as they grew into adulthood and came to understand the meaning of death, tried to seek out images of the lost parent—voices, faces—as a crucial part of finding their own identity. The other eleven had some definite memories to ease the process of coming to terms with parental death, although this could be equally prolonged, and for some was again clearly unresolved.

Nevertheless there were possible resolutions. Some were remembered as never fully available as parents, and hence perhaps a little less of a loss, like the five mothers who were invalids, 'always ill, she had a bad heart'. At the opposite extreme were three parents who in memory seem strongly idealized, and still provide a fundamental life inspiration. Thus Tony Dickson succeeded in fusing the images of his father with the stepfather who followed him, for this stepfather too had married a foreigner, and his wife had also died of a brain virus, 'so there were a lot of similarities there.' In terms of character again, he was 'mild-mannered . . . very similar to my first father' and both would tend to 'spoil the children'. It was as if his father still lived on in the person of his stepfather; and indeed, when his stepfather later died, he mourned him more than he had his father. Equally effectively, as we have seen, Harry Bolsover felt himself a living continuation of his father: similar in manner, in feeling, in his skills and in his love of dogs and woods. 'I would have liked to have been like my dad. . . . I still go to me dad's grave, now.'

Half of the parents who left the home, yet remained alive, were as we have seen in Chapter 4 also effectively totally lost, six leaving no memory at all. None of these parents was idealized. On the contrary, the presumption against them was negative. Either they were always bad, or it was bad of them to leave. This was especially true of those who totally disappeared. Some left black memories of 'a pig', drunken, violently assaulting mother or child or both. Others were resented because they had always seemed withdrawn; yet others because of hopes broken later. 'It's the fact that she never bothered to get into contact. If I left my children, I'm sure I'd stay in touch.'

There was less chance, when a parent had withdrawn altogether from contact, for the child to come to understand the parental split as a complex mutual failure, rather than the sole respons-ibility of the parent who had gone. The remaining parents were physically absent, but not lost. And as we have seen, the child could come to know them as real people in relationships devel-oped over time. They thus remained part of the child's world, and exceptionally, could grow in significance and prove an important resource later, for example in work.

Most often, however, the contact was irregular and infrequent. Nevertheless this allowed a gradual mutual detachment, in which the child came to interpret the parent as self-centred and emo-tionally hard, if not also physically rough. Again, this not only helped towards the acceptance of loss, but in the longer perspect-ive reduced it. Alan Downs summed up his evaluation of the departure from the household of his violent womanizing father: 'A lot of children may say that losing their father, for whatever reason, was not good for them, but from my point of view it wasn't a bad day at all, because things were actually easier. . . .

Life became better. . . . I was not sorry to see him disappear over the horizon, quite frankly.'

There were just seven of the 'absent' fathers who were known more thoroughly: four because they were seen regularly throughout childhood, two often but with breaks, and three with whom the child also lived at some point after the parental split. Only one is described as having a strong relationship with his child: typically the others were remembered as never very close. None of these fathers was thought of as 'lost' at all: simply as fathers who, like many others still in the home, had always been peripheral.

The point is a wider one. If we measure loss against ideal parents, we exaggerate what children suffer when their parents separate. Real parents are rarely ideal. This becomes, indeed, abundantly clear when we look, in turn, at the parents with whom these children remained: their primary parenting resource. As we have seen earlier in Chapter 3, the custodial parent could, in fact, be as serious a source of difficulties as the parent who had gone. If we look at memories of these fifty caretaking parents, at least eighteen gave their children, at best, material caring. They lived with mothers or fathers who were unable to talk closely with them, unable to show affection and usually stern disciplinarians too: four of them 'hard' even to violence. These children thus struggled against a double deprivation; but the worst was not because their parents had separated, but because they had not provided good enough parental care.

Of the remaining caretaking parents at least half, if on balance positive, were certainly remembered ambivalently. Three were powerful women, described as 'strong' or 'beautiful' or 'charismatic', strongly emotional yet difficult to be at ease with. Two were at the same time both emotionally close, and also deeply deceitful. Four were physically affectionate, but never available for talk 'in depth'. Three others were both uncommunicative and also physically unaffectionate, yet sufficiently mild and practically caring to give some sense of security; 'a very loving, very caring person', as one daughter described her father, 'I feel very close to him'. 'She was always there', recalls another of her mother, 'I always felt very loved and secure.' The phrase 'always there' is one which recurs with other adults whom children found supportive, but in a relatively unobtrusive, or even passive way: in terms of good enough parenting, perhaps the bottom line.

Fourteen children, by contrast, described 'very close', 'very affectionate', confiding relationships with 'gentle and understanding' parents, whom they portray as 'great', 'wonderful', 'lovely', 'easy-going', 'loving', 'super'. A few fathers were able to win this closeness through what they did, rather than verbal intimacy. Thus Sid Western's father was 'very easy-going, he never bullied us . . . a very quiet man, he doesn't bark and shout'. Sid feels that 'he did a remarkable job . . . a lot of the bringing up'. Rather than play, 'he would build things for me'; above all a train set which filled the lounge all winter. 'Trains, Trains, trains, trains': his father and grandfather were both railwaymen. The family holidays were by train; and in between, his father and grandfather 'used to take me train spotting. So it was trains! To the exclusion of all else!' And Sid has followed his father's tracks into adulthood: he too works for the railway.

It is equally striking that these close relationships are frequently conveyed as more than parent–child bonds. One son described his father as like 'a brother' to him; other children speak of mothers or fathers as 'good friends'. As one daughter put it, 'I have always been close to my dad, but I think I've been a friend with him as well. I could say anything to him and he would take it.' And a son says of his mother, 'She's my best friend. Always was.' In fact it is highly unlikely, either for him or for others of these relatively fortunate children, that their relationship 'always was' so close. The experience of separation, and especially of lone parenting, could bond parent and child much more closely than was common when parents remained an intact couple. As Jamsie Noble put it: 'I've always been protective towards him. It's like a lifetime effort. Because my mother died, and so I've only got my father, in my eyes, my father's always done right. I've never really resented him in any way, whatever he's done. He's always tried to help me as well.' The first potential compensating resource for a child who had lost a parent was, in short, a closer intimacy with the parent who remained. But the parent had to be both strong enough to provide security, rather than becoming too emotionally dependent on the child; and at the same time, sensitive and gentle enough to be fully open to the child's needs. Only a minority—scarcely more than one in three—had these qualities.

In all these families, sooner or later, the child experienced a relationship with another adult, a stepparent. As we have already seen (Chapter 3) for many this offered nothing positive. The stepparent was either thoroughly disliked, or at best a marginal figure, in the household physically but never part of the child's emotional circle. Of the remainder, on the other hand, twenty-five stepparents are remembered either positively, or with at least some positive characteristic as part of a mixed memory. However, with only five exceptions it was the more supportive parents whose new spouses also left the most positive memories. A successful stepparent, in other words, was more likely to reinforce a good parent than to provide compensation for one who was lacking.

It is hardly surprising, in view of the differences between stepfathers and stepmothers which we have encountered earlier, that these positive memories were less likely in stepmother than in stepfather families. Only three stepmothers are remembered as having quickly become significant and positive adult figures in the child's world. In each instance the father was also close. It is also striking that two of them are explicitly described as not being stepmothers: one man commented, 'I don't see Gwen as a step-mother', while a woman who called her stepmother 'mum' never-theless said, 'she's been a big sister.'

Stepfathers by contrast, who were not expected to be central figures in the household, usually aroused less strong feelings. Although eight men were accepted by their stepchildren as true substitute fathers, three of these had been led to believe that they were natural fathers. A marginal role was more typical, positive in minor ways: providing presents, leisure outings, 'talking to me perhaps more than my father did, taking an interest'. Some of these men saw themselves as taking the role of a father: 'he looks on us, I suppose, as his kids.' But the children were less likely to reciprocate, thinking of the stepfather as 'more of an uncle' or 'as a friend'. This was partly because often the child had no clear idea of what to expect of a father: 'I didn't really know what a dad was.' They speak as if unaware that describing a natural father as 'just there', or 'always there', or still more 'as a friend', would have been distinctly approving.

Siblings, Half-Siblings, and Stepsiblings

Nearly all of these stepchildren had, in addition to parents and stepparents, another possible source of support within their immediate households: siblings. Despite the obvious importance of sibling relationships, there has been remarkably little research on them in intact families,[1] and virtually none on siblings in stepfamiles.[2] In our families, although thirteen children had no full brother or sister, even these all had either half or stepsiblings. Siblings—and especially half or stepsiblings—might be living elsewhere: but, in fact, only one of all our stepchildren never lived in the same household with at least one sibling for part of their childhood.[3] How much help could they find in these brothers and sisters of different kinds?

Relationships with siblings were as varied as those with parents, ranging from indifference to intense love or hatred. Behind each relationship lay a mixture of influences—demography, family dynamics, and personality. Looking at the patterns in our families overall, it is immediately clear that the emotional pitch was highest with full siblings and least intense with stepsiblings. This partly reflected whether or not they co-resided, and if they did, for how long. As a result, while siblings as a whole were three times more likely to be loved than disliked, full siblings were somewhat more often loved than half or stepsiblings, and also, perhaps more surprisingly, they were much more often disliked. Indeed, the tendency emerges still more strongly when we take into account that some of the disliked half-siblings were believed by the child to be true brothers or sisters. Intense hostility, while a common form of relationship among full brothers and sisters, seems to have been very rare indeed towards half or stepsiblings: there are only three instances in all our families. Step-relationships were thus, on balance, less often close, but when they were close they were much more likely to be good: otherwise they were usually simply marginal. But they were again measured against an ideal which could be painfully elusive.

The ideal was of a closeness based on common upbringing, which continued into adulthood: 'we've always been together'; 'oh aye, we're close. Every day we see each other, like.' But many children remembered constant antagonism: 'my brother who I—hated—I argued and argued with him continually, we fought and fought like anything as children'; 'my sister and I used to fight all the time.' Sometimes, however, an intensely hostile relationship would change to become a gain in the end: 'we're very close now, but as children never. . . . For a long time, I resented her.' Other siblings both loved and fought from the start. Martine Brabourne was close in every way to her younger half-sister, Sheba, whom she believed to be a full sister, sleeping together for many years in the same bed, and helping to bring her up: 'I had to look after my sister always.' She describes Sheba today as 'skinny, talkative, very, very lively, very animated, good actor, very loved. . . . People tend to flock towards her.' But as a child, she responded with 'outrages, temper and violence towards me'; 'it used to be physical, because I always had to parent her, which I think she resented, and she used to fight me physically, like scratch me, and I bear the scars still!' And it was as bad at night: 'the bedtimes were a bit of a fight as well, because she was very bony, and I didn't like her legs on me, and she didn't like me touching her!' Still today, 'we've got a very strange relationship. Very strained. We're very close, but we fight like hell, verbally and emotionally.'

Protectiveness between older children and siblings is quite often recalled as an important element in a close relationship, and typically as straightforwardly positive. The strain here seems to have been rooted in a personality difference: the younger sister was already asserting a forcefulness which would have been an asset had their roles been reversed. Interestingly, Martine had no problem in later playing the 'big sister' role with her much younger half-siblings by her second stepfather. Mandy Pope, who again grew up believing her half-sisters to be full sisters, distinguished still more sharply between her elder sister, 'a very, very good person' to whom she was particularly close, and her younger sister whom she disliked from birth: 'I hated her. I resented her as being alive, breathing on this planet. I hated her . . . I used to belt her.' There were also other children with more than one full sibling who remembered love for one and hostility towards another. One man describes himself as 'very close' to two of his sisters, but 'as different as chalk and cheese' from his brother. Doreen Gower, who was 'closer to me younger sister', describes her 'jealousy' for her older sister, who was 'like a swot and she was always in her room doing homework . . . and maybe I was jealous that she was clever. . . . I didn't speak to me eldest sister for about seven years. . . . It was a long time not to speak to your sister. It's something I always feel guilty about.' Differences in personality also explain why in another family a woman finds her only sibling 'boring'. 'He's not very talkative. I mean, I feel uncomfortable if I go round his house even, and he's my own flesh and blood. . . . He won't start a conversation, and the answer you'll get back is "Yes" . . . or, "No" . . . We're not very close, but then we're different, like chalk and cheese really.' Personal compatibility or incompatibility could not be preordained, even between natural siblings.

The quality of sibling relationships did, however, to some extent reflect that of the household culture as a whole. It is noticeable in general that children much more often found a supportive relationship in a brother or sister when they also had a good relationship with at least one parent. Although the interviews do not bring this out, we can assume that some of these parents deliberately fostered good sibling relationships. Conversely, in those families where the child was relating to both full and half or stepsiblings and there was conflict between the groups, this was invariably where parental support was inadequate. Good sibling relationships thus again tend to reinforce good parenting. Nevertheless, there were important exceptions: seven children who each lacked a supportive parent did find a close relationship with a sibling. Siblings could, indeed, help to fill a vital gap. As Ann Highfield put it, 'we all got a little bit of strength from each other. . . . I think we all helped each other through it, because my dad was no help.'

How far this was possible, and also, more generally, the shape of sibling relationships, was also partly dependent on the family life cycle. Children who entered stepfamily relationships relatively young were more likely to have half-siblings, and those who entered as teenagers to have stepsiblings.[4]

Half-siblings in our families were normally much younger, born some ten or more years later. This made jealousy less likely. Only two recalled the birth of half-siblings as making their situation 'a lot worse', a cause of later conflict. The others have positive memories. It made them feel more complete, 'a proper family', it was 'great', 'tremendous', it 'brought us closer'. For girls

especially, it could provide a new positive role in the family—'I
used to look after her, feed her.' Yet boys are just as enthusiastic:
'Oh, I was excited.'[5]

It was unusual for half-siblings to be strongly disliked, although
some certainly were not close—'like chalk and cheese'. But more
typically, those brought up together did bond. Those who feel
closest think of them like full siblings: 'a normal brotherly relationship', in one man's words, or as a woman put it: 'I look upon
them as my brothers. As far as I'm concerned, they are my
brothers.' In this they contrast strongly with half-siblings brought
up in other households, with whom there was little contact. These
are not seen as part of the 'family', to the extent that at the
extreme the kinship is totally denied. One man said of his half-
siblings who were brought up in Canada, 'I've met them, I've met
them. . . . But there's no blood like. . . . I didn't think it was like a
brother.'

It was more common for there to be little or no contact with
stepsiblings if they were non-resident. Many stepfathers especially
were—intentionally or not—out of contact with their children by
a previous marriage. As a result, they rarely took on a significance.[6] One exception, however, is Bee Potter, who did not at first
realize that her four stepsiblings existed at all, but once they began
to meet developed quite strong feelings for each of them. She
didn't 'get on' with three, describing one as a 'big-mouthed sod',
but with the fourth she soon had 'a great realtionship. It's more
like a brother and sister relationship—or is it? I mean, we can talk
to each other about anything and everything.'[7]

Twelve families also took in, at least temporarily, stepsiblings.
In three families this resulted in severe conflict. One boy dismissed
a stepbrother with whom he fought bitterly as 'a little whimper';
while a girl still feels she 'can't forgive' a trouble-stirring stepsister
who proved 'a compulsive liar . . . I don't class her as my sister'.
But these were rare exceptions, and in most families the relationships were non-conflictual or positive, even 'great'; and when the
children were together long enough, they might become deeper.
Such close feelings could sometimes be recalled with some puz-
zlement, as if stepsiblings ought not to be felt as real brothers or
sisters. One man describes his stepbrother as like an older friend
with whom he 'went around together'; another as 'friendly lads'.
A third, by contrast, who has completely lost touch with his full

brother whom he regards as 'totally different', comments of his stepbrothers, 'I still say they're me brothers now.' Conversely, Richard Hammond explains a relatively detached but amicable relationship with his stepbrother with the comment, 'You don't class your stepbrother as your normal brother . . . I always relate to Simmie as my stepbrother, I wouldn't class him as blood brother. To me, there's always that distinction, yeh.' But he goes on to remark also of the full sister to whom he is least close, 'I've never classed Bella as being a sister really.'

Friction with stepsiblings was most likely to be a danger in the teenage years. This was because of a cumulation of a gradual change in full sibling bonds. From early childhood onwards older siblings quite commonly related to younger brothers or sisters in a quasi-parental fashion. When children were young, this was typically encouraged by parents, and it could continue to be at their behest later on. Stephanie Rogers, for example, described how her older brother took on a disciplinary role, which he maintained even after he had left home: 'even after he was married, our Bill, he was still there. "If you don't behave yourself, I'll phone Bill!" . . . I was frightened to death of our Bill.' But there were some families in which, partly in response to the inadequacies of adult parenting, such child-parents began to act in alliance with their siblings against the wishes of the adults in the family. We have seen (Chapter 3) how the older Gordon brothers attempted, and ultimately succeeded, in frustrating the attempts of their stepmother to reform their younger brother.

The most striking instance, however, and still more catastrophic, was described by Albert Black. Caught between two inadequate parents who separated when he was 7, he took it on his own shoulders to prevent his two brothers, sister, and himself from being separated into institutional homes: 'That's a part of my life where there's a lot of dark memories, a lot of hurt, a lot of pain, and a lot of crying, but I kept my family together. I fought and fought, I fought to keep myself, Evan, Steve, and Mandy together . . .' When his stepmother arrived with her two daughters, Albert was now 12, already with battle honours on his side. He found the stepmother 'domineering' and hard, and particularly resented her favouring of the stepsisters (her own daughters) who 'had the biggest bed' and in her eyes 'could do no wrong'. As for the two girls, he disliked them 'immensely and I still do'. Along with one of his brothers, he counter-attacked immediately, fighting both stepsisters and stepmother 'hammer and tongs. . . . It was an experience I wouldn't go through again. . . . Very sordid memories of violence.' There was to be no resolution until, as a delinquent teenager, Albert was forced to leave home for an Approved School: 'it was always two families.'

Siblings, in short, could certainly provide emotional sustenance. But there were households in which the very failure of parent–child relationships meant that too close a bonding to brothers could aggravate difficulties, rather than soothe them.

Grandparents and Kin

Beyond the immediate family household at the moment of parental loss there were often grandparents, aunts and uncles, and other kin. As with siblings, they have been surprisingly little considered in stepfamily studies.[8] How far could these provide support for a child in this time of crisis?

Both the ideal and the normal practice of the English family today, and at least for several centuries back, has centred on the nuclear household of parents and children rather than the extended family network. Newly married couples have expected to set up independently as quickly as they can, and take full responsibility for their children. In tune with this attitude, grandparents normally prefer and are preferred to live separately, occasionally giving a helping hand with a treat for their grandchildren, but taking care not to 'interfere'. In the past, because they died earlier, most grandparents did not even play this marginal role: two-thirds of children grew up without any significant memory of a grandparent. They were more likely to matter when a parent had died, but even then not many were alive and available to play a more important part.[9]

This ideal still shapes attitudes to stepfamily life. Other studies[10] have suggested that couples who remarry typically wish to start afresh like new and independent nuclear families, resenting intrusions from their own previous marriages. Clearly some stepchildren also feel similarly, welcoming the reconstruction of a 'proper family'; 'we were a family then'. But they tend to remain much more ambivalent than their remarried parents. This underlies the difficulties they find in naming the stepparents and half or stepsiblings to whom they become close. Children also often carry into the stepfamily very strong attachments to grandparents or other kin which remain of central importance to their self-identity right through into adult life. The relative weight of this emotional attachment to grandparents and the lived experience from which it is derived sets them apart both from the typical experience of English children, today and in the past, but also from their parents. Probably most parents who remarried hoped to make a new enclosed emotional world;[11] but their children, more often than not, still held other kin in their hearts.

Most often these kin were also positively important for their parents, such as grandparents on the custodial parent's side. In any case, when a parent had died there was no reason for cutting off other kin, and in these families three-quarters of children had contact with both sides. But with those who had divorced, on the other hand, this was true in under half of the families. Many children seem to have accepted such a loss without questioning it, commenting passively, 'I only know me dad's side'; 'my real father's parents I never met. . . . That side of the family was never really contacted . . . I understand that it is a fairly large family, but I've never met them.' Others felt there had been good reasons for the breach: as with a grandmother who had been directly involved in facilitating a mother's secret plans for departure, having the children to stay that weekend, but 'denied all knowledge when he [the father] confronted her with it. Later it transpired that she did know.'

A child could, however, sense an independent need to stay in touch. Bee Potter, whose father left when she was small, comments that she saw her paternal grandparents often, 'especially after my parents divorced. . . . As far as I was concerned, they were my grandparents, and I was gonna keep hold of them.' In Celia Newton's family the 'rift' had its origins in divorces before her own parents married. 'As a young child, I tried to find them desperately, and found them, and spoke to my grandfather one day, and explained who I was: and he said he didn't want to talk to me.' She persisted, nevertheless, and 'got to see him, and spend time with him, and I went to stay with him and his wife'. And two other children sought out lost grandparents as adults: 'recently, I found them'.

But typically, the significance of other kin for the child stemmed directly from the crisis in which one parent had departed.[12] In altogether 44 families—all but six—at least one grandparent, aunt, or uncle had played an important role in the child's life. In over half of these instances, the child lived for some time in the same household as this relative, and in some others visiting was daily. The part played could be in practical caring, or emotional, or both. There were aunts and grandmothers who played, at least temporarily, key caring roles, but to whom the child never became closely attached; and in just one instance, a co-residing grand-mother and granddaughter openly disliked each other—'we just didn't get on.' But very remarkably, out of altogether nearly 60 relatives recalled playing an important part in these children's lives, three-quarters also became closely attached. They were, in fact, much more likely to be close to them than either to their stepparents or their natural parents. The emotional significance of the wider family is not only distinctive to children who have lost a parent, but provides their most reliable resource to mitigate that loss.

Although there were a few important grandfathers and uncles, overwhelmingly these significant relatives were women. Men might be an influence, offering a character model or a glimpse of a work-world, sharing a skill or allowing a visit to the signal-box; or as a special source of fun. One granddaughter recalled how 'I loved to play cards, and we'd sit for hours, just the two of us'. A grandfather could indeed be accepted as a substitute for a missing father through doing little more than this. As another granddaughter put it, 'I took to my grandad as though he was my dad, and I was spoilt rotten.' Sylvie Higgenworth was brought up living with a classically unhelpful grandfather, who regularly drank too much, and 'he were very dominant with my mum . . . I remember him swearing and expecting his tea on't table at five o'clock'. But he was 'pretty good with me', and she 'thought he were wonderful . . . I think I got really ruined by my grandad . . . I think that's probably why I never really missed having a dad, because I had my grandad there.' Of these men, only three grandfathers also took on an active domestic role in the home. 'He was a great help. . . . We probably couldn't have coped without him', a grandson says of one; another puts it, 'he was a great chap. . . . He took a lot of the housework on, cooking and washing.'

It was much more frequent for a grandmother or an aunt to become the everyday mainstay of a child's life. It perhaps helped that the traditional image of a good grandmother, providing constant support and encouragement and sustaining food, encompasses this practical domesticity.[13] Dawn Lynam, who saw her grandmother daily, indeed describes her as 'a story-book gran', always baking, who had been a domestic servant when young: 'she'll do anything for anybody.' Another 'very loveable' co-resident grandmother would also 'do anything for anyone'.

Such practical caring was easiest when the grandmother or aunt lived in the same house, but there were also striking instances when they lived close by. Carol Stevenson's grandmother, for example, had lost both her daughter (Carol's mother) and her husband by death, and as a lone widow 'really I was all that she had left. So she made a lot of me, and I spent a lot of time with her. She'd come over and take me to school in the morning, and pick me up in the evening.' After Carol's father remarried to a stepmother to whom she was never close, she continued 'to spend a lot of time at my grandma's, so it wasn't so bad as when I was at home.' Characteristically, her grandmother cooked her dinner daily, and often tea too, because her stepmother 'wouldn't keep dinner for me until I got home. So my grandma said I could go there for my dinner. So I went there every day for my dinner, and also for my tea at least three times a week.' Lorna McLean's grandparents also 'treated me more like one of their own. I was their first grandchild.' She frequently stayed overnight with them, and each summer they took her on a caravan holiday. They would also take her shopping, and instruct her in domestic skills: 'she would let me do the washing, and baking, and she let me hang up the dripping wet things all over the kitchen—the sort of thing Mums don't let you do! At my gran's I always had sandwiches and hot drinks for supper, I liked that.' Although her parents were together until she was 12, 'I've got more memories of being with my grandparents, actually.'

Such grandmothers and aunts were, however, normally as much an emotional as a practical support. 'We were very close to my nan. My nan was like another mum. . . . We used to see her every day, because we only lived round the corner', recalls one

granddaughter; and another, who would stay with her grandmother for weekends, describes her as 'a great influence . . . a
real loving grandmother. If there were any problems, granny was
always there for me.' Some played, as we have already seen
(Chapter 3)[14], an especially crucial part in maintaining communication about absent parents, keeping 'the memory alive' about
the past and explaining what was happening in the present: 'I
always relied, I always felt me grandmother told me the truth.'
And Ann Highfield was able to talk about her mother both to a
cousin whom she knew as an aunt, and to a great-aunt: 'she had a
lot of photographs of my mum, and she talked about my mum'.
In addition, even when they took on some disciplinary role
towards the child, none of them were harsh: instead, in contrast
to many natural parents, most seemed able to combine firmness
with gentleness (Chapter 3). All these qualities recur in memories
of them, sometimes linked with the image of an ideal parent:
'lovely . . . very like a mother'; 'great, terrific . . . never seen him
with an angry face'; 'great, bubbly . . . used to come over and help
out . . . smashing woman, I loved her dearly'; 'she spoilt me . . .
she were mum'; 'wonderful . . . the kindest, most gentlest'; 'soft
. . . really wonderful . . . very gentle'; 'she was just very patient,
very kind, considerate, listened—so, all of those'; or—of a 'very
close' aunt—'she's always made a lot of me. . . . She's more like a
mum. I can talk to her.'

Although very close attachments were most likely to develop
with kin who lived within the household, they were also frequent
with those who lived nearby or were visited regularly. And it is
notable that in their teenage years several children found a special
resource in a relative who was not actually living with them. One
woman with a stepmother chose to talk about puberty to a nearby
aunt, and she remains 'really close to her. She's more like a
mother to us. . . . I even send her mother's day cards.' Another,
who had felt her grandmother—who lived next door—'was always
there, instead of me mum', preferred to confide in her first about
her pregnancy. A woman who started work at 16 lived all week
with her grandmother, going to her mother and stepfather only at
weekends: 'when I was at my mum's I always felt that I didn't fit
in, but I felt at home at my nan's.' Another used her grandmother's as a secure half-way house when moving home as a
teenager, so that she remained 'always there' in both a psychic

and a material sense: 'she's always been somewhere I knew that I could always go and stay.'

In a few instances relatives were indubitably the strongest influence in a child's emotional life and search for identity. Albert Black described his grandfather as the one stable point in his turbulent life, 'a rock in a whirlpool. . . . He was there, and he was solid'; another grandson said of a grandmother, 'my granny was—really became my mother, as such'; and a third—'she guided me'. A granddaughter recalled of her grandmother, that she 'worshipped her'. Such relatives could provide models against which these now adult children still measure themselves: 'if I could be half her—half of her personality and strength'. And to lose them in childhood might prove the most bitter blow of all.

Dick Pembridge had grown up as a village child, aware of his absent father at work nearby, and also of a great-grandfather who had been a cabinet-maker; but he felt closest to his railwayman grandfather, also retired, who kept the church in repair. This was a family in which the men never talked deeply to each other, but Dick would 'go and give him a hand making something'. His grandfather, a 'practical type', was for Dick the touchstone of a family tradition of men as makers: 'it's just a bent, a family bent. . . . It runs in the family.' It was not in fact when his father left home, or when his stepfather moved in, that his most serious difficulties began. He got on well enough with both men, and spent a phase working with each in turn, picking up different skills. But it was when his grandfather died that he broke down. 'I seemed to lose me marbles after me grandfather died. . . . I remember the day as if it were yesterday. . . . I just couldn't handle it.' He then started on a path which led to a very troubled time in the big city; and only after an interval found his way back to a more fulfilling life: significantly, as an inventive craftsman.

The extent to which a relative could provide such support, or indeed any support at all, depended partly on position, and partly on personality. Grandparents were turned to more immediately than aunts or uncles. There were twice as many significant relationships which came from the maternal side as the paternal side of the family. Still more noticeably, it was very rare for stepgrandparents to prove significant—whether they were the grandparents of a stepparent, or the spouse of a remarried natural grandparent. In this sense remarriage, which in principle amplifies the choice of

relatives to whom a child can relate, in the 1960s and 1970s bore
few gains in practice. This may be one important change today,
when the evidence of children's gain from new step-relationships
is markedly stronger.[15] But then, on the contrary, family disruption more often cut them off from natural grandparents with
whom they would otherwise have been in contact.

There were, nevertheless, three exceptions which hint at the
potential gains which other children missed. One woman calls her
step-grandmother as 'nan', while a man comments, 'I ended up
with three grandmas—step-grandma, step-grandfather, and then
two of my own grandmas'. And another woman describes a
stepfather's mother as 'the best thing to come out of that
change'. She was 'a real character . . . total eccentric, but really
nice . . . larger than life, and always happy. Every time she
descended, she had a different man in tow. . . . She definitely
brightened an otherwise dull afternoon . . . That's the only advantage, I think: getting an extra set of grandparents.'

It is clear, however, that some of the most influential relatives
were also very strong personalities. Four grandmothers are
described as 'powerful', 'very strong', or 'very dominant' women
who, in many respects, led their families. 'She dominated us. . . .
She liked to take that away from me mum, being the mother, that
she was the mother influence in the house'; 'she likes to feel that
she's still running the family'. Some aunts played similar roles in
their families. Mark Laithwaite lived for a time in the 'cosy' home
of his Aunt Lizzie, an 'old-fashioned' woman who was 'just like
the old queen of the family . . . I've still got a soft spot for her.'
Martine Brabourne, whose grandparents had remained in Jamaica,
found a parallel figure in 'Queen Bee', a childless great-aunt
married to a policeman: 'extremely upright', 'a bit stiff, and sort
of pouty', but also 'very kind, very generous'. It was she who
conveyed the family's history, kept old photographs, and provided
advice on crucial matters such as abortions: 'even though she was
tiny, . . . it seemed to me that people had to ask her permission to
do everything.' Like Mark, she was not very close to this aunt, but
she played a significant role in her life, and 'in many ways I did
like her.'

These two aunts, however, lead us towards a final form of
familial support. So far we have looked at it in terms of significant
individuals. But each of these aunts was also important as a gate-

keeper to the wider family network, which, for some children, could offer a more diffuse yet nevertheless highly reassuring form of security. Tom Rice, for example, had a tough role as an eldest child, who had to cope not only with the disappearance of his father but with an acutely depressed mother. It must have been a crucial help to him that when his mother went into hospital a cousin came to stay, and that one of his aunts so often took him to stay for the weekend that he came to call her his 'nan', and that when he played football on Saturdays, they 'all turned out on the touchline to cheer.'

There were altogether eight children who grew up within such a supportive wider family network. But they came from two very different social contexts, each a minority pattern in the contemporary British family scene.

Two of these families were migrant from the West Indies or the Indian sub-continent—and a third, it should be added, was cut off by divorce from such a network. We have already encountered the Hassans, whose transcontinental family branches, re-knitted by cousin marriages and by work opportunities in the family firm, operated in Pakistan, the Middle East, and Britain: their family feuding and solidarity was both the main source of pain and its principal resolution in Yasmin's own life. The Brabournes lacked their financial resources, and also their intense feelings about family integrity, but they too moved over wide distances, between the West Indies, Britain, South Africa, and Canada, to seek work, spouses, and holidays. Whereas the Hassans were dominated by their men, however, with the Brabournes the men seemed essentially transient figures, physical fathers but rarely much more for long; it was the women who held the family together. And this pattern could be traced back at least to the maternal grandfather in the islands, a white travelling cattle salesman, who was never more than intermittently at home: but 'he obviously used to come and go, which is how he got the ten!'

The other six instances are from provincial British families who, because they had not migrated any distance for at least two generations, were exceptionally well-rooted in their localities. They were all of working-class origin. In two Lancashire families, in one the father was a busman, and in the other he had become a publican; another father, who had started as a farm labourer, lived in a small Scots market town; a fourth was an ex-miner in an industrial hamlet in the Midlands scattered with siblings, cousins, nieces and nephews. Just one, a technician, lived in a southern town. The most extraordinary instance, however, was the Bolsover family, who again had a farm background, but had subsequently colonized an isolated group of council houses built out in the countryside in County Durham. Harry Bolsover spent much of his childhood living in the household of his grandmother, who was the lynchpin of this network. Her own household also included a great-uncle and a niece whom she adopted; and other descendants of great-uncles and great-aunts still fill almost the whole estate of houses. 'Apart from five in the thirty houses, we're all still related.' There are so many relatives around, indeed, that much of the time they ignore each other—'sometimes we can just pass each other in the street, and just walk past each other'—but when help was needed, 'they were always a tight community'. They made sure, through a petition to the council, that when his grandmother died (when he was 20), he could take over her house. 'They were going to give it to someone else, but at the time no one down here got a house unless you were related to the street.' He still lives there. And he can never have questioned, from boyhood onwards, that at a pinch there was always someone nearby with whom he could find a home.

Neighbours, Friends, and Environment

These unusually stable neighbourhoods could also provide a child with a sense of security, and sometimes also direct support, from outside the family too. When Gary Butler walks around Hanging Hill, 'if we go anywhere, somebody'll know my father or me, we just—we can't go anywhere literally, because that's the way we work, or the way the family is, because obviously in the village here everybody knows me and everybody knows my family'; similarly today, when his wife goes out, 'people will stop her in the street and have a chat because they know me.' A South Welsh family preferred not to move out of their own small town for similar reasons: 'we were settled there, all our roots were in the same area, our schooling was the same, there was no point in uprooting.' In a small Scots town too, there were not only close kin but also a welcoming neighbour, Bridie, who would cook for the child after school, give her 'special treats' and have her to stay at weekends—'a family feeling, really.' Similarly, a Lancashire girl, when hurt, would run not to her mother, but to her grandmother or a neighbour known as 'Auntie Tessie': 'she was always there as well, she was a friend of me nanna's'—and it was she whom the family used to tell her that her father had died. Another Lancashire girl comments on the safety brought by neighbourly cohesion: 'You couldn't breathe in the street without somebody knowing what you were doing. But I never resented it. . . . It was a close-knit community. You couldn't do anything without being seen, and having it reported back to your parents. None us us could. If any of us went out, there was always big brother looking over our shoulder.' Such neighbourhood communities were much less common in the south. There is one North London instance of neighbours who rallied round when a mother died, and one 'showed us a lot of affection'; and another example of 'a really rough area' in a Kent town, where when a neigbour died, 'they would club together and buy flowers': here too there was 'that closeness. . . . Everybody talks to each other. . . . I loved it. Oh, I loved it!'

There was a much less attractive side of neighbourly solidarity, in an intolerance of those who failed to fit in. It is likely that this affected some stepfamilies as such, because of the way in which parents and children had come together. Among our stepfamilies, however, it was felt most acutely by two who suffered from racial intolerance. Martine Brabourne recalls how at school in London, 'lots of children were actually told not to play with us'. And Gill Deighton, whose mother married an Indian, and has herself married an Indian, was told by her mother how in their northern city neighbourhood 'she was a bit of an outcast where they lived, and people used to spit at them: there were not that many Indians here, in 1958 . . . and people would spit at her'.

For most children, however, the sense of being rooted and known in a neighbourhood was important on one level simply because it provided a sense of continuity, at its simplest, physically: a known, familiar environment. A house could do this too, providing both a continuing physical shelter and also a symbol of a child's 'safe, secure little world'. For some children it was also a setting for pleasures and play in which parents were also involved: model train sets and winter parlour games, sports in the garden or yard, keeping chickens, budgies, a cat or dog, or gardening: all of which could be important continuities in their lives. Most of these children moved house, despite the disruptions in their family life, no more than three times before their late teenage years, and a few never moved at all.[16]

Some parents were determined to stay in the same home, and children too might be conscious of the importance of their 'roots': 'I've been here ever since'. Becky Armstrong's mother no longer needed a detached four-bedroomed house, and she could 'have made life more comfortable by selling the house, and going to live in a council house, but she just—she didn't want to do that'. Gary Butler's father did sell his house, but to move in with his grandmother, 'in the village still'. Linda Clarke moved into her grandmother's nearby council house so that she spent her whole childhood 'in the same road'.

Even a single move could be difficult for a child to accept. After moving to a gardenless terraced town house, Arthur Fisher continued to miss the garden, the friends, and the surroundings which he had enjoyed for his first nine years. 'When I first moved here, I didn't know anybody. . . . Living in the country where we were, we were surrounded by heathland and things like that, and it's great when you're a kid to go exploring. . . . I must admit I did like it down there. Lovely garden and that. That's got some good memories.' A father now himself, he has taken his own children to see this childhood home which still has such a strong hold on his imagination. 'I took the kids back, I've not actually been inside it, I just drove up and had a look round. Just showed them where I used to live when I was a kid.'

Fifteen children, however, experienced no such stability, moving between four and ten times. Sometimes these moves were resentfully blamed on incoming stepmothers, who insisted on a move to a fresh house: 'she wanted everything'; 'we wanted to stay in the other house, but she wanted to move, so we did'. The worst moves, however, were those following the breaking up of a family when loss of a parent was exacerbated by a sharp drop in living standards. Middle-class children might carry with them idyllic memories of a 'beautiful' house as their lost home: a seaside house with a huge garden, a playroom with a big doll's house and a wooden rocking horse, where a 'back door opens onto the pebbles'. For others, the changes might bring real poverty, living in a series of rented rooms: 'we moved in with lots of different families'; 'even, sometimes, one large room divided with a curtain'—'living in rented accommodation, it was always a bit iffy, because if they didn't like kids . . .'

Even when a lasting new base was established, there was quite often simply not enough space for the growing children. A lone parent often lacked the resources to rent sufficient space, while a stepfamily might have too many members for an ordinary family house. Consequently siblings had to share beds as well as rooms— 'she'd put her legs over me, and grind her teeth'. If they were of mixed sexes this became impossible as they became older. One girl grew up in a one-bedroom flat with her brother, her mother, and from middle childhood, her stepfather. For a while, her brother slept in the bathroom, but as teenagers both he and she were forced to sleep out on weeknights with friends—and she 'used to resent it, being pushed out'.

Conversely, one of the most obvious gains of entering a stepfamily, especially for middle-class children, could be a substantial increase in living space. 'So, all of a sudden we had our own room', remembered one girl, in 'the biggest house in the street', complete with a built-in theatre organ, Daimler car, and thrice-weekly 'treasure' of a cleaner. They had moved from a small bungalow where 'my grandparents had slept in one room and my mother, sister and I had slept in another, together. . . . Having an upstairs was a great luxury.' A boy felt himself moving 'quite up-market'. Another girl lovingly described the new pleasures of a 'big house, a lot of land, a dog, a cat, a nice area to live in'; and a third girl, equally fortunate, found herself soon living in 'a most magnificent house' in a Kentish village, a 'chocolate box house, to me, as a child'. It was ancient, tile-hung, with a big old wooden door with 'a latch and a thong to open it', and antique glass windows which 'went out on little wrought iron hooks that were all hand-forged'. Beside the house was a little river, which 'then ran through the garden. So it was like fairyland to me.'

Nevertheless, just because the loss of parents so often carried with it removal from home, a house was a less adaptable base for security than a wider physical context. Equally important, neighbourhoods, along with schools, were the setting for peer group play. It is striking that while these children often had many local friends, they are rarely singled out individually as long-term sources of support: at any rate, not until as teenagers they began to make serious relationships with boy or girl friends.[17] An interesting exception is one older friend made through a stepfather's brother, who would provide advice, and later became a workmate; but he was known as 'Uncle Fred', incorporated as an adult relative rather than as a friend. Another boy as a teenager singled out a fellow-stepchild, 'a close friend who was in a similar position to me, that I still see on a regular basis, now. He's just down the road.'

For most of these children, however, and especially for boys, friends are remembered more in a collective sense: 'I had my gang.' For some of them, what seems to have counted for almost as much as the friends themselves in the long run, was the context of play: streets, or still better, for those close enough to the countryside, woods and fields, for makeshift football and cricket, tobogganning and sledging, camping out and cooking, biking, stealing fruit and bird-nesting. A girl from a small Lancashire town 'used to walk bloody miles' with a group of boys and girls, 'all the neighbours over't road', following railway tracks: 'there used to be a whole gang of us. We all used to go off tracking—we used to take jam butties and a carton of milk.' And Nigel Griffiths as a village boy 'never felt I'd go off the rails', above all because he 'managed to live in a boys' world'. His mother—

always encouraged us that we would go out, outside. She was very much one for saying, 'Get out in the fresh air and not hang about the house.' And she kicked us out after breakfast, and we were called in for lunch, kicked out again, and then brought back in for tea. . . . We played a lot outside—in the snow, and— . . . made a lot of friends . . .

I have always had very good friends. . . . Life went on, and, as boys—just played.

Professionals and School

For boys as well as for girls, school could also provide a sense of continuity in both physical context and friendships. The schooling of thirty-five out of our fifty children was not directly disrupted through the family transitions which they experienced. One boy and three girls indeed thought of school as being for a while an important refuge from family: 'I remember enjoying school, I hated home life at that stage'; 'I tried to involve myself in other things'; or as Lily Beck put it 'I used to really enjoy school. I thought school was wonderful. I couldn't wait to get back on a Monday, because school was an escape, not being at home where I was bashed about, and the tension. I didn't do brilliantly at school, but I used to really enjoy school.'

Altogether twenty of these stepchildren—boys slightly more often than girls, and those whose parents divorced also slightly more often than those bereaved—have some positive memories of schooling. This might be expressed in a generalized way, or as a place where they picked up particular skills, or where they found 'good friends' and fun: 'school was great. I had three very good friends, who are still friends now'. Two boys who did not distinguish themselves educationally found a pride in excelling at sport: 'I was always into sport.'

There are, however, an equal number—this time slightly more often girls than boys, and those whose parents died rather than separated—who had strongly negative memories of schools which they disliked or 'hated'.[18] These sufferings could be a direct consequence of parental loss, and understood as such: the humiliations of free school meals and free uniforms, or the depersonalizing rigours of boarding school at an early age. One boy mentioned the embarrassment of being different, because his mother's surname was not the same as his own: 'it is hard. People don't accept it, and you have to explain.' A girl living with a single mother also 'felt different at school. . . . In them days, it was quite unusual. I felt a lot different, especially—especially at school. You have letters addressed to "Mr and Mrs—", you know, and mum all on her own; but they just ignored that. I found that they didn't really acknowledge it.' Sylvie Higgenworth vividly remembers her confusion and embarrassment when she was specially called out from class: 'she wanted to know, she sent for us to ask us, this headmistress, and she said, "I want to know who your father, who are your mother and father" . . . And I—I didn't know what to say. . . . And I can remember blurting out my granddad's name, and I got home, and I said, "I think I've told them a lie"!'

Five children remember becoming rebellious at school, and at least seven took to truanting: 'I just got fed up with it. . . . I thought there were better things to do.' Some deceived both school and parents, presenting forged parental notes; but one girl was deliberately encouraged to miss school while her mother was on her own: 'You'd be asked to stay home for all kind of things, for—if my mother was sick, or if the gas man was to come, or if the electric man, or whatever. Or if your aunt was ill, we'd have taken a week off to look after her. At the drop of a hat you'd be kept away from school.'

A few were alienated by the sheer number of moves between schools. One girl, who went to seven different schools before leaving at 16, 'was never there in the last year, I was always skiving'. A boy, who also 'lost interest in schooling for a while' after a parental death, exclaimed, 'What school did I not go to! We moved a lot.' Another girl recalls bitterly, 'I can remember thinking, "I've only just made a friend, and we're moving again". I hated starting new schools. I used to make myself sick about that.' Or the impact could be more felt as simply internal; several echo the phrase, 'I lost interest'; 'just after my mum died, I just had no interest. I couldn't seem to—nothing sunk in.' After Harry Bolsover's father died, 'I just didn't have any interest. I'd rather go sit in the wood all day by meself. You know, watching the birds; and thinking. As I say, I still miss him now.'

We can assume that for Harry, as for many other children who 'lost interest' in school, the primary reason was the impact on their spirits of the loss of a parent, especially after a death. But another factor was that some parents were less active in their support, some because they were too preoccupied with their own problems, others, especially with teenage children, because financial needs made them more anxious to see the children in immediate work than continuing in education.[19]

Teachers were the only professionals with whom all these stepchildren came into contact. Many must have also seen doctors, but none recalls finding a support from them. One or two have been helped in adult life by some kind of therapy, but the few who found themselves the child clients of social workers do not recall this positively. The police impinge only as a disciplinary arm of the law, except for the policeman's orphan whose school fees were paid for: 'it was a case of looking after each other. Obviously with him being in the police, she was all right financially, she got a house and everything.' For almost all these children, therefore, schoolteachers were the front line of the helping professions.

Institutionally, the schools at that time showed little understanding of the difficulties these children were encountering through living in single-parent or stepfamily homes.[20] The insensitivities which many children experienced from teachers took place at a time when scarcely any advice was available on stepchildren in schools. Two children who were sent to boarding schools were cruelly cut off from what was left of their past, forbidden from talking about it, deprived of a favourite doll's clothes, prevented from receiving phone calls. One day-school made some concessions on school uniform after a mother's death; while at another, after a parental death a girl was held back a year 'because they said I'd had a lot of trauma'. But as a whole very few schools are remembered as being 'aware of the family situation', and it is clear that many failed to find out why pupils were truanting. One boy who went through a rebellious phase in a state school was caned so hard that a doctor had to be called in. Clever children in state schools were allowed to under-achieve with no apparent effort to encourage them, and in the case of one black girl, an active discouragement mingled with racism: in career guidance, 'all of the black girls would be told that they couldn't do what they thought that they wanted to . . . You'd be told, "well, no, perhaps you couldn't really think about physiotherapy, but you could be a nurse". There wasn't that encouragement.' A small number of children do have strongly positive memories of enjoying some of the skills which they learnt at school, especially music and craftwork. One boy remembers an unusually imaginative primary schoolteacher, who would send him 'off down the village to find something to write a song about'; and an older girl, a teacher who 'made history come alive'. But it is very striking that although altogether half of these children have risen in terms of occupation to a higher level than their parents, only in six cases is this directly attributable to education. They include some children who went on to become teachers themselves. The most remarkable, however, is a boy who took up modelling houses at school, where one of his creations was put on display: he became a surveyor.

Equally strikingly, astonishingly few teachers became close to their stepchild pupils. A few children singled out a teacher of whom they were 'terrified' or especially 'hated'. At the other extreme only six children—five of them girls—have strongly positive memories of an individual teacher. One girl liked an art teacher, another a history teacher, and two others liked maths teachers; but the feeling seems to have come mainly from the child's side. Another recalls attempting to make friends with a PE teacher: 'it was always wanting to be special to someone . . . I wanted a mum at school.' Yet another girl did make an adult friend at school—in the cook! But only two really close mutual relationships are remembered with a teacher. One is between a girl and her form teacher, who 'called herself my "Dutch uncle", . . . If there were any problems at school, I would find her and tell her. . . . She knew just how to talk to you, and how to make you feel that you could tell her anything that was a problem.' The other is the exception that does prove the rule, brief though it proved: a 15-year-old boy, already truanting and on the edge of serious delinquency, who took out his PE teacher at lunchtimes as a girlfriend.

Stepchildren were then a small minority of those in school. Twenty years on, we hope that professionals are responding more imaginatively. But for that generation, support was to be had almost entirely through friends or family. If we sum up the patterns, we can see that what needed to be made up for these children was as often parental limitations in the face of grief and change as outright loss; and although some did gain from the advent of stepparents, this was most often those who already had good enough parents. Half and stepsiblings, on the other hand, were a more widespread gain from stepfamily life. But the most powerful resource of all was the unconventional new intimacy which so many of them discovered with the grandparents, aunts and uncles in their own wider family.

6

Gender

GENDER as a theme is everywhere and, at the same time, opaque and elusive. In devoting a separate chapter to it, we acknowledge that, while it is embedded in all the other themes we discuss, it is also so crucial to making sense of different experiences of step-family life that it needs to be considered on its own. Stepfamilies provide a particularly useful context within which to understand gendered experience because, in the transition to stepfamily life, men and women act out their roles in the absence of one biological parent. This means that the biological role too is experienced differently because of the presence of a non-biological stepparent; such families therefore offer an ideal forum in which to explore the processes whereby gender roles are shaped and maintained.

Our understanding of gender from the perspective of our different disciplines leads us, while recognizing it as a—many would say the—key organizing principle of social life, also to explore how it is socially constructed in different contexts. For our project, gender provided a key to understanding many step-parenting dilemmas: suggesting how we may 'unpack' the meanings given by interviewees to their experiences, and highlight the overwhelmingly important role played by women in helping children to cope with loss and transition.

Feminist critiques of the family constantly point to the short-comings of conventional descriptions of 'The Family' because they do not do justice to the differences between men's and women's experience and the frequent or, many would argue, inevitable tensions between men's and women's needs. Many studies of marriage draw attention to the fact that there is 'his' marriage and 'her' marriage[1] and recent studies have commented on the different realities of 'his' and 'her' divorce and stepfamily life.[2] The work of feminist theorists has produced much illuminating research into men's and women's different ways of constructing and experiencing intimate relationships.[3] At the same time, while

using these ideas, it is important to remind ourselves that just as
gender patterns contextualize family life, they are also contextualized by idiosyncratic patterns in particular families.

A family systems model enables us to address the complex
interplay between these different levels; on the one hand, those
aspects of men's and women's belief systems and relational styles
which are influenced by societal beliefs and myths about gender
and, on the other, the patterns, rules and beliefs that evolve over
time in particular families. The life story method has proved a
powerful means of exploring how these levels converge in
women's and men's own subjective experiences as they express
them in narrative.[4] In looking here at gender themes, we address
three interconnected levels. First, the macro level of socio-
economic factors, including those disparities and inequalities in
education, job opportunities, and income levels which shape
men's and women's lives generally, and are frequently amplified
following family breakdown. Secondly, gender roles within specific families, their effect on behaviour in different relationships,
and their development over time. Thirdly, the subjective level:
how experiences of loss, transition, ambiguous, or conflictual
relationships are made sense of internally and represented in
the narratives.

In the interviews, we sometimes hear gender addressed overtly,
as when gender roles are identified by informants as having been
important factors in family breakdown, family conflict, or indeed
in promoting family cohesion. More often, what we explore is
implicit, an interpretation of gendered beliefs, or a gendered
narrative which we have ourselves drawn out from the interviews.

Hence, as well as seeing how the views of our informants,
looking back at their parents and step-parents, are coloured by
gender expectations, we also need to acknowledge how those
issues we chose to highlight or ignore are also inevitably affected
by our own beliefs about gender roles. Thus in the interview itself
a mother's failure to look after her children following the loss of
her spouse might have evoked more curiosity in our interviewer
than if she had continued to function competently as a mother.
For fathers, by contrast, effectively taking over domestic responsibilities might be deemed more worthy of comment than failure to
manage. In analysing the transcripts, the theme of gender thus

especially challenges us to be aware of the processes through which we construct meaning.

Gender Roles in First Families, Stepfamilies, and Current Families

The interview guide included a very detailed set of questions about who did what in the household, both in relation to chores and to different aspects of childcare. This made it possible to get a clear picture not only of these remembered details but also of expectations about men's and women's roles and how these affected the subsequent allocations of domestic tasks. Since we are looking back on marriages formed in the 1950s, it is not surprising that most of the informants remembered the intact family as being organized by 'stereotyped' gender roles. However, informants varied considerably in whether they understood these roles as a particular gender pattern, or just accepted them as the way things were. Women were more likely to take the former view: as Becky Armstrong put it, 'I think he was a fairly selfish man, like he would go off and play golf on the weekend, you know, and wouldn't ever really help with the children, but I think that tended to happen then. I would imagine if he was around today, that he would probably have been different.'

Some informants thought that conflicts over gender roles had been specific triggers for their parents' marriage ending. Thus Emrys Hughes reflected, 'I think, my mother, you know, the responsibility she was under . . . working full-time, and having eight children to look after. . . . I think it just got on top of her really, and she couldn't take the strain.' And Nigel Griffiths comments of his parents, 'My mother wanted to pursue other hobbies, and he was very much, "I'm doing a good day's work, and I've got my football at the weekend", . . . and he expected my mother to be at home. And that was the big conflict.'

While the majority of our interviews show some shift over time from stereotypical household arrangements to a more equal sharing of tasks, there are many factors which indicate a much more complex picture. In particular, there was no clear correlation between women working and more equal sharing of household tasks, even when women worked full-time. This pattern was as likely in stepmother families as in the first family. Eileen Moriarty remembers how her stepmother 'was thrown into a situation where she had two young children. . . . She always worked full-time. I think she did most of it.' Thus while some informants clearly identified progress on their mothers' part from a less to a more equal marriage—in one case on the third marriage—others moved in the opposite direction. Indeed partly because going out to work was not necessarily viewed as a positive source of status and independence but more as a regrettable financial necessity, remarrying a wealthier man could provide a welcome opportunity to give up work and concentrate on home and children. The arrival of further children would reinforce such a move.

Conversely, men who were unemployed and undertook domestic chores were not necessarily doing this as other than a temporary expedient and it rarely indicated a change in beliefs about gender roles.

Another factor which impeded the shift towards less stereotypical patterns was that many fathers chose to remarry women who were more malleable, younger or financially dependent and willing to take over the running of the household. Thus Nigel Griffiths contrasts his mother's independent spirit and her refusal to 'toe the line' with his father's marriage to his stepmother, whom he describes as 'very, very, very much a woman about the home. Really quite dull and boring, I think. No interests, no hobbies really as such.'

Other children seem to have been much more critical of any deviation from stereotypical gender roles. Harry Bolsover saw the difficulties in his parents' marriage as partly caused by his mother working. 'I mean, my mother used to go out to work and bring money into the house. But me father used to work long hours as well. . . . Um, it was just—she was never there to listen to me dad.'

When we heard how informants describe task allocation in their present relationships, there was, not surprisingly, a greater emphasis on equality and sharing. However, whereas in describing their parents' roles, they were trying to recall actual practice, in speaking of their own role divisions they seem as likely to be presenting an ideal than what was happening in practice. Hence questions about detail generally revealed a somewhat different picture, as with Chloe Pargeter and her partner:

How about household chores in the family?
Oh, shared.
So he does cooking, cleaning and—
He, he, well he doesn't clean the house very much. He will do cooking and—
And what about looking after children, is that something that you've shared?
Oh, yes, yes.
But you stayed home?
I stayed home, yes.
And so, generally would you say that if you think about feeding the baby and changing—
Yes, mainly me.

Emrys Hughes's answer has a similar flavour:

How do you manage household duties?
Well the majority we probably share, no, share is wrong. I help where I can. When I'm home, I'll do the dishes . . .
So you don't have an idea about women's jobs and men's jobs?
Oh no.

These responses are similar to those commented on by other researchers who observe how a belief in equality is often maintained even when questioning about detail reveals gross inequality between spouses participation in domestic chores.[5]

Parenting Alone

The experience of parenting alone presents many challenges, but especially when the former marriage had been based on a rigid division of labour. Later we highlight the ability of the remaining parent to cope as one of the protective factors for children; and an important part of that appeared to be the flexibility of that parent in taking on all the tasks of parenting in the absence of their previous partner. From the child's own point of view, on the other hand, women's coping was generally taken for granted, because their mothers had always been so much more central to their everyday lives. In descriptions of parental coping, gender assumptions were crucial. Let us first consider the fathers.

From the sixteen stepmother families, only ten fathers spent any significant time as a single parent, and of these only five waited more than two years before remarrying. Yet only two of these five were remembered as coping well, and even then with some ambivalence. Eileen Moriarty, whose mother disappeared when she was 7 and is fiercely loyal to her father, is eager to play down any shortcomings: 'I think he found it difficult because it was just him, and I can recollect never being cuddled or anything. . . . I think he was in a very difficult position. He tried to keep us together, and it was just thrown on him to look after us and do everything all of a sudden. I think, you know, its not a situation I'd ever like to put him in. I think he achieved it admirably.'

Carol Stevenson too was full of understanding for her father's struggle after her mother died:

They married quite soon after. I think my dad was finding it difficult to cope with me on his own.
In what way do you think?
I think it must be difficult for a man on his own with a little girl of 7 years old.

In the same spirit Lorna Maclean, who describes her father as 'panicking' and thinking that he couldn't look after a 12-year-old on his own, nevertheless also says that while she lived with him alone he was 'good about the house', a compliment that it would be rare to hear made of a woman.

Men on the whole made fewer evaluative comments about their fathers as single parents, tending to see arrangements through which other women took over as natural. Mark Laithwaite and his father went to live with his father's sister, Auntie Jeannie, after his mother left. Mark assumed that outside work and domestic chores were incompatible. *Would anybody else help her in the house?* 'No. Me dad was working and Uncle Jim was working.' Gary Butler also recalls being received, at the age of 7, into the bosom of female relatives when his mother died, and it is interesting to note how totally his concept of being parented is tied up with the female role:

We were lucky—for want of a better word—that we got somewhere to go because, like I said, we got my grandma, my two aunties who mothered us for three years anyway in that respect. . . . Because I'd got three more Mums, like I say. It was pressure taken off my Dad. I think it would have been totally different if I hadn't had my aunties and my grandma there, but it was—we didn't need to talk [about his mother's death] because I'd got a ready-made family again.

Both he and Jamsie Noble, who also lived with relatives after his mother died, clearly had very strong and close relationships with their fathers, although it often appeared to be of the nature of a silent bond rather than a closeness expressed through open displays of affection or much mutual talking.

Three other informants give vivid accounts of fathers unable to cope and households disintegrating after mothers had died or left. Albert Black, whose mother left when he was 8, remembers his father 'going to pieces' and he and his brothers and sister being received into care for a short time until their grandparents took over. Brian Carter's father was a heavy drinker who could not hold the family together in any emotional sense after his wife died. Brian became delinquent and started taking drugs. Rosa Daniels, whose mother died when she was 10, also recalls how her father 'used to come home drunk and that was it, really. I just used to fend for myself.' All of these fathers were men who had taken a very traditional role in the marriage and were therefore little prepared for learning the new and complex skills of parenting and managing a household at the same time as suffering the trauma of loss. As we shall see below, in many stepmother families this was to have profound repercussions for family relationships.

If we turn now to consider women as single parents, we find that most faced a double challenge: to hold the family together emotionally, and to take over the responsibility of being the main breadwinner. None of the mothers broke down following the death of their husband, and only two failed to cope after the break-up of the marriage. Tom Rice's mother appeared to have the most difficult time. She became very depressed and after several suicide attempts was hospitalized. Hers was one of the most traditional marriages. Tom's father was a 'chauvinist' whose life was very much focused on his work, and the social life that went with it. His mother did all the domestic chores. She gave up her part-time job because her husband objected to it. The marriage broke up when Tom's father left to set up home with his 19-year-old secretary. Despite his resources he also failed to support the family, so that Mrs Rice suffered serious financial difficulties. After such a traditional marriage, where even her own attempts to be more self sufficient were thwarted, it is not surprising that she felt overwhelmed.

For most informants, however, the loss of a father was not experienced as cataclysmic at the level of household functioning. 'I felt quite secure with my mother, really'; 'she'd always been the one that was there'; 'she was always there and remained so', were typical comments. Many mothers, of course, faced the prospect of going out to work for the first time since they had had children, but as we have seen (Chapter 5), as a result many grandparents became more involved in child care.

For some mothers, the necessity of change provided an opportunity for self-development. Camilla Jefferson's mother, who had been an outworker, went back to school and college after her husband died and developed a career in teaching. 'She's done very well when you consider, you know, what a life she must have had with no money and me dad dying. . . . She's probably the person I most admire: she's fought against all the odds.' But having a mother who coped heroically could also be a burden, as Stephanie Rogers, whose father died when she was 8, suggests: 'She brought four of us up single handed, but don't we know it. . . . Her attitude is, she's got four children and we owe her something because she brought us into this world, you know.'

The gender differences in this single-parent phase fit clearly with some of the reasons for remarrying which informants recalled. No doubt their parents might have given different explanations themselves, but informants were often aware of highly pragmatic reasons for settling down with a new partner. These were typically economic security for women, and help with the children for men. Not surprisingly, informants were more likely to explain their parent's remarriage as a pragmatic decision if they disliked the new partner. However parents too, where they communicated their decision at all, also appeared to find it easier to explain it to their children in terms of some direct material gain. Doreen Gower's mother exemplifies this. She told her children, who were opposed to her remarrying that it was partly for financial security and partly so they could have a nice house, which represented a long-thwarted ambition. 'We didn't want to go. . . . She just said, "Well, you"ll have a lovely house, and I'll have no worries about money."' Another woman described her mother's choice of partner in the following terms: 'She once said to me that, as he was six years younger than her, she thought he would work longer and look after us. But whether she married him for love or need, I don't know, but I never saw any love between them. . . . He's very self-centred and arrogant.'

If a second marriage was entered into for financial security which failed to materialize, this might also end in divorce, as was the case with Becky Armstrong's mother. She saw her mother's third marriage as much more based on equality and mutual interests. However, when women took husbands for pragmatic reasons, there were generally less serious repercussions for the children than when men remarried primarily to provide a wife to take over childcare and manage the household.

Gender and Stepparenting

When we come to consider how gender differences influenced the stepparental relationship, we see a complex interaction between constraints from the wider societal context and the gender roles that developed in intimate relationships. Entering an already formed family may either open the possibility of creating a new and different relationship with the children, flexibility negotiated over time, or at the other extreme, entail taking on a prescribed replacement role which may or may not fit with the needs, wishes, or talents of the participants.[6] Clearly, when men and women remarried, they had different economic and emotional resources at their disposal, and this affected both their expectations of the new relationship and how much power the incoming stepparent would have. But to a greater or lesser extent the biological parent will actively shape both the relationship that the stepparent can have with the children, and their role in the household generally. And mothers and fathers differed greatly in how they managed the entry of their new partner into the family, the tasks they expected them to carry out, the emotional space they made available, and the support they gave to them.

Stepmothers

As we have seen in Chapter 3, much more was expected of stepmothers than of stepfathers, and stepmothers also appear to have
expected a great deal of themselves. It is not surprising, therefore,
that most descriptions of stepmothers were highly emotionally
charged, with at least four informants conveying irredeemable
dislike. These devastating condemnations need to be seen in the
context of the higher level of parenting demanded of women.
There are much less caring, much more violent men in these
recollections, but they are not vilified in an equivalent style.
Despite the denial by our informants of preconceived ideas about
what life in a stepfamily would be like, it would seem that the
background presence of 'wicked stepmother' myths both made
the task more daunting and also offered a handy frame for making
sense of hostile interactions. The origins and influence of stepmother stories on the experience of stepfamilies has been widely
commented on.[7] But to understand the meaning of this cultural
myth only in terms of women's experience is too limiting. It
obscures the part played by fathers in creating both the constraints
and the possibilities for the role. Our interviews powerfully suggest how the lack of experience of most men in the most rudi-
mentary skills of parenting left them hopelessly adrift after the
death or departure of their spouses, and with very few resources
to offer their children. When men had care of their children, they
thus were frequently only too eager to offload this task onto a
woman, no matter how uninviting the task or how unsuited she
was to undertake it. Having done this, they were also likely to
distance themselves from her relationship with the children.

The descriptions of stepmothers which were most damning
were primarily in those families where the father took a very
stereotyped role in the family before and after the remarriage.
This meant, as we have seen in Chapter 3 that there was then no
adult who actively held together the ongoing family routine and
culture, providing a sense of continuity and space and time for
children and stepmothers to get acquainted with each other's
ways. This lack was typically apparent right at the start, with
fathers failing to communicate to their children what was going

to happen, and in one instance delegating this task to the step-mother herself.

Once stepmothers had joined the family, they almost all took on the major responsibility for domestic tasks, either because they did not work, or they earned a great deal less, or because of unquestioned assumptions about gender roles. Certainly many stepmothers were financially dependent, so that they appeared to have had little option but to take over the role of housework and childcare. But Eileen Moriarty described how her stepmother took over most of these tasks even though she worked full-time, and this was the source of many rows. She presented the conflict, however, as if the choice was only between two women: 'I suppose she did lots of the chores that I would have been expected to do.'

When stepmothers gave up work to look after a new partner's children this could be recalled as natural and inevitable: 'She was with us all the while because obviously she had to look after us. When my father got married there was only him working, so obviously she was looking after us. She had to pack up work, she didn't work at all; only on a part-time basis, and that was it.' Gary Butler saw this as part of a hugely positive relationship. Other stepmothers, however, were often remembered as carrying out their new tasks stripped of emotional connotations. Thus in Mark Laithwaite's family close relationships free from feelings of exploitation never really seemed to develop: *'Are there important things you learnt from her?* No, I wouldn't—she didn't really spend that much time with us. She just cooked and washed and ironed for us. That's more or less all she did. She didn't really show us any affection.'

Whereas for some stepmothers, taking on the main responsibility for the household seemed to fit with their expectations, for others it was a part which did not fit at all with their own needs, wishes, or talents. Girls were much more likely than boys to remember how they themselves came to feel exploited because they bore the brunt of the resentment and the burden of helping with the despised tasks. Thus Victoria Wickham, who 'absolutely hated' her stepmother, notes of her that 'she didn't want children, a very self-centred person.' Victoria recalls: 'We hated living with my stepmother, we absolutely hated her. . . . We were like unpaid servants. . . . We used to have to clean the house from top to bottom.' However, although Victoria does not criticize him directly, her father's contribution to this unhappy situation is worth noting. While the stepmother is accused of keeping the father from his children, we also learn that 'Saturdays, he was off playing golf.' It seemed therefore that, unfitted to the task of childcare as this stepmother may have been, it was also important to Victoria's father that his own routine did not suffer any radical change.

For some women, marrying a man with children was seen as a good opportunity to gain financial security, and this did not automatically require them to have any emotional commitment to the children they were supposed to be caring for. Both Ann Highfield and Rosa Daniels had stepmothers who were apparently married simply because it was cheaper than paying them to be housekeepers, and both of them also appeared to have viewed the arrangement opportunistically. Ann Highfield's father married two successive housekeepers, both equally disastrous from the children's point of view. 'I think it was a matter of convenience, more than anything else. That's why he got married.' Rosa Daniels recalls bitterly that her stepmother used to offload all the domestic chores onto her and saw her father as powerless to intervene on her behalf.

It is striking that, while these women were loathed and detested, the fathers who had introduced such unsuitable women into the household were largely exonerated; they were either seen as vulnerable to exploitation, easily duped, or preoccupied by the need to work. The fathers, too, frequently acted as if they were not themselves responsible for what was happening. Moreover if fathers who were coping alone had let the household lapse into chaos, either because they had abdicated parental responsibility or because they lacked the skills to cope, an incoming stepmother might feel that she had no choice but to step in to restore order. This was likely to be deeply resented, especially if it was a household of adolescents as Jim Gordon's recollections in Chapter 3 testify. If stepmothers were expected to take over discipline, fathers would generally see it as their duty simply to back up the new rules, which again caused some severe resentments.

However alongside the resentment that fathers failed to challenge stepmothers' rules and disciplinary procedures, there was another powerful factor. This was that when a stepmother moved into the home, fathers often withdrew from any active caretaking role they might have had. This seemed to exacerbate the difficulty for many children, especially boys, of finding a means to express their emotional bonds with their fathers, and increased the hostility towards stepmothers. Given that generally we found that the bond between parent and biological child was the most durable and powerful within the stepfamily, then it is significant that in many cases the biological relationship with the father was a bond that could not find an overt means of expression.

Some fathers, for example, handed over the entire responsibility for the child to the new stepmother and ignored the child's point of view. 'He never, he never would consult me. He'd just get a report, a run down, and that was it. And then I was punished. . . . He was more on stepmother's side, really,' complained Nigel Griffiths. Others conspicuously failed to intervene even when the children got into violent conflict with the stepmother. 'He'd be a fly on the wall' was how Albert Black expressed it. Often it seemed as if the socially constructed gender role of 'mother' took precedence over the pre-existing relationship between father and children, although for some fathers and their children, this had never been a very expressive one. In some families, however, the stepmother's entry disrupted a developing closeness between fathers and children which the father may not have had the self-confidence to protect.

Thus Carol Stevenson remembered poignantly how 'after my mum died, my dad used to sing me to sleep every night. And when she came'—all that stopped: she had to cry herself to sleep on her own. 'She wouldn't let my dad give in.' Here, several factors contributed towards Carol's highly ambivalent relationship with her stepmother. Her father showed a loving nurturance which was interpreted by the stepmother as over-indulgence, and so probably triggered her to feel she had to intervene quickly to set limits. Carol's father may not have been sure enough of what was right for his daughter to stand up for his way of dealing with her. This Carol naturally understood as her stepmother trying to keep her father and her apart. Other women also explained conflictual relationships with stepmothers in terms of rivalry over their father. Both Joy Carmichael and Rosa Daniels who expressed loathing of their stepmothers had the strong conviction that they were trying to keep them from their fathers.

Rosa remembers complaining to her father, 'You don't like me, do you?' and being told, 'I do love you, but she doesn't like me talking to you.' When this marriage broke up, Rosa's father was anxious to make amends: 'since he's got rid of her, he's absolutely brilliant. . . . He thinks he knows now what he did but, I mean, at the time, when you're with somebody, you don't . . . '

Even those women who did not describe especially conflictual relationships with stepmothers almost all expressed some rivalry over their fathers. This often took the form of worrying that their stepmother might not understand or care for their father as well as they could. Caroline Herbert looks back with some surprise at how protective she was of her father: 'I must admit, I can remember at times, thinking, you know, she hadn't washed his shirts properly, or hadn't cooked his meals, and I'd feel at times, you know that she wasn't doing things right and I almost wanted to take over, like, the role of caring for my father. I don't know why.' Sandra Carstairs, whose mother had died when she was 5 and whose stepmother entered the family when she was 8, said that even at that age she worried that her stepmother would not understand him well enough, or as well as she did herself. All of these women expressed in some form the anxiety that their father would no longer put their relationship with them as a very high priority. Eileen Moriarty's father, by contrast, did clearly manage to convey to his children that their relationship was inviolate despite the stepmother's arrival, for example by taking separate holidays alone with them; 'he was always there for us, he'd always put us as equal to her.' Although this caused jealousy and ructions in the short term, family relationships remained close and sustaining in the long term, and Eileen and her stepmother were able subsequently to joke about the jealousy between them.

Men, by contrast, remembered conflicts with stepmothers more easily than jealousy of them, and their memories poignantly highlight the emotional absence of fathers. Albert Black remembers his father going off to the pub when conflict between him and his brothers and their stepmother and her children became too violent: 'When there were all the arguments and fights between you and Sian [stepmother], what did your dad do? He'd be a fly on the wall . . . callous, sometimes, pulling his hair out, or he'd go on a binge.' We could perhaps understand some of this violent behaviour as an attempt to engage a father and define a relationship with him in some other way than as a 'fly on the wall', or 'referee' as Emrys Hughes described it, which must have been confusing ways to understand the link with their biological parent.

Thus, while men primarily described conflicts with their step-mothers in terms of issues of authority, women saw them much more overtly as conflicts over relationships and their loyalties towards their natural parents. These gender patterns suggest that rivalry over the father was a more acceptable and admissable experience for girls, and thus made for a more coherent story of which they could make sense in retrospect. Girls were also per-haps given more opportunity to get close to fathers, to comfort them, to see themselves as useful during the single-parent phase. Men rarely reported this experience. For them, the possibilities of closeness with fathers were often so hedged around with ambiva-lence and emotional constraint that rage with the stepmother emerged as the most powerful emotion recalled. Furthermore, some men may have needed to understand such strong emotions in ways consistent with their images of masculinity.[8] Talking about rows and fights with stepmothers appeared to be one such way. Girls, on the other hand, were far more likely to be left with feelings of being exploited and of having to bear the brunt of the stepmother's own feelings of exploitation.

Stepfathers

How do accounts of stepfathers compare with those which we heard of stepmothers? The most striking overall difference is that in general stepfathers were remembered with far less intense feelings than stepmothers. When they were disliked, moreover, it was usually because of violent or cruel behaviour towards the mother, or because of feelings of displacement, rather than for attempts to intervene in their stepchildrens' daily lives. We heard surprisingly few reports of violently conflictual relationships with stepfathers.

Like stepmothers, some stepfathers appeared to have been married in order to fill a vacant role, but typically it was more in terms of what they were expected to do for the family, rather than within it. Certainly taking over as the breadwinner could be onerous: 'at one stage he was having three or four jobs to keep us all going.' But it seemed that the entry of many stepfathers to the household created an almost negligible difference to existing relationships, especially in men's recollections. Alex Plumber said of his stepfather: 'He could have been anyone really as far as I was concerned.' Richard Hammond's attitude was more affectionate and appreciative but somewhat dismissive: 'When Bert came in, he never sort of took on the role of being a father, so he never sort of imposed himself on us. . . . He was just a typical working man, he's happy just coming home, like—quite happy if he's got enough money in his pocket to have a pint, you know. That's all.'

When mothers and their children moved into the stepfather's house, they were more likely to have to accommodate to his rules. However setting the rules did not necessarily mean a stepfather became closely involved in the children's lives. Doreen Gower's mother, who had explained to her children how by such a move, they would all gain 'a lovely house and . . . no worries about money', accommodated to many of the stepfather's rules, such as not watching ITV—'it always had to be BBC 1'. But he apparently had no wish for closeness with the children and this clearly suited their mother. 'He didn't involve himself with us. . . . So he was just someone who came home for his tea, but he had his funny little ways.' In contrast, one of the most successful relationships was that of Camilla Jefferson and her stepfather. Here the adults had negotiated an equal relationship, and the stepfather allowed himself to be close while respecting the boundaries of the relationship: 'I think me Mum was lucky in many respects, because Keith always shared the domestic chores, always went shopping with her, always took his turn in cooking, so to me that was normal. . . . She'd always looked upon herself as being an equal breadwinner and equally responsible for her children, so she didn't look upon him as a sort of saviour, you know.' The relationship comes across as relaxed and very friendly, but her comments also capture its inevitable ambiguity: 'Everybody he works with thinks he's my actual father and in fact it's quite amusing, because people quite often say, "you look like your father". And he loves that [laughs]. . . . He was [affectionate] but he was always careful because he wasn't our real father. I think he held himself aloof sometimes from us.'

As we saw in Chapter 3, being an acceptable stepfather seemed generally to be much easier than being a good enough stepmother; it could even be achieved by the avoidance of certain behaviours, especially any stern disciplinary role, or violence. Some stepfathers were specifically contrasted with a drunken or violent father. Thus Lorna Maclean said of her stepfather, 'He's got a dry personality, very dour. . . . At least he doesn't hit her.'[9] One stepfather who was particularly adored was David Evans; he was described as 'lovely', 'quiet', 'affectionate', and, above all, 'sober', which was a welcome contrast to his heavy-drinking father.

Positively, a child might also be won over by being taken on outings, given presents, or by simply the stepfather being a 'friendly bloke', open, 'talking to me perhaps more than my father did, taking an interest'. In these recollections, especially from men, there was more uncertainty about how the relationship should be understood with stepfathers than with stepmothers. While some saw their stepfather as trying to take the role of a father—'he looks on us, I suppose, as his kids'—children were more likely to think of a good stepfather as 'more of an uncle' or 'as a friend'.

It seems clear then, that the relative acceptability of stepfathers is related to the lesser demands made of them, and beyond that, of fathers in general. They were therefore less likely to impose on the child. Although one-third were called 'dad', there is a sense that few of them were expected to fulfil a parental role except in the most limited ways. They did not often get emotionally close enough for the child to confide. The lack of expectations of stepfathers and of urgent hopes for them to fill an emotional gap has to be seen in the context of the parenting skills and experience of the natural mother. Since most mothers were the main caretaker, both practically and emotionally—'She's always been the one that was there', 'I felt quite secure with my mother, really'—there was rarely much of a vacuum to be filled. Conversely, however, this brought with it the potential difficulty that, because the mother was so emotionally central, 'losing' her to a stepfather could be experienced as particularly painful.

These narratives suggest that men and women experienced relationships with stepfathers very differently. There were no reports from men of violently conflictual relationships with stepfathers, in contrast to many such accounts of conflicts with stepmothers. The most characteristic pattern for boys was to distance themselves, physically or psychologically, from a relationship with their stepfather and this also suited the stepfathers who were used to taking a marginal role with children. And when emotional bonds did develop between stepfathers and stepsons, they were rarely described as in conflict with relationships with the fathers; and indeed were not easily expressed at all.

Thus Tony Dickson challenged the interviewer's use of the word 'affectionate' in a way that illustrates assumptions about men and fathering:

Did he ever show affection to you?
Well it's difficult to say. . . . Like affection . . . it's very difficult for him to take the place of an actual father. . . . He looked after me, I would say, but I think the word 'affection' I would put as between a father and daughter. . . . That type of affection is shown when you're a young child. . . . When you're 15, 16 . . . I'm more grown up.

Richard Hammond also struggled with this question, revealing how difficult it was for him to think of what a close relationship with his stepfather would be like, and indeed his tentative ideas about what any father should do:

Was he an affectionate sort of bloke to you?
Bert?
Bert, yes, when you were a child? Did he show you affection?
What, like kissing and things like that?
Yes, or were you aware of him as a loving parent?
I don't know, really. I don't know. I think one thing that you miss—I know this sounds weepy—but what I missed really—is, as a kid I could have played football. . . . You do miss having a father who can show you the right direction, you know, and some sort of role model to look up to. That's what you do miss.

For women, the picture was somewhat different. They were more likely to struggle with understanding their relationship with their mothers in the context of a difficult relationship with a stepfather, and to be unsure about where to allocate responsibility. An extreme example of this was the violent and abusive behaviour of Lily Beck's stepfather. In trying to understand how her mother could have stayed with him, she acknowledges her mother's fear: 'it was, she was just petrified of him. . . . I don't think that side of him showed till after they were married.' But she also blames her mother both for not protecting her—'I feel she was never there'—

and for choosing her stepfather over her and her brother: 'I remember feeling how awful that she chose him instead of us. . . . I really did resent her for that, that she was going to kick us children out for him.' For Martine Brabourne, whose second stepfather sexually abused her, there was a further twist through her understanding of his disempowerment as a black man, and also her own experience of her mother's tyrannical behaviour. 'I feel that about his stupidity and tolerance of a bizarre, crazy life with this woman [her mother] and also about the way he has dealt with issues of racism. . . . I now see the abuse as part of that . . . sort of about power.'

For many women, experiences of domineering—if less violent—stepfathers were closely linked to the painful experience of displacement from the relationship with their mother. Many struggled with whom to blame for this. Some, like Sylvie Higgenworth, focused on the intruders, who in her case included a stepsister. 'I resented it so much that these people were, not just taking up time of my mum's, but prising their way between me and my Mum.' Her deep sense of loss is made more poignant by her wish not to pressurize her mother by expressing it too openly: 'I felt like I couldn't talk to my mum at that stage, because like she were in this situation, and I couldn't impose on it. . . . It were like—talking to a daze that's not there any more.'

When a rare stepfather did try to develop an active relationship with a child, they could be bitterly resented. Yet even so, the mother who allowed this would often end up being resented more. Yasmin Hassan fiercely resisted her stepfather: 'He could never accept that he wasn't our father . . . I'd throw tantrums, kick and scream and get upset, and it was all because of this, I didn't want him as a father.' Yet later in the interview she reflects: 'I wish we had been closer, and I blame my mother for that. Because in any marriage that has a stepfather, whoever's children they are they are the ones who have to make the effort to bring the family together. . . . I think my mother had an important part which she didn't play, to make him realize that he should talk to us more.' Thus the clearer expectations of mothers' roles and the greater closeness of children to their mothers contextualizes stepfathers' roles in a number of ways. First, it often allowed them a marginalized life on the periphery of the family, which may at times have been lonely, but meant lower expectations and thus less disappointment and fewer loyalty conflicts. Secondly, it created the danger, especially for girls, of a highly resented disruption of intimacy with the mother, precisely because of the mother's greater emotional centrality. Thirdly, even when stepfathers behaved monstrously, a mother was generally condemned too, either for being weak, or for being selfish in putting her new husband before her children. Regardless of the gender of a resented stepparent, women were most likely to be seen as primarily responsible.

Thus the memories of stepmothers and stepfathers differed greatly in terms of the expectations that were placed on them, reflecting not just pre-existing family patterns but also the wider social expectations of men and women. Caroline Herbert, who lived successively with both a stepmother and a stepfather, sums up her experience of the difference:

Did you have any ideas about how stepmothers would be?
Yes, because I'd had a stepfather, I'd seen the situation. But, it's funny, moving in there, I had this feeling that she'd do more than my father, because girls, or children, do still at that age [11] need their mothers and so it was more difficult for me in terms of having another woman looking after me, because my dad wouldn't look after me. It would be Gwen looking after me, I felt.
So you felt more that Gwen would be a replacement, or a kind of replacement, for your mother than you did with Dick, trying to be a replacement for your father.
That's right, yes. That's right, yes.

Gender Constructions and the Child's Perspective

As well as underlying the contrasting accounts of the roles of stepmothers and stepfathers, gender was also powerfully present in the different ways in which men and women told their stories and recalled their emotional experiences. These differences lay in the language they used, in the meanings they attributed to their experiences, and in the extent to which they incorporated these experiences into an ongoing narrative of self.

Losing a parent in childhood through death, being separated from one through divorce, and gaining a new parent through remarriage, are all experiences which are replete with confusion, helplessness, and ambiguity. Men's and women's memories differ not only in their depth, detail, and tone, but also in the characteristic responses to the experiences which they narrate. For example, in the single-parent phase, a common experience for children was that of being faced, not only with the loss of one parent, but also with a remaining parent who was unhappy, distracted, or struggling to function. Feeling the need to take care of a vulnerable parent in the absence of another trusted adult is an especially ambiguous experience for children. It carries the potential for developing strengths and resources that can be useful throughout life, but it also involves the long-term risk both of an acceptance of always denying one's own needs, and of being especially wary of the entry of another adult into one's intimate life.

Wanting to take care of a parent is probably always a double-edged experience. At one level, the child feels the parent's distress and wants to give comfort. At the same time, children's own developmental needs lie in having a parent who can nurture and look after them, so that much of a child's caretaking efforts may be intended to restore the parent to a point when they can parent. This may lead the child to such 'caretaking' behaviour as attention-seeking or acting out, which is unlikely to be appreciated and leads to blame and guilt. This only highlights the discrepancy between the magnitude of the task and the limited means at the child's disposal.

The extent to which these experiences were remembered by our informants depended on a number of factors, including how far they perceived their parent's vulnerability, on the availability of other forms of help, and, very noticeably, on sibling position. Older or only children remembered it most powerfully. But again, gender was also a key variable. When we asked the question, 'Did you feel you had to look after him/her?', virtually all the women answered the question in the affirmative, immediately understanding what the question was getting at. For some, like Martine Brabourne, the experience was overwhelming, yet accepted as inevitable. 'I haven't really had much of a childhood. I had to take care of my sister always, but I also in a way looked after my mum . . . making sure she was protected. . . . I was really her companion rather than her daughter.'

For women an expectancy of taking responsibility for others is a characteristic part of their socialization from an early age. Hence, undertaking this in childhood may be extreme, but is likely to fit an ongoing self-identity.[10] The burden is felt therefore not so much as of a false role, but of its premature weight. Girls typically spoke of remembering this as a sense of uncontrollable responsibility expressed through what may be described as 'helpless worrying': being acutely concerned about a parent, often more so after remarriage, but being unable to do anything about it. Lorna Maclean remembers: 'not long after I had moved in with mum, there was that big electricity strike, and I used to worry about my father because he was on his own, because everything he had was electric.'

Talking about these experiences seemed to make immediate sense to most of the women. We can probably assume that many boys also worried helplessly about their parents, yet most of them struggled with the question, and many dismissed it. Tom Rice, for example, took on a substantial caring role when his mother had a breakdown after his father left, and yet seemed uneasy about acknowledging it:

Did you feel you had to look after her at the time?
I didn't feel I had to look after her, no. It's just, I mean, she's your mum and you look after her, like.
Yes, but within the family, would you be the one?
On no, no one said, like . . .
But you felt most responsible though?
I would have thought, being the eldest, yeh, yeh, . . . didn't think about it at the time, you know. Just one of them things, you know.

Tony Dickson, who felt 'I wasn't really old enough' to take over his father's roles, interestingly was able to make a clear connection between lack of feelings and lack of action: 'I don't think I was ever responsible for her anyway. Like I say, I wasn't really at an age where I could do much in that respect. Like I say, 9 to 15 years old, you're really too young to have any kind of impact or help in any major happenings.' Because he couldn't do anything, he seemed not to have allowed himself to own the feelings.

Conversely, the power of some memories may lie in their maintenance for the informant of a sense of agency in an otherwise terrifying time of turmoil and transition. We can speculate that, for many men, a sense of agency can only be acquired by doing, and that memories of helplessness in the face of parental failure therefore tend to be screened out. Thus Albert Black, who had vivid, if fragmented, memories of his childhood struggle to keep his family together when his father was unable to cope alone, found it hard, even twenty-five years later, to acknowledge that the task was beyond a 9-year-old's capacity: 'but I kept my family together . . . I fought to keep the four of us together, because Mandy was still a babe in arms. . . . We was in homes, yes, but I fought and I can remember shouting at a warden or something. . . . And I can remember having Mandy in my arms.'

For several other men, coping through doing emerges as central in holding their lives together. Dick Pembridge's intense connection to his grandfather, 'a practical type', to whom he would 'go and give a hand making something', is a good example of this. A masculine emphasis on identity through doing is even deployed by Jack Finlay to explain his very lack of memory. 'Like my memory is, when it's going back to things like that, it's not too good. . . . Probably more important to remember what you've got to do rather than what you've done.'

Women, by contrast, seemed able to maintain a sense of agency through valuing feelings of worry, even if they were unable to do very much; they absorbed those feelings into an ongoing experience that made sense to them, even if it often cost them dear. This differentiation in ways of coping relates in part to the different expectations that adults held of boys and girls. We could speculate that many of the men who explained their inability to connect with feelings of worry or helplessness in childhood with the phrase, 'I was too young', had found few opportunities to do anything that also allowed them to stay emotionally connected or that seemed to meet the needs of the occasion. Because more expectations were placed on girls to take responsibility in the household, they may have found more familiar ways of being useful or comforting, and thus needed to 'cut off' less because they were not faced with such terrifying feelings of powerlessness. Being told to 'go out and play', as Jim Gordon was by his father when his mother died, was not only a message about it being best to deny feelings, but also that there was no useful role for him in the house. Alongside this, girls were also far more likely than boys to be provided with models of same sex adults who coped and provided support. As we have seen, these female models could be offered not only by mothers, but from the extended family and the community, where it was overwhelmingly grandmothers, aunts, or female neighbours who played such roles.

We also noticed striking differences in how men and women remembered difficult or traumatic experiences. At one level it is hardly surprising that, with some notable exceptions, we found the women's narratives to be fuller and richer accounts of changes in relationships, and of the feelings evoked by events in childhood. Other studies have indicated that women's memories of emotional events are generally fuller, more detailed, and vivid than men's.[11] In researching experiences of family life, we are operating within what has traditionally been a woman's domain, and in probing for information about relationships, we rely on skills and expertise that women have been expected to demonstrate more than men. We were very struck, however, by how often we had to work hard to coax stories out of men, whereas women would anticipate the kind of information the interviewer might want. It was also notable that very often men would present their narrative in a more 'sewn up' way, with phrases like 'and that was it', or 'that's all really', or 'it was as simple as that'. Women's narratives, as well as being more detailed, seemed to be more open-ended. This tallies interestingly with findings from research into men's and women's narratives in therapy, suggesting that while women give accounts which could be interpreted in different ways, men tend to give versions leaving less room for ambiguities or differences.[12] We argue in Chapter 8 that men were likely to present a coherent life story at the expense of reflecting on ambiguities and differences, while women were more likely to try to incorporate different points of view at the expense of a coherent story.

When asked to describe crucial experiences from earlier childhood, many women recalled emotionally-laden events with immediacy, detail, and feeling. Men, by contrast, even when able to give quite detailed accounts, such as of a father's death at 9, distanced themselves by insisting that they were too young to realize the implications. Still more strikingly, many men claimed not to remember similar events at all. 'I was too young' was a frequent response. Even for men who were in their teens when a parent died or left, the lack of recall could be very remarkable, with some saying they can remember no details about their childhood. As Gary Butler put it, 'Whether I've just blanked out or not . . . I can remember Christmasses probably from 13 to 14. But before that I can't.'

How should we understand these differences? At a closer look, we see that we have not simply memories themselves, but also narratives about memories. Let us compare how a woman and a man told us about the deaths of their mothers. Rosa Daniels' mother died when she was 10:

And can you remember when your mother died?
Yes. Yes, I remember it dead clear. What, you want me to tell you about it?

Well, come home from school, I just remember this girl saying to me on the way home from school, 'Your mum's died.' Of course I didn't believe it. Went to my nan's straight to my nan's, and they never told me. They just said she'd gone in hospital. And then my dad came home and, he told me. He come home from hospital and he just said she'd died. And that was it. It just doesn't sink in, does it? You just can't believe you're not going to see them again.

Jamsie Noble's mother died when he was 13. He began by asserting that he 'canna remember that much about my mother, you know. . . . My childhood seems to have been blacked out, you know. . . . I can't really remember much about it to be honest. . . . I can only remember once my mother died.' But it soon emerged that he did have earlier memories. *'And how about school, can you remember going to school?* Oh, yeh. Yeh, I remember going to school.' Gradually, as he talked, his narrative became more vivid and emotional:

Do you remember when she died? Do you remember what . . . ?
Oh yes. And I actually, I don't know, a sixth sense or whatever it was, I knew, when they came back into the house after coming back from London, you know, I just knew. . . . Even at 13-year-old, you knew what it was, like, yeh. It took a few days to recover, but you kind of forget, I suppose, a little bit, being a child, you know.

Here are two clear memories of feelings at the moment of a mother's death. However, Rosa has an immediate connection to the event which suggests—as she later confirms—a continuous relationship to her memory of her mother. It emerges as a central and acknowledged part of her emotional life. Jamsie, while not obviously defensive or unwilling to speak to the interviewer, claims that he cannot remember when he clearly can, and then, having recalled his mother's death, trivializes his own emotional response to it.

We do not assume, however, that though they may have employed different mechanisms for coping, men were less affected at the time by painful experiences than women. It is easy to talk of denial and to make sweeping generalizations about men's 'inability' to deal with their feelings. But we can equally well address ourselves to the question, 'How were so many women able to remember events so well?' To answer this, we need to consider how both men and women learnt their models of communication. For some men, acknowledging the strength of childhood feelings may have conflicted too much with their sense of masculinity and agency to be remembered; and not remembering may lead to a self-definition as 'not emotional' which makes memories of emotions still less accessible.

Women appear to have found it somewhat less difficult to incorporate these memories into an ongoing self-narrative and were thus more able to give them meaning and emotional space. Rosa Daniels, who, as we have seen earlier, experienced a profound depression when she reached the age at which her mother had died, has a powerful and consistent, if rigid, story of her life as one dominated both by loss—'I didn't have my dad. I didn't have a mum'—and of exploitation by her stepmother—'I had to do all the housework.' She links the experience of loss to her depressive episode and that of exploitation to her currently being 'soft' with her own daughter; and gives the impression of understanding very well the connections between past and present, despite not having been able to voice these feelings publicly.

Finding space for painful experiences in their life stories seemed to enable our informants to engage more fully in their relationships with their own partners and children. For men, especially, this often depended on the crucial role played by a female partner. Thus Harry Bolsover talked movingly and reflectively about the loss of his father: 'There is no one to compare to me dad. I mean, if me dad had been alive I would have been a much better person than what I am.' Unusually, he is also able to make links between this loss and subsequent losses, and to reflect on its impact on other close relationships, describing intensely his turmoil after the death of an infant child: 'I thought I'd, you know, like, "Get back,

Christine [wife]," and that was a lot of the fighting, because I
thought that, "If I love you as much, I'm going to lose you as
well."' The interview shows clearly, both in his wife's comments
and in what he says about her, that she played a major part in
helping him express his feelings more easily. He holds a clear
expectation that this should be her role, unlike his mother who
'was never there to listen to me dad'. Although he belittles his
own contribution—'Christine's always there if I wanted to talk, in
fact she complains because she'll be talking to me and I'll not be
listening! But she is always there, if I've got anything on my mind I
can say it to her'—he shows an impressive openness in exploring
and expressing his own feelings.

In nearly half of the interviews with men—ten out of twenty-
two—their wife was present and played a part in the process. This
was in marked contrast to the husbands who, if in the house at the
time of interview, typically excused themselves from it. The part
played by the women present varied. Some made only the odd
interjection, or were called upon to supply information: one
informant asked his wife to give his own mother's date of birth!
But more often they joined the interview to make insightful
comments, and to encourage their husbands to expand upon
answers or to interpret and link events. Mark Laithwaite's wife
provides a good example of this when her husband is embarrassed
by an intimate question:

*How would you describe the sexual side of your life? I realize this is a very
personal question . . .*
Wife: I should think it's improving, as the older we get, it's improving.
Is it an important part of your marriage?
Wife: [laughs] I'll let you answer that!
Mark: Yeh. I think it is. Yeh.

Mark's wife then gives a detailed account of the effect that having
a child has had on their sexual relationship. Mark comments,
'She's just come back from her college course so she can answer
all these questions.' To which she answers, 'No, I'm not, I'm just
thinking about it.'

Both Harry Bolsover and Mark Laithwaite are instances of men
who found in marriage partners who helped them to engage at an
emotional level and drew out this potential in them. There were
other men, however, who preferred to allow their wives to 'carry'

the responsibility for emotion in their relationships. Yet others found no close partner, and so lacked this ongoing context for reviewing early experiences and were therefore more likely to discount them. The four men in this position showed enormous difficulty in expressing or reflecting on their feelings. This was not so with the women who had no close partner, perhaps because friends or female relatives fulfilled such a function. Once again, the expected role of women as emotional experts and interpreters seems of critical importance.

Although, since no husbands were present at the interview, we were unable to observe their relationships directly, several women commented on how much they owed their sense of emotional security to their husbands. Two women in particular, Camilla Jefferson and Lily Beck were fulsome in their praise of men who supported and encouraged them. Lily, who had an atrocious relationship with her stepfather, a man who physically and sexually abused her, felt that this cast a shadow over the early stages of her marriage, but her husband's love and support helped her to overcome it. 'Without Dylan, I wouldn't be the person I am today. . . . He's the best thing in the whole of my life.' Camilla, who enjoyed a warm relationship with her stepfather, but suffered from 'night terrors' as a child, and anxiety and depression in her early adulthood, also attributed her self-confidence to her husband. 'He's everything. I mean, he's wonderful, he really is—he's kind, he's considerate, he's honest . . . ; he's generous, he's loving.'

We also looked at what men and women most looked to for fulfilment in adulthood and whether this connected with child-hood experiences. While most mentioned both work and family life, there were some clear gender differences in emphasis. On the one hand, children appeared as salient for only one-fifth of the men, but for one-third of the women. For two women a child had become a fundamental anchor: 'he's all I had'; 'my shadow . . . I wouldn't know a life without her'. On the other hand, with regard to their work, while some women were certainly ambitious, many more—even if successful—spoke of it with dismissive phrases—'a little bit of everything, and not a lot of anything', unrewarding or 'boring', 'drifted into it'—and much less often than men as 'great'. And at the extreme, one-third of the men—four never married—and only one woman focused on work to the exclusion of relationships.

Equally strikingly, women much more often reflected on how their present lives connected with their past. For some, the past was primarily a warning sign of 'what not to do'; 'it's been hard to be happy all of my life . . . and is it worth trying to bring a child into it?' Jean Wheeler described her past as haunting her in times of difficulty: 'Usually there's been a problem at work, or a problem at home, if you're feeling bad anyway, that's when the ghost comes and kicks you. It's biting a bit at the moment, which is part of the reason I said "yes", I would do the interview.' She was among those who spoke of aiming for her own marriage to be different from her parents'. Another put it as wanting 'to settle down, and do the cooking', but the theme which recurs most often is of a determination to hold together a marriage for the sake of their children. 'I've always said, "I'm not going to split from Joe. My children are not going to come from a broken home"'; 'no way was she going to go through what I went through'. This resolution was sometimes reinforced by choosing a partner who had also experienced stepchildhood:

I know that there are a lot of people that have happy relationships in stepfamilies, and their kids grow up happy, but I have no faith in stepfamilies being good things for children to grow up in. So it's made me more determined to make a go of my own marriage, and to choose a husband that has the same ideas that I have, that one marriage is for life, and that's it, there's no divorce. And Robin is like that. He thinks marriage is sacred. So we're here together till death us do part.

For men, relating past and present was less likely to be in terms of a precept or rule for the future, but as a connection made when faced with an actual problem or dilemma. Thus when Alan Downs found that his own marriage had become conflictual, he recognized a pattern to avoid. His anxiety that his children would not witness conflict between him and his ex-wife such as he had with his parents led him to leave the marriage. His memory of his father losing touch with him made him equally determined to stay close to his own children. So Alan looks after them for alternate weekends, and telephones regularly. 'I hope the children will always phone me up and ask me, if they want to talk to me about something.'

Other men were able to draw on their own childhood experiences when they found themselves becoming stepfathers as adults. Ben Carlisle, who became a stepfather said, 'I think that having a stepmother certainly helped me with the children. I realized that I couldn't go in there and be hundred per cent right, demand what I wanted.' Dick Pembridge had also formed a relationship with a woman who had children, but had less clear memories than Ben of steparenthood, and had never found it easy to talk to his stepfather. He eventually decided to tackle him at a wedding. 'I suppose the alcohol was getting at him, like. Barriers go by the way then, don't they? . . . I've asked my stepfather, "How difficult was it for you to get on with me and me sister?" "It's fucking difficult", I think he said.'

While men were more likely to acknowledge the relevance of the past in relation to a current problem, some dismissed it altogether. This was especially likely if the man was partnerless. One, a successful professional, who feels himself both too busy, and too 'shy' and 'introverted' to make relationships, does not talk about the past, partly to avoid 'upsetting' his stepfather, but also because 'I'm a quite independent sort of person'. The other, who found his 'family' at work on the railway, does not even see himself as a stepchild: 'no, not at all'. Some men indeed saw it as strength in themselves to do this, valuing it as independence.

There were no women who explicitly denied the relevance of the past to the present in this way, even when their present circumstances did not appear to challenge them to make connections with the past.

To sum up then, whilst gender is so closely interwoven with other facets of intimate human relationships as to make its identification as a separate contextualizing variable always problematic, we see it as a fundamental theme in understanding how individuals adapt to changes in relationships over time. But gender needs to be understood, not as a biological determinant leading to fixed and essential roles, behaviours and emotional responses, but as a fluid and dynamic social construction, always experienced within the context of particular family relationships and beliefs as well as wider societal expectations.[13] The rich biographical detail in these narratives enables us to explore how boys' and girls' experiences of separation and loss were shaped by their parents' own gendered expectations both of themselves and of their children. The roles of stepparents were similarly shaped. And finally, gender also deeply influenced how the memories of childhood were incorporated into an ongoing life story, and so self-identity and relationships in the present.

7

The Continuing Capacity for Change

THE criteria that have often been used elsewhere to measure a 'successful life', as in epidemiological research or cohort surveys, seem inadequate in the face of the complexity of people's own understanding of how their lives have evolved.

An interview in young adulthood reflects ongoing processes of change rather than an end point. We have therefore looked at the 'outcome' of a stepfamily childhood for our informants in their early thirties under headings which reflect these ongoing processes; on the one hand in relation to achievements and thoughts about work, and on the other to their families, parents, partners, and children. We have looked at success in relationships as indicated by marital state and mental health at time of interview. In evaluating the latter, we drew on both the interview transcripts and the self-completed health questionnaires.[1] Where informants had had children, we look at their beliefs about bringing up their own families, and the influences they perceived from their own childhoods. Examining the in-depth inverviews can thus offer some indications of the impact stepfamily life is likely to have on the next generation, for better or worse; and their testimony can be placed alongside the statistical evidence of the wider cohort sweeps, and the questions that these have raised.[2]

In particular, the retrospective life story interviews enable us to examine what happens to stepchildren in the long run. Thus in this study, although we found a serious impact of disruptive family life on education at school age, so that few children did well academically in their teens, some did return to further education or training in their twenties. Nor could the high rate of early marriage necessarily be deemed a 'risk' factor. Whereas a very high proportion of the group married at 22 or under, many more of those were still married at the time of interview than had separated. There was in fact no significant difference between the rate of divorce of the stepchildren whom we interviewed and that of NCDS cohort members from intact families who married at any age.[3] And where separation did take place, it appeared to be more clearly connected to parental divorce and stepparental hostility than to age of marriage. Nor was the relationship with their childhood families static. Many of them were re-evaluating their families in positive and appreciative ways through witnessing the parent–stepparent relationship withstand the test of time. In addition new bonds had formed between step-parents and grandchildren, which were creating strong intergenerational links.

What factors in life contribute to adult well-being, other than success in education, work, or marriage, the criteria most favoured by researchers? Some that began to inform us from the interviews included good connections with an adequately support-ive social network; inner contentment or peace of mind, curiosity about others, and the capacity to reflect or think about one's own experience and that of others; the capacity to nurture one's chil-dren, and to allow and enjoy their development. In our own thinking about the quality of people's stories about their lives we have also looked at how their stories were told, and at the meaning they made of their own experience. This has brought home to us how qualitative research, by drawing upon informants' own subjective experiences, can challenge researchers to rethink their own favourite categories.

Careers and Work

Some earlier studies have suggested that the children of divorced parents under-achieve occupationally. Wallerstein conveyed a dis-mal picture of her clinic sample ten years on: those who had left education were either unemployed, or 'had a history of low-level jobs and frequent change of employment'.[4] Less dramatic under-achievement was also found in the small numbers of such children in the 1946 cohort and, most notably among women from middle-class backgrounds, with the NCDS cohort at the age of 23.[5]

In contrast to such suggestions, our own interviews revealed that by the time that they had reached their early thirties, almost all these young people had succeeded in coming to terms with the world of work, and indeed, that more of them were thriving in it, rising occupationally above their parents' level, than were under-achievers.[6] They certainly were not drifting aimlessly. Only one out of the fifty, a man who had been through an earlier phase of severely disturbed behaviour when he had been in prison, was involuntarily unemployed.[7] Some of the women had deliberately chosen not to work while they had pre-school children, but all the others were in regular work at the time of interview.

Equally strikingly, none of them were now, and very few had ever been, frequent job-changers: typically they had been in up to three jobs over a period of fifteen or more years, and at the most, no more than five or six. Some of the women described a more unsettled earlier phase during which they had learnt what kind of work suited them. One had worked for four years in a bank before becoming a local government administrator: 'I don't think my face fitted—I was too outgoing, too noisy.' Another started as a factory worker and 'had a number of jobs, because at that time, jobs were great. You could go for one week, and then if you didn't like it, go to another.' But then in her mid-twenties she trained as a secretary, and 'I never looked back . . . I've finally found somewhere I like.'

At the other extreme, several informants seemed to conceive of their jobs as anchor-points in their lives. This might be in eco-nomic terms: another upwardly mobile woman, whose manage-rial husband was unemployed at the time of interview, emphasized how in the present 'industry and job situation' her own administratvie post was 'not a rewarding job, whereby a doctor saves a life. But as I say, there's not many jobs around.' But work for some was an emotional anchor too: like the rail-wayman's son, whose childhood leisure had revolved around trains, and who has always worked for the railway himself. He not only says that work there was 'good fun', but that for him the railway 'was a family'. And he wants to stay with it: 'paper pushing. That's all I've ever done . . . I like it . . . I'll stick with the railway.'

We have noticed earlier how this kind of emotional attachment to work is much more typical of the men than the women.[8] There was, however, also a class difference to these contrasts in empha-sis. On the one hand, there were four informants from middle-class backgrounds who had under-achieved occupationally, but who had strong marriages; on the other were ten from work-

ing-class backgrounds who had not formed stable intimate personal relationships, but who had succeeded occupationally. No
doubt this contrast partly reflects the contrasts in economic situation which class imposed. For working-class stepchildren, many of
whom had experienced material poverty after losing a parent, the
need to succeed economically must have more often seemed a
primary task: a struggle which left no time for nursing their
psyche. Children from more privileged backgrounds, on the other
hand, especially those who married, could more often afford
without much discomfort to concentrate on relationships at the
expense of careers.

Nevertheless, one of the most striking features of the group as a
whole is their occupational achievement. Although some of their
parents had not reached the peak of their careers until middle age,
almost half of these young men and women had already risen
higher than their parents by their early thirties; while on the other
hand, only ten were in a lower occupational stratum. This is
particularly remarkable since so few of them had been successful
educationally. Many had left school as early as they could, and of
the only two who went on to university one withdrew without
finishing the degree. Five others did complete professional training courses; while another would have gone to an art college if his
non-custodial father had not refused to pay the fee. Another eight,
often at a later stage, took a vocational course such as in typing or
a skilled manual craft.[9] Thus three-quarters of them had no post-
school qualifications. They were certainly fortunate that it was
much more possible when they entered the labour market than it
is today for those with few qualifications to find jobs and to rise
through work itself.

What then were the processes through which they found their
present occupational positions? We can separate them where we
have sufficient evidence into four groups, beginning with the least
successful.

First, a very small group of four men remain occupationally
below their parents. Two of them have distinct psychological
problems. On the other hand, a third, well-adjusted man, despite
being pushed into a skilled apprenticeship by his foreman father—
'You don't wanna be like me, have nothing'—has deliberately
chosen unskilled work where he can enjoy 'messing about' with
'all my mates'. He feels 'peaceful' in this less demanding situation.

His attitudes are somewhat similar to those of another man, now back in manual work like his parents, who earlier rose to a managerial post, but gave it up because he disliked the 'hassles' it brought.

Such undervaluing of occupational success is the main characteristic of the second group of twelve women, who include almost all of those working below or at the level of their parents. They saw themselves as 'not really a career person'; and in this spirit had been prepared to give up good chances, to nurse a sick sister or to follow a boyfriend, to stop working when their children were small, and subsequently to find a job which 'fits in' with their family needs: 'I just wanted something so that I was there for the children.'

A contrasting third group of five women and men, all of whom had risen occupationally beyond their parents, described the influence and support of one parent as crucial to their own achievement. Their upward movement was co-propelled. One described how her stepmother had 'persuaded me to do nursing'; and another how her stepfather intervened at a critical moment by telling a shop to withdraw a job offer to her, and buying her a typewriter instead. 'And I literally had to sit for three hours a day at this bloody typewriter. But I look back, if I hadn't done, I'd have ended up in Woolworths. So he was good to me, even though I hated him then.' Two who became teachers had mothers particularly committed to education: 'she brought us all up to have a good education and get a decent job', one man said, 'me mum's always stressing having a nice house'. More unusually, one daughter rose almost parallel with her mother, who herself returned to education when she was nearly 40: 'she's an incredible woman, very charismatic. . . . She's probably the person I admire most, when you consider what she's been through and how she's fought against all the odds.' A similar sense of closeness in ambition infused the pride of a son who continues in the same industry in which his father had risen from worker to manager. His father had wanted him 'basically to achieve more, than he did. I think that's every parent's ambition, isn't it? Well, I own my own company, whereas he didn't, so I suppose in many ways I have.'

We can set against such parental support the explicit regrets of one woman who, although occupationally successful, failed to carry through her earlier wish to become a nurse: 'It's the one regret I've ever had. I wish my mum had just pushed me a bit in that direction, because I still have a gut feeling about nursing. . . . I wish I'd been pushed a little bit more in a project that I were on with, rather than swapping and changing, just fluttering about and doing what I wanted to.'

Lastly, there are thirteen men and women, most of them already successful, whose dynamism seemed to be more independently generated. They spoke of work as a primary focus of their fulfilment in life and dreams for the future: for some of them, indeed, as explicitly the 'best thing' in their lives. Some described intrinsic pleasures and possibilitites in the work process itself: thus a life-raftman imagines designing and building improved new models, while being a detective brings another man 'interest, variety, and the chance of something more exciting'. For others, what counts most is independence—'being my own boss'—or being in charge. Several had developed very clear strategies of working their way up, either through an innovative business enterprise or professionally. 'I didn't want to stay on the shop floor', one man explained, 'I realized it was going to be a dead end, so I got into drawing.' In the same spirit a woman who had left school at 16 rose through clerical work into administration, and then deliberately went for an administrative post where she knew she would be seconded for further training: 'it was quite strategic. I thought, "Well, I've got to move. I've got to get back to education."' And above all, more than half of them explicitly describe the hopes they had for work success in the future, often calling themselves 'ambitious', and certainly conveying the inner drive which fuelled their achievement. As one woman, now a secretary, put it, 'I could never be a housewife and stay at home . . . I'll be the practice manager there one day . . . I've decided I will.' And as our interviews show indisputably, such ambitions are not mere dreams. Many stepchildren can and do thrive in their working careers.

Attitudes to Relationships and Marriage

Many of our informants however saw relationships as more important than careers in reflecting what they had achieved. Interest in upward mobility was less often voiced as a matter of concern where a successful relationship or happy family life with children had been achieved. Women in particular were more likely to emphasize relationships, although they also appeared to have suffered more difficulties in them. There was also a tendency for those who had lost a parent through a marital break rather than a death to be both less confident to enter a marriage, and readier to abandon it. Nevertheless, for many of these young people who had survived parental divorce and unhappy stepfamily relationships, to create a good family through their own marriage might in itself constitute a 'successful' adult life.

It is crucial to keep in mind that these young adults were working out relationships in a social world transformed from that of their parents. Both divorce and illegitimacy had then been relatively rare. Even cohabitation before marriage was unusual. Today it has become normal for unmarried young people to cohabit, one-third of all births are outside marriage, and nearly one-half of all marriages, including a quarter of those with children, are predicted to end in divorce. It is no longer surprising for any man or woman, whether a former stepchild or not, to have an illegitimate child or a broken marriage. This makes for a special caution in evaluating our informants' relationships.

In fact they clearly did not bear out the most pessimistic predictions which had been made of their futures by some moralists or researchers. All but seven of them had married. And of those who had married, almost three-quarters were still married, often for long periods reaching up to seventeen years. Both figures are very close to those in the NCDS cohort coming from all types of family.[10]

It is striking how close some of these well-established marriages are. The most vivid descriptions come from the women, who speak of their husbands as 'very loving', 'kind, he's considerate . . . generous', an 'ideal man', 'a really wonderful person . . . gentle, caring, understanding. He's very sensitive.' Almost all such marriages have children, and typically the role of husband and father are seen as intertwined: 'a family man . . . very loving man. He loves his children. He loves the home'; 'a really good husband, and a brilliant father'.

Although many of the husbands play an active role in childcare, there is little sign in these long-established marriages of any shift in other domestic roles. Among the relatively newly-married with young children there are more instances, including three men who cook regularly. But of these, only one marriage, where one notes there are not yet children, is described as a 'partnership' in which the husband plays an equal role in home tasks, shopping, gardening, cleaning, and cooking.

What is perhaps most distinctive with a few of them, especially when their spouse had also been brought up as a stepchild, is a joint determination to stick together despite any difficulties. 'We're here until death us do part, as far as we're concerned. The only thing that will split us up, is death.' 'My children are not going to come from a broken home.' The husbands who share such a pact are the most praised of all. 'The best thing I ever did was to marry Dylan.'

The Intergenerational Transmission of Divorce

Because the minority of our informants who divorced are those for whom disrupted patterns of relationship are evident for over two or more generations, we discuss these families in some detail here, and also later in Chapter 8. We especially highlight the relationship between the context of these young people's earlier family experiences and how they do, or do not, make connections between events and their potential meanings.

The issue of transmission can also be examined by looking back to the grandparental generation. The degree to which divorce and remarriage were part of the larger family pattern in certain families prior to the significant parental divorce in this study, and the degree to which this differs from the population as a whole during the 1960s is an interesting, but unanswered question. Nine of the families where there had been a parental divorce had experienced a divorce or remarriage in the grandparental generation (as compared to two in the stepfamilies created by death). This legacy of in-built family disruption did not relate to any higher proportion of those divorcing in the current generation. If, however, we take those who divorced and those who had children outside marriage together, we find that over half had grandparents who had themselves experienced marital changes. It may be that in these families the idea of 'family' itself, more readily included variety in patterns of cohabitation and child-bearing.

While diverse responses to marital disturbance can be seen at more than one generational level in some of the accounts of childhood, they do not offer enough of a coherent picture to justify the idea of specific intergenerational influence in the direction of divorce. Indeed for some informants it laid the foundation for a determination to remain married which was accompanied by a particularly careful and conscious assessment of the parallel commitment of their potential partner.

In considering the impact of divorce or death, subsequent family transition and later, parental remarriage, our informants described a wide variety of influences that they considered important in determining the current life choices they themselves had made. Whereas influential American researchers have stated that the young people from families of divorce in their sample believed that one marriage and lifelong fidelity should be their own life aim, we did not find this to be so with nearly half our own sample.[11] Their life stories need to be understood in the context of a triangular interaction between changing wider social norms, particular family traditions, and individual experience. Each plays a part in influencing adult beliefs.

There were some marked differences here between this group and those who had lost a parent by death. Eleven of the twenty-nine young adults whose parents had divorced had themselves divorced at time of interview; as compared to three out of twenty-one where a parent had died, as well as two who had children outside marriage. Of those who had divorced, seven had remarried, seeing this as the marriage that was to last for the rest of their lives. Their accounts of the differences in the quality of relationship experienced in the two sets of marital relationships were vivid and detailed. But the capacity to reflect on the experience of change, and on differences in nuances of relationship, was a notable feature of the accounts of all informants who had been through transitions of intimate relationships in their own lives, whether or not they had remarried.

The accounts of the young people who had been divorced at time of interview offer no single key influence from their own families that unites the group. There are, however, shared clusters of negative experience. All came from households marked by high degrees of quarrelling, violence, or turbulence at some sustained period during their childhood. While this was also true of those from stepfamilies formed by divorce where the informants had not themselves divorced at time of interview, most who had divorced had felt particularly threatened as a result of their own parents' divorce and remarriage, and had not been able to form any kind of alliance with their stepparent during their teens.

The boys and the girls, as gendered groups, share different dimensions of negative experience. All but one of the boys recalled continuing further quarrelling and violence in their stepfamilies. None had been able to form positive relationships with their stepparents. In one family there was a drinking problem accompanied by violence, in two others inappropriate discipline towards the child, in a fourth continuing rowing and hostility between the original family and the stepfamily. For the fifth boy a loyalty conflict between his attachments to his stepfather and his own father caused him great personal confusion, especially when his mother decided to break up with his stepfather.

With the girls, by contrast, the emphasis tended to be on other powerful experiences which had contributed to loss of security and self-esteem. Half had also suffered further quarrelling and violence in their stepfamilies, often directed at themselves. In addition, two had, through a parent leaving the home, lost the parent with whom they believed they had the closest relationship. Two had formed very close and intimate relationships with their mothers during the lone-parent phase, and deeply resented being displaced by the intrusion of their mother's new partner. Seeing this solely as a loss, they continued to regard their stepfathers as rivals for their mother's affections rather than having any possible parental relationship to them. A further girl had an intolerable relationship with her abusing stepmother, and another had discovered at the age of 16 that she was not the daughter of the man she thought was her father. Two girls who came from stepfamilies formed by death had also divorced, and one of these families was also marked by high degrees of quarrelling and sustained verbal conflict.

A more diffuse but also important shared factor, which emerges from several of the women's accounts, is the destructive effect of a high degree of sustained critical comment received from a parent or a stepparent They associated this with their own sense of low self-esteem. Critical comment as a factor might well have a negative effect on its own, but combined in memory with the loss of a parent who was felt to be the child's ally, or who in fantasy became the parent to whom the child would have been closer, left children feeling highly sensitive and vulnerable to family acrimony.

It is striking to compare their experiences with those of the six women, whose parents had divorced, but who did remain in long-term first-time stable marriages. Three had lived with their mothers, two had lived with both parents and one had lived with her father. All but one had witnessed quarrelling and violence between their parents and for three this was repeated in the stepparental marriage. Thus they had not experienced more supportive childhoods. Their success seemed to depend rather on having taken positive lessons from their negative experiences. Some had consciously chosen or developed a different way of managing from their parents, for example by having an explicit contract about how they talked to each other as spouses, or managed discipline for the children. Others regarded the fact that they had achieved a good marriage almost with incredulity, and with an ongoing awareness of potential legacies of marital relationship that needed to be borne in mind. As Maureen O'Nally said, 'My marriage is nigh on perfect. . . . It frightens me if you want to know, because I'm highly superstitious.'

Evaluating Early Marriage

It seems important to note, because of the special concern of researchers that youthful marriage exposes stepchildren to a higher risk of breakdown, that it can also be viewed as an appropriate and protective move in many instances. Early marriage can offer a supportive intimate relationship at a time when young people are not finding such needs met at home. It needs emphasizing that early marriage does not necessarily lead to marital instability. Equally important, even when the marriage proved short-lived, it may have been beneficial, providing a relationship context which could be left later on, just as families of origin need to be left. It was of course a more serious problem if there were children of that early marriage, and how they were then regarded.[12] Of the small number of young men and women overall who had divorced, half had married before they were 20, and all but one before they were 23. But we found that the dissolution of a first marriage was not necessarily viewed as a bad thing. Many people regarded their own divorce as a positive part of their own development. To isolate a single marriage and no divorce as a criterion for the most successful outcome in relationship terms, may not be adequate as a representation of how people subjectively assessed their own lives. A first marriage had often been used as an available intimate context for mutual development at a point in time when both parties needed it; but from which both subsequently grew away without regret. Where children were born to the first marriage, they had in each case stayed with their mother.

Certainly there were some for whom the choice of an early marriage was subsequently seen as mistaken. 'I was looking for security and he was looking for a replacement mother. . . . I know that now, I didn't then. Two very lost and very frightened young people got married. The biggest mistake they ever made in their lives.' Sometimes the decision was precipitated by a major row with a step-parent.: 'I was just 19 and I left home and I think it was because my dad and I had a big row and I said, "Right, that's it, I'm leaving home . . . " I vow to this day that if I hadn't had that row with my dad [her stepdad], and I got on with my dad in my earlier years I'd never have married that early, and I'd never have left home.' Others simply wanted a secure social niche: 'I wanted to get married, I wanted to be Mrs Somebody, I didn't want any children at the time'; 'I wanted to be secure . . . just security more than anything.' In a number of instances it seemed that the marriage was primarily to the family of the person being wed, which was seen as offering a better base than the unhappy situation at home. Not surprisingly, for some whose initial move into marriage was above all part of a search for security and recognition, commitment to the marriage faded when the security diminished or the sense of recognition faded. As Tracy Sims wrote to her husband, 'The only thing we've got in common now is the house and the goldfish.' The decision to leave might correlate with a recognition that the marriage was re-creating feelings of insecurity that had developed in childhood. As Yasmin Hassan said, 'My mother didn't expect anything better from me and I think that's affected me for the rest of my life. . . . I always felt a failure, and I myself began to believe that I wouldn't be able to do anything better, and that later affected my marriage: . . . a vicious circle.'

Sometimes the ending of a marriage came with the formulation of the wish to have a child. As Jean Wheeler said, 'By the time I felt secure enough to consider [having children], it was sort of time. I found him playing around. So there went security and without that I wasn't going to have a child. I didn't want to do to a child what was done to me.' With others it was the possibility of another relationship developing, for example at work, that brought out the awareness that something was missing. As Sylvie Higgenworth said, 'Meeting Sid I suddenly felt different, very special again, very important. . . . We had a lot in common really. . . . It made me realize that I just did not want the marriage any more, whether anything you know, anything developed with me and Sid or not.' In half the marriages that had ended, the belief was that the partner had been unfaithful. Perhaps not surprisingly the reasons why this might have happened were not explored in depth in the interviews, although it was generally framed in terms of 'lessening interest', or 'growing apart', or 'going our separate ways'. What was clear from the accounts of those who had remarried was that the sense of coupledom had not developed in the first marriage: in ways that they could identify through the different experience that they were now having.

A small number of those interviewed were in ambiguous arrangements with their marital partners; the arrangements for living together having ended, but clarity about future arrangements still not achieved. Mandy Pope, for example, was neither divorced nor living with her husband, who was currently living with another woman, but expressed her belief that he would return: 'breaking up, its totally destroyed everything I ever thought, dreamt about, that marriage was going to be forever'. Her relationship with her child was markedly intense, 'my shadow, my little doll, my baby', and the interview obviously came at a time of unresolved turbulent experience. For Albert Black recounting the experience of divorce to the interviewer was also highly charged and resurrected traumas of earlier childhood separations. In his own account the amplification of a current life stress by an earlier experience of loss was both vivid and painful, leaving the interviewer concerned about his well-being. Having experienced no continuous or protective care when younger from either his mother or his stepmother, the current experience of separating from his wife and child was acutely felt, particularly in that it had left his son in a position that reminded him of his own childhood vulnerability.

Repartnering or Living Alone

Altogether, following the ending of a first marriage, seven out of the fourteen had not remarried, often by choice.[13] Three were in positive relationships. Two who were not in sexual relationships were well connected to their family networks and to satisfying jobs, and expressed contentment that they had found their way through the upheavals of their own divorces into a calmer life. As Tracy Sims expressed it, 'I wouldn't say, I'd like to never want for anything because I think if you don't want for something you get selfish. . . . So I'd still want to have to, not struggle, but appreciate things, you know like I am now. I'd like a child. Someone to love me and me to love them.' In thinking back on what she most valued, she cited her best friend from childhood who is still her best friend now. 'I see her every other day. In fact I probably see more of her than I do my mum. . . . So when you come back to saying who do I talk to, who am I closest to, I am closest to her, my best friend.'

One alternative pattern described by three women was that of serial cohabitation, in which marriage was just one of several steps in intimate relationships. This appeared to be associated with informants who when adolescent had experienced themselves as raised to the same generational level as their parents by being treated more as adults than as children, perhaps thus diminishing their awareness of key transitions. Two were also positively encouraged by a parent to develop early sexual relationships.

Joy Carmichael's father encouraged her to smoke, and to share his cigarettes from an early age, and used to take her to the pub with him. In the context of her unhappy relationship with her stepmother this camaraderie was welcome if confusing. He encouraged her to have her boyfriend in the house and brought them tea in bed. Moving between two sets of parents and feeling at home with neither, she grew very independent as well as mistrustful and chose to have a number of long-term live-in relationships, including one marriage that lasted five years. She described herself as loving the idea of marriage, but finding the experience awful, 'a sudden terrifying realization that life was going to be like this for the next fifty years'. As with the previous cohabitations she had left, she left the marriage; always feeling she needed to be in control.

She had not as yet remarried. She was in a relationship characterized by 'open talking'. She and her partner ran a business together. She hoped to avoid things she has seen go wrong in her parents' relationships, 'how not to be from the experience of living with people who have no consideration for others'. She was in no rush to have children.

Joanna Austin had married at 22 and had a child, but did not wish to live with his father. Altogether she mentioned nine sexual relationships, none of which had lasted very long. Earlier as a pre-teenager she had been elevated to a parental caretaking position while her mother was severely depressed, and suicidal. Her mother's subsequent relationship with a man she could not respect filled her with distaste, and she had resented 'being put back into the kids' role having been earlier taken out of it'. Her mother also encouraged her sexual relationships when she was young. At the point of interview she still did not seek or value marriage, placing honesty in relationship as of a higher moral order.

She described herself at time of interview as in a stable living-out relationship with a man whose child was the same age as hers, and held a demanding job which she enjoyed. She reflected:

I don't know about marriage. . . . I would get married again if I was very confident about the relationship and—if a partner seriously felt it made a lot of difference to their sense of security, but otherwise I'm not at all religious these days. . . . I don't see a moral need to legalize it—its all just taboos and things. . . . But I don't feel a deep personal need at the moment to get married. I don't find it a romantic idea.

Her ideal of a partnership was based on 'things I've never really had. . . . Honesty emotionally'.

In considering how informants viewed their own marriages and family life, comparisons often arose with the marriages of their parents and the family lives of their childhood. While some people made comparisons for good or for bad in a direct manner (see Chapter 8), the influences from parental figures were complex and subtle and sometimes emerged obliquely in attitudes towards relationships rather than in direct telling. Stephanie Rogers, for example, who had loved her father and was obviously loved by him carried this love of men forward into other relationships: with her stepfather and with his extended family. 'I never thought, "Oh he's me stepfather", never thought like that. He was more a friend. I thought of him as a friend because we used to laugh.' However the fears and anxieties of her childhood also travelled. She never felt that she could settle down in marriage, and preferred her 'freedom', always fearing that if she made a commitment she might be 'let down'.

Others were more explicit about their mistrust, originating in childhood relationships, but often confirmed by relationships of their own which they had discarded. As Doreen Gower, with a child but deliberately without a partner put it: 'Men, I've never respected them I don't think. . . . I've been able to walk all over them in a way and get me own way. I like being on me own. . . . Like it doesn't bother me that I'm a single person. I don't feel I have to be in a couple. In fact I hate being in a couple. I don't like to feel I'm tied to one person.'

Becoming Parents

For a number of women, however, the primary relationship, whether or not they had men in their lives, was with their children, and for them this clearly provided the key context for change. Twenty-six out of the twenty-nine women had already had at least one child. It is striking not only that our informants were more likely to have had children than were their age group as a whole, but also that this was especially so with the women.[14]

The women's reactions on discovering their pregnancy differed partly because not all children were intended. Some of those unplanned were nevertheless quickly accepted: 'a little accident, but I love her dearly'. For others, the hoped-for birth was eagerly awaited: as bringing 'something of my own, something I had'; or feeling 'very excited, dying to have children'.

For the women, only four of the births were mentioned as notably difficult. At least half of them had their husbands present throughout the birth and none was ambivalent about this: one described it as 'a wonderful feeling'. Some of the men too were clearly deeply moved. One remembered 'I felt over the moon'; another called it 'brilliant'; and two the best moment in their lives.

When we look at the emotional impact on fathers at being present at their child's birth, there is one instance of a man who missed the birth of his first two, but after being present at the third became a participant, taking his part in feeding, changing, and dressing the baby. Of the other men, the five fathers who did least had all been present at the births. As a whole, half of the fathers were active co-carers for their infants. With older children, although the evidence for this is thinner, it looks as if their roles, apart from concerning discipline, were mainly in playing or taking to sporting occasions.

In terms of discipline, almost all these mothers and fathers believed in occasional smacking, although often also mentioning the context of a loving relationship. There were no discernible differences in the patterns towards boys and girls. Only the two single mothers had completely renounced physical punishment. One couple claimed that their children 'basically rule us, rather than the other way round'. Of the others, most suggested that they rarely resorted to physical discipline: 'I can't remember the last time I smacked them.' Only two hinted that they punished regularly: 'If they don't, still don't do it, then I'll give them a backhander'; 'I think a good whack doesn't do any harm now and then.' Because parents always tend to give a softer view of discipline than children do in interviews, it seems probable that they tended to underestimate their own severity here. Nevertheless the evidence does strongly suggest that as parents they were handling their own children much more gently than they had been treated themselves as children. Certainly there was no sign that any was as uncaringly harsh as many of their own parents.

As parents they also varied in what they thought the most important qualities in child-rearing. Some described a striking commitment: 'we should give one hundred per cent to our kids during the time that they're here, and after that, that'll be our time.' Most often they emphasized the need for a mixture of love with guidance and discipline: 'love, affection, and knowing where you stand'; 'to show them love, and hopefully guide them'. Only two emphasized physical affection. Three mentioned encouragement 'to better themselves', but another 'would never push' his daughter 'into anything'. Although there were two who were already keeping important secrets from their children, another four stressed the importance of talking to their children. One was Martine Brabourne, who saw the key to helping her son to develop 'his freedom to express himself' above all in her

listening. . . . Being there is important, yes. . . . But I don't think in order to be a good parent you've got to be there twenty-four hours a day. . . . Being able to listen and able to provide the answers, or at least find the answers. . . . People say that he runs rings around me because I'm soft but I don't quite see it that way. I mean I think he actually feels safe to explore lots of different things being with me.

Like so many of these stepchildren become parents, Martine was helped by being able to reflect on her own early experience, and her wish to offer something different to her children.

Two Divorced Men with Children

Two of the men who divorced had children from their first marriage. One had fought to stay in touch with his daughter and the other had decided not to. Since the question of what helps men retain contact following marital breakdown remains a challenging one, even though fewer fathers now lose contact after a divorce, their different thinking about their own connections to their children are worth describing in some detail.

Nigel Griffiths had married at 25 to a woman he had lived with for two years and with whom he had a daughter. They separated within a year, and he attributes this to the incompatibility of their jobs. This repeats one aspect of the relationship between his own mother and father, in which his mother was more ambitious than his father would have her be. Nigel says his own wife followed a similar path, moving away from him towards someone more compatible with her interests.

And I was very upset about it for some time afterwards, because of the fact that coming from divorced parents I never thought it would happen to me, and then of course it does. And because there were children involved I didn't like it at all. I wanted to start again. . . . But as much, you know, as much as you try, and hope there might be some reconsideration, there wasn't.

He then attempted to continue with contact arrangements, but these proved too painful.

Whilst I tried to carry on for a little while, having Anna at weekends, it gets to the point where in my own mind, I had to cut it to a certain degree out of my own life as well to start again afresh. And my wife and her new chap were making it very uncomfortable for me. And there came a time, when you know I just had to walk away from the whole thing and start again. Which is what I did. And I don't think it's really affected us at all [turning to his second wife next to him], has it? I don't really, we don't really ever talk about it at all. I started again, fresh as if nothing had happened.

In further discussion he shows that he had no further contact with his daughter, but believes that one day 'she might turn up. I've spoken with Marilyn, we know that one day that may come up, but then hopefully she'll be old enough to understand what really happened'.

The sharp separation of his first and second relationships is also seen by Nigel—and presumably by his second wife who does not comment—as an important aspect of their own relationship's success. 'She's never had to worry about stepchildren, or any problems of a previous wife, or anything like that. I don't think you can hang her up in the past. We had time to develop as a couple without the hindrance of other pressures around us.' Although unvoiced in the context of his own second marriage, the shadow of his father's second marriage in which he had accompanied his father as a child unwanted by his stepmother must have influenced his current choice for a 'fresh start'.

His second wife has also been important in teaching him how to show affection, and allow her independence.

Looking back on my parent's marriage, one of their biggest faults is the fact that my mother didn't have the opportunity to develop her own interests, and I've always tried to allow that to happen. . . . I don't think my parents showed enough affection to each other so I never saw any kind of love being shown either between themselves or to us as children and I want to improve that. And certainly Marilyn's shown me more the way to do that.

In his first marriage he does not believe he was mature enough to realize that. Marilyn's parents have also been influential: 'I've seen

that there is another way to family life, very much so where she is
much more open with her parents . . . and they take very much
more interest in her life, and our lives as a couple. . . . My own
parents, although they are there, I wouldn't say they are really.'

In thinking back on what would have been helpful, Nigel is able
to describe the way he wished his biological parents could have
conducted themselves after the divorce. 'If they had been a bit
more open with us, perhaps explained things a little bit more it
might have made things easier. And if they had helped us as
children to come together more and you know if my father had
delivered me more to my mother or whatever so that life could
have continued without the bitterness between them.'

Alan Downs also had children from his first marriage which had
lasted ten years, and ended because his wife was having an affair
with a neighbour. Unlike Nigel, he was determined to maintain an
ongoing connection with his child. He did not wish to repeat the
pattern set by his father following the ending of a marriage
marked by severe domestice violence. He speaks to his own
children twice a week on the phone and has them for the whole
weekend every other week. He remembers the end of the marriage as having echoes of his own childhood.

We were getting into the same stage as my father and mother were
twenty odd years previously. So at that point I said, 'Right', you know
I'm not getting to this stage, and my kids are never going to witness this,
and so we went our separate ways. And it was bitter for a while, but it
got better, and we're all relatively friendly now. . . . Her and the little
girls have been here numerous occasions, and you know she can pop in
and say this, and she'll phone us up if she's got a real problem.

Alan has a clear idea of how he wants to be different from his own
father. 'It's a view I've had from a long time ago, that I was always
going to try and be better than my father was. I try to think that I
can learn from the mistakes he made. . . . Just that do completely
the opposite to what he did. . . . I always wanted them to know
that I was there.' He explains very specifically how he does not
intend to be a father that only give them treats. 'You see my
father, even now he's gone from me and my brother to his
grandchildren, and he treats them as novelties.'

What enabled Alan, whose background memories contained
more frequent and vivid images of violence than Nigel's, to

manage a more continuous image of fathering following divorce? Unlike Nigel he was raised with his mother who doted on him, and when his father went life 'actually became better—easier'. Although his dislike of aspects of his father is intense, his images of him as a man are much richer than Nigel's are, even though Nigel lived with his father. It may be that the experience for Nigel of being cut off from his mother without explanation for two years at the age of 9 created a trauma, which remained unresolved because it was never discussed and no explanation evolved. The fact that Alan's mother seemed happier following the separation and that he experienced that happiness is also important. In addition, when his father married again, 'My stepmother was always very pleasant and . . . I used to quite like her.' But unlike with Nigel, this stepmother was never his primary caregiver. Although things got tough when Alan's mother remarried, due to his stepfather's excessive drinking and accompanying violence, it seemed that the relationship with his mother combined with ongoing knowledge about what was happening, allowed for the development of a more coherent and positive story.

Stepchildren as Stepparents

It might be expected from general trends in the population that eventually at least six of these former stepchildren will themselves become stepparents in turn, and indeed, already nine had partners with children from a previous relationship: seven women and three men.[15] Of these, however, all the women and one of the men played no significant role in the lives of their stepchildren, none of whom were resident with their partner. Only two of the men were able to play active roles as stepparents, and both of them were interestingly reflective about it.

Ben Carlisle is an active stepfather of three stepdaughters. His own mother had deserted the family when he was 11 and he had never heard from her again. This made it painful for him to accept that his stepchildren still had loyalties to their father who, as Ben saw it, had deserted them. While acknowledging that 'I would never try to interfere with that', he admitted that he felt a little hurt when he heard them talking about their father. In viewing his stepchildren's wish to stay connected to their father, his own decision to cut off completely from a mother who had left was being silently challenged. In dealing with his stepdaughters, he drew on his own experience of a stepmother. 'Let the parent stay in charge, and back them up. Don't make your own rules. . . . Talk things over with each other away from the children and don't disagree in front of them.'

Dick Pembridge, who had recently begun a relationship with a divorced mother with two boys, was also trying to draw on his own childhood experiences, and to supplement his own rather sketchy memories by talking to his mother and stepfather.

The third stepfather, Brian Carter, had significantly chosen to marry another former stepchild so that he and his wife had comparable pasts, but by contrast, it was a past on which they both preferred to turn their backs. They had only occasional contact with her three older children, who had stayed with her ex-husband. After a very problematic early adulthood Brian had now found a new stablity in his self-enclosed family of marriage, with his wife teaching him to parent their two children, and the whole atmosphere based on 'sharing. Plenty of love. . . . Very close. Friends, like, lovers. We've just got a great relationship.' Stepchildren must have seemed a threat to this ideal new family world.

Of the seven women who had the position of stepmother, the role brought none of them direct responsibilities, and rarely even occasional contact with their stepchildren. However, they took very different attitudes to the absence of these potential children from their active lives. Thus, on the one hand, Gill Deighton, who only became a stepmother at a point when her stepson was already of an age to leave home, strongly believed in contact with him. For her, however, the importance of parents keeping in touch with their children, which she had missed and longed for herself, was highlighted in the advice she constantly gave to her husband who had fallen out of contact with his son through a dispute over family loyalties. 'I tell him, "You've just got to forgive. He's your son, it's not worth not seeing each other for."' she had no desire for children herself. 'I think, "Are there any perfect families?" That's how I feel. Maybe that's why I haven't got the desire to have children straight away. I don't have this family impact. I've told Bill that if we start arguing and squabbling, I'll move out. I won't live in that situation.'

Sandra Carstairs, on the other hand, already had a daughter of her own aged 8 when she married, and she saw her husband's daughter by a previous marriage as a potential threat. 'I said to him the best thing he can do now is just forget, because he's not going to see his daughter—because she just won't let him.' This appeared to conflict with other information she gave, including that the ex-wife had invited them to stay, which Sandra dismissed as 'weird'. It seemed she had glimpsed relationships that she wanted for herself, in her husband's family. 'I love his dad dearly, he's a darling. . . . I look on him more as a dad than my dad.' But although seeing the needs of her own child as of great importance in relation to her decision to remarry, she failed to see her stepdaughter in the same way, for it seemed that she was frightened of anything that risked rocking her new-found stability.

Partnerships and Family Life

In listening to the accounts of marriages and the developing family relationships both within the home and with the extended family, there is a strong sense of having arrived, often after careful and extensive scanning and planning. Celia Newton said of her second marriage:

Over the weeks before we decided that we were right together things were discussed and he would make his opinions about me and I would make my opinions. And then in those days we could go out for dinner, and people would discuss things about their children, or education, so things like that soon became apparent if we were on the same wavelength or weren't.

Celia continues, 'He's good all round. I suppose you would say Tony is the perfect carer. You would find a man, you would find it very hard to find a man as caring as he is, about whomever.' The marriage is perceived and described as teamwork. In the same way, first-married respondents see the marriage and family as the resting place where their journey has brought them. Partnership and solidarity are the keynotes. 'We're very supportive with each other. We do nearly everything together.' The recognition of family life itself as an end point is expressed as a relief. 'He is quite a secure person you know, and his mum and dad are very together and did everything as a family, and I that's how I want it to be for you know for my kids, which it is.' In considering those who were in settled marriages this sense of openness, sharing, learning, and changing in the context of the current family comes through strongly. 'There's more openness, more communication, more questions, and more curiosity. She keeps me young—keeps me on my toes. . . . We talk about anything under the sun.' He speaks of a sense of 'pulling together' and facing difficult things as a pair: 'we pulled right through and we done it and we didn't need anybody to help us, we done it all by ourselves.'

Many young men contrasted their settled married lives with a 'wild' period which preceded it. Arthur Fisher, for example, met his wife when he was 19 and she was 16, and her mother was opposed to their going out together because of his wildness. Both sets of parents subsequently approved the marriage three years later, and he was now very close to his wife's family, 'closer than my own'. He sees his marriage as helping him to be closer to his children than his parents were to him; and values the way his wife has taught him to be with the children.

The sense of learning together, and especially of men learning from their wives, about family intimacy is a strong theme of the interviews. Thus Alan Downs, now recently remarried to a woman he met four years earlier, who feels his own children are 'quite happy' with her as a stepmother, says of himself: 'I didn't know how to go about being a good parent, and I'm not sure if I am a good parent . . . I mean you've both come with a second chance based on your own experience; things you want to copy and things you don't want to. You definitely want to get away from, but its learning to be parents together isn't it?' He spoke as someone who, after initially resenting his own stepmother joining the family, had subsequently appreciated the climate of order and routine she created, and the patience she showed with her step-children; a virtue which he listed as high on his own list of what good parenting is about. Others, still caught up in the context of larger family acrimony, described their own marriage as a refuge and a relationship which has eased the pains of the past. As Mark Laithwaite reflected, 'I would say it's as though I'm in such a good life here, it makes me look at everything that's happened in the past, and it just doesn't bother me. You know it's just as though in a way it never happened.'

Harry Bolsover was even more explicit about the importance of his marriage to his mental health. He still cited the death of his father as the worst thing that happened to him in his life, and his baby daughter's cot death some fifteen years later brought the old grief out in a new form, leading to a severe depression which his wife helped to get him through.

If it hadn't been for having her and that it was the one time when I could honestly have said I could've just went out and topped meself. . . . Because it felt like everyone who I loved. . . . You know it even got to the stage where . . . I thought, 'If I love you that much I'm going to lose you as well.' I still go to me dad's grave now. And as it happens, me daughter's buried just down from me dad.

Reworking Old Relationships

For all those who were either parents or stepparents, the rearing of children inevitably reawakened unresolved questions from childhood and posed dilemmas about models for parenting, which many were eager to discuss. Some also voiced their wish to find an opportunity to unravel and perhaps resolve past misunderstandings. Typically the role of men as both fathers and stepfathers came in for the most open scrutiny, although some positive re-evaluation and affirmation of stepmothers also took place. Jean Wheeler made the point, relevant to many others that 'specifically for us who had no father role, we had no expectations of what the father role was, it was very difficult'. Very often these re-evaluations were directly related to subsequent painful personal experiences. Thus Albert Black, recently separated from his own wife and children, had come to much more of an appreciation of what his father had done for him.

Since I've grown up and I've got a family, I've had a family of my own, it's only in the last three or four years that me and my dad have got really close. Because, I don't know, it seemed like there was a barrier between me and him, because we were so much alike, that even people say today, 'You're the bloody spit of your father.' But it's only the last couple of years that I've been able to sit down and talk to my father. As you get older, you get wiser. And I can understand what my father went through, because I went through the same.

Periods of long depression, my father had a nervous breakdown. But he kept the four of us together. There's a lot to thank the man for, you know. He's my dad.

Dick Pembridge had come to reconsider fathering through sensing that there was something missing for his partner's children:

You feel the need for them to have what—there's three boys. One is 15, 12 and 7. . . . They can be a little bit—like—getting thrown out school and you can see exactly yourself, you know. And some things they do, I was exactly the same, and they blame things on this, that and the other and you can see—it's useful to have a man about the house when you are a boy, cos you need that don't you.

At the same time he expressed the need to sort things out with his own father.

I don't really know him, I don't think you know because I don't see him, I feel I need to. I feel—Boxing Day evening I think it was or the day after Boxing Day. I went into a pub with an ex-girlfriend, went for a drink and he was there, and I had had a few by then, and I said to him that we ought to—I'd get down and drag him out and have a head-to-head, get it sorted sort of thing.

Camilla Jefferson, who had always felt comfortable with her stepfather, perhaps captured the quality of the experience of 'father' that Dick was attempting to describe, seeing the role as a sense of a continuous presence: 'part of the house really, and because I didn't really remember me own father very well, it just never occurred to me to sit down and think, "This is going to be my stepfather." He was just there.' In discussing a 'dad' she says, 'I didn't really know what a dad was. . . . In one sense I never thought of him as me dad and never called him dad, but then again, I thought he was me dad, do you know what I mean? Because he was there, and he took us out and we went on holiday together, and he brought us things home on pay day and things like that.' She makes a valuable observation about the nature of successful stepfather entry into family life: 'He's been there so long, since I was so young that it seems natural. . . . I mean possibly if he's come into our lives when we were teenagers, then that would probably have been a different scenario, but because he was there from such an early age, we just accepted it.' The importance of 'being there', a presence which gradually came to be depended upon, although often unacknowledged at the time, was voiced by many men and women. 'He were always there to help me, you know, he's there, you know, he's just there.' The absence of a biological father's presence at significant life events gave viability to the closer trust in stepfathers as a continuous reliable presence. 'He [my father] didn't come to my wedding, so then I wrote and let him know about his granddaughter. And he never bothered.' 'I don't know how you would define him [stepfather], I just, he's just been there, he's always been around. I keep saying if I needed anything, I think I could have gone and said, "Look, help me".'

Many accounts are characterized by the revaluation of an adolescent relationship with a stepparent. From adulthood there was a different recognition that the person who had been violently fought as a teenager nonetheless represented a parental figure to whom the respondent felt truly connected. There was a tendency for women who had divorced to remember stormier relationships with their stepfathers in their own report than those who had stayed in a stable marriage. Their own mothers' first marriages had also been characterized by violence, and the conflict was often carried into the second relationship, not only through the interactions of mother and second husband, but also through the behaviour of the child. Thus Tracy Sims felt that the relationship between her mother and stepfather had been a stormy one largely as a result of her own behaviour: 'my mum was always in the middle of arguments. I mean, I went two years without speaking to my [step]father, you know in the same house, so that must have pulled that woman apart.' But looking back now, she also remembers him as the person who by rights represents 'father' in her life. 'He was good for me, even though I hated him then, he was still good for me. I can remember, I mean, everything I remember about him now was all really good, for my good, for me you know, and he done everything for me which was, you know, good.' Strictness, which had previously been fought against, was now recognized as offering security. 'Then I would have said I missed out, but I don't think I did, because as I say whatever he done, he done for

me. I knew a lot of girls that ended up really bad, like prostitu-
tion. . . . So he was strict and good for me.'

Other women realized that their relationship with their stepfather had also been connected to their relationship with their
mothers, and the false expectations that the mothers had imposed
upon them for their behaviour as stepchildren. As an adult, now
separated from a hostile and alienating relationship with her
mother and living with an aunt, Yasmin Hassan revised her image
of her stepfather in the light of her now more critical image of her
mother.

I didn't realize till then that it wasn't myself, it was my mother, and
[then] my relationship with my stepfather improved. I respect him when
I meet him, I talk to him, and if I phone and he answers I have a little
chat with him. . . . Basically he's a nice person. He's never commented
about the past, and he always says, "If you're happy, I'm happy" . . . I
like that about him, and I wish we had been close. And I blame my
mother for that.

Some of the informants had already lost a stepparent through
further parental divorce. Some felt that they could only overtly
stay in touch with their stepparent at the expense of loyalty to
their own biological parents. Thus Mark Laithwaite regretted
losing his connection with his stepmother when he had to
choose between taking sides either with her or with his father
when they separated. He was subsequently attacked and got into
a fistfight with his stepmother's brother-in-law for not taking her
side. 'I used to call her "mum" . . . She was probably everything
that a mum would do. . . . But I'd still go with my dad before
Stella.' In other instances, however, many women expressed their
delight that their mothers had finally separated from the men
they themselves had disliked as children, and their pleasure if
their mothers had settled into better relationships. But by now
some were witnessing their mother's third or fourth unsuccessful relationships. Boyfriends or 'toyboys', who were simply personal sexual intimates, were distinguished from third husbands,
who had a relationship with the family and in particular with
grandchildren.

Death had also visited some of the second marriages, triggering
memories of old losses and in some cases amplifying them. When
Tony Dickson's stepfather died, 'I would say it got to me more

than when me father died, because like I say, being 9, you know you have a completely different outlook.' For him, it provoked a new evaluation of the man and the relationship: 'me sister turned around and said, "He was really proud of you and what you've done."' And then came a sense of opportunities in the relationship that had been missed: 'blimey, you know, damn; you kinda think, "Oh if only he was still here, we could have found the time to have a chat." There was always some form of invisible barrier that was there.'

Grandchildren provided another context for the relationships with stepchildren to develop, in two main ways. The first was renewing the relationship with the stepparent through the grandchild, and so developing a new appreciation of what they themselves had experienced as children. As Bee Potter described it, the stepfather who had always 'been there and all . . . always laughing, always got a joke for somebody, always treat you as though you're number one', is also—

great with the children. . . . He was great with Camille. Really was, he used to be standing over the cot sometimes, and he'd think nobody was listening to him, and you'd get all this baby talk. He's as loving towards the children as my own grandparents were. And I think the children love their granddad . . . Ernie, yes, they love him, I think, just as much as they would if it was their real one.

Ernie's capacity to take the children and grandchildren seriously is contrasted with her own biological father, and his assumption of 'rights' after deserting the family many years before.

He come through the door, and he said, 'Well, what do they call me?' I said, 'They'll just call you Horace.' I said, 'As far as we're concerned and as far as the children are concerned, Ernie is their granddad.' And he said to me in front of the kids, like, he said, 'Do they know anything about me?' And I said, 'No dad'. I said, 'As far as they're concerned, you don't even exist.'

Secondly, the baby could provide a relationship in which new practical and helpful tasks were offered. Eileen Moriarty remarked,

I am much closer with my stepmother now, and she actually adores him, I think, because she never had children of her own. When I had Ben, probably six months ago, we're even closer than we've ever been . . . I think, in affection, she never really gave us much, but probably she didn't know how . . . I think because she never had children of her own, there's nothing she likes better than being left alone and wanting to take him for a walk. I think that's making up for something she never had, which is really nice.

While some of those telling their story about parents who had left had found their wish to re-meet them aroused by the arrival of their own children, this trigger also brought an opportunity to review, mourn, and close a relationship that could have no meaning in their current lives. Rachel Colman reflected, 'I'm not interested in them meeting him as their grandfather, because he was never interested in my sister and I, so why should he be interested in our offspring? My sister and I never even talk about him, because he's not been part of our lives for so long now, over twenty years.' For Lorna Maclean, however, the fact that she received much of her parenting as a child from her father made his loss in adult life particularly sad. Her frequent attempts to reinvolve her father had been criticized by her husband, who felt she should give him up: 'It's him that's missing out; he's obviously decided where his loyalties lie. . . . His own natural grandchildren don't know who he is . . . Archie to them is their grandfather and he is very good to them. Archie held Hamish when he was only 6 hours old so he has always been very close to Hamish.'

Thus while memories both of childhood and the transitions of the teenage years and early twenties created openings to reflect on family life, it was the more current aspects of family life, partner- ships and parenting in which the past was most powerfully brought into the open to be reworked: 'you've both come with a second chance based on your own experience: things you want to copy and things you don't want to.' It was a conjunction of reflecting on the past with thinking about its implications for the present, and for future actions and relationships, which seemed most often in the interview to open up a wider rethinking about constructions of family and everday family living. Many inform- ants engaged in an open scrutiny, in fresh ordering of ideas and some positive revaluation and confirmation of relationships and family values, as well as sometimes reliving painful and unresolved experience; relating these to possibilities of change in their own roles as members of a family in the future. In the next chapter we explore further the relationship between lived experience and the way it is remembered and subsequently narrated, looking in particular at the ways in which informants either felt the power to change what they had perceived as negative experience in their own lives into more workable relationships in the future, or did not.

8

Looking Back and Looking Forward: Legacies and Narratives

EVEN today, despite the rapid rise of divorce, three out of every five children grow up with both of their original parents, and expectations of normal childhood are still seen in terms of intact nuclear families. For those whose experiences were different, how do memories of transition through death, divorce, and remarriage create a remembered story of childhood, whether happy or unhappy? How far do stepchildren perceive themselves as a deviant and disadvantaged minority group? Do transitions and new experiences also offer new definitions of self that can serve in positive ways in adult life? How, in particular, do memories of childhood affect children's sense of what is important in family life; what is good or bad and what values are worth holding on to for themselves and their own children?

Recent research from psychoanalytic perspectives has suggested how an ability to reflect on one's past life in psychological rather then merely factual terms—and especially to take into consideration the mental states of self and others—can provide a good prediction of success in making relationships, and for those who become parents, of how securely attached their children will be.[1] Peter Fonagy has developed a nine-point scale of reflective self-functioning and considered this alongside Mary Main's measurement of the earlier childhood attachment of adults, in which their coherence in narrative was found to closely reflect their successful attachment to their own children. A coherent narrative here is one that contains few internal contradictions and constitutes credible, spontaneous discourse. Fonagy and his colleagues argue that 'the predictive power of coherence lies in its close association with reflective self function': that is the capacity to reflect and appraise events and their implications for future action, rather than to react without reflection.[2]

While this impressive research has influenced our own thinking and confirms our view that the way an adult thinks about his or her life story may in itself be a moderating factor in the way connections are made between one generation and another, there are some different ways in which we think the concepts of reflectiveness and coherence may need to be explored. In particular they need to be understood in the context of a realistic awareness of those aspects of life that may be irreconcilable and at times in acute contradiction. Such conflicts may be a product of former childhood experience which is held internally, but may also continue to be experienced in ongoing everyday life. A further dimension is that, while most of the adult attachment interviews on which the concept of coherence is based were carried out with middle-class samples, our own sample was of a cross-section of social classes and contained a proportion of people for whom poverty was a major feature of their lives. Many of our informants thus with good reason emphasized external influences in life events as much as psychological ones, and for some of them physical survival itself was wisely given a high order of priority.

There was also the question of how informants felt that their story was their own or whether they were still caught up in the drama and conflict of their parents' competing stories. The question of who controls, selects, and shapes memories, and when and where new memories can be allowed to emerge, are critical here. In families as in the wider society the same memories may be held more or less in different contexts so that children may have to re-edit their memories for different ears in order to ensure the survival of crucial relationships.

Adults can also impose their power to trivialize memories they find uncomfortable. This may be by scorning the typically idiosyncratic and 'trivial' details, especially easily discountable by an adult who would prefer the child not to recall painful or shaming events. Tracy Sims, who went to visit her father after twenty years absence, describes her pain and disappointment when he dismissed her memories:

He wouldn't own up to things that I knew about him that he'd done. Like silly little things. Like he, he used to suck his thumb—and like dunking your toast in your tea which he used to do. . . . But he said, he denied it, so if he denies the silly little things, so he's certainly not going to own up to the major things, is he? Such as he used to beat my mum up, you know.

Children, in other words, may be acutely sensitive to the power of an adult narrative, and suppress or keep secret memories which do not seem to fit, or which may be too challenging to a parent's position. In families as well as in society, a context of violence will especially constrain the possibilities for holding memories which challenge a dominant story.

We were interested both in the context of the narrative and in its complexity, in the continuing life stresses that may have amplified early experiences of loss and the moderating factors in relationships both at different points in time and over time. We were also interested in how accounts were given and how the story was told. For some people the recounting of past experience offered a way to move between past, present, and future; so that in the act of talking old events took on new meanings, and possibilities were considered for different actions developing in the future. For others the story was expressed as a legacy which had binding qualities from which they felt unable to escape. There were very varied ways in which the interview process could offer an opportunity to change positions in relation to a past self or to have a fresh look at how contexts, both past and present, related to different aspects of self. These were all different ways in which people's sense of freedom to take charge of their own stories could emerge.

Family styles of communication and managing conflict and family patterns of relationship were another important context within which to evaluate the narratives. These could hinder or facilitate the development of a coherent narrative, particularly around emotional issues: above all where a child had been caught between apparently irreconcilable stories about the parental separation or remarriage. Such children had to live with not only a dual official version which changed depending on which home they were in, but also an unofficial version which they usually had to hold silently in their minds. As Lorna Maclean said, 'I think a parent should never forget that the child has two parents, the original parents. My mother totally cut my father off from her, and I felt she wanted me to do the same as well, but they were still my mother and father.'

However it was not only active war between parents which made remembering difficult, but also deliberate silence, the elision of memories, or the destruction of traces of a person's existence, the refusal to speak about emotional relationships in periods of the past. Thus for Eileen Moriarty, whose mother left her father when she was 7, her growing closeness with her mother-in-law has made her think again about her own mother. The idea of asking about her or looking for her nevertheless remains still taboo. 'I'd have to ask my father things, and I don't think—I should imagine if I ever asked about her, he'd just completely blank the issue, he wouldn't talk about it. Or he'd get very cross with me, I can imagine him getting cross about that.' In this there was a strong intergenerational pattern in the family of maintaining secrecy about people who went missing, with her father apparently never questioning the story behind his own mother's disappearance.

We paid attention to current relationships and their potential to create a resource which enables rethinking about the past to take place. For our informants, it was often the spouse who played this interactive and reflective role, although in some cases a sister or a close friend would also be mentioned. In principle however, we noted that, from the new context of a secure relationship, people could now look at their own past lives in ways which are impossible for those caught up in the same repetitive patterns. Nevertheless, the relating of accounts of childhood in a different context, typically with a spouse present, did not always bring positive reformulations. In some instances the presence of another adult simply added to the confusion and pain evoked by describing continuing hostilities between their parents and unresolved questions of 'truth' and 'falsehood'— or public and private versions of the past—which had preoccupied them as children, and still continued to entangle their minds in their current adult lives. For them, the telling of the story increased their own emotional confusion as its complexity emerged. The degree to which they had been not only subject to falsehood as children, but also to a subsequent falsification of memory, which at times amounted to negation of their own experienced reality, related to the degree to which they felt currently entangled.

In addition, gender is again a powerful mediator of all these experiences, with women perhaps tending to accommodate to a multiplicity of views, and men being more likely to diminish the importance of reflectiveness and to hold rigidly to a restricted story. While there is copious evidence of the differences between men's and women's ways of talking and of describing past events, the effect of gender on narrative seems to have been curiously neglected in the literature on attachment and narrative.

Coherence and Reflectiveness in Narrative

The question of how, in the process of an interview, experience remembered and narrated could transform private and sometimes secret memories into an account that created a sense of continuity and a positive construction of identity was a powerful aspect of the interviews as a whole. In considering them, we raise some questions about the connection between reflective and coherent narratives. A coherent narrative can be seen as one which is characterized by an absence of internal contradictions and a reflective one characterized by evidence of having thought about how different experiences connect to each other, and by an ability to see other people's point of view. In many of the narratives we did not see these two features co-existing.

Thus some of the most impressive narratives in terms of their accounts of surviving traumatic events also contained many contradictions. This may be particularly characteristic of our informants, since they frequently had to grapple with competing and apparently irreconcilable stories, or stories where a public truth and a private belief contradicted one another. The desire to see other people's points of view, particularly when these have belonged at different points in the child's life to parents or stepparents in conflict with one another, may in itself lead to contradictions in narrative. Where an adult continues to try to accommodate to competing, hostile relationships to which a connection or loyalty is still experienced in the present, these contradictions will continue to be lived and witnessed and may be less availabe for revaluation.

Conversely, some of the most coherent narratives lacked evidence of much reflectiveness, and some informants, mostly men, conveyed the strong impression that they were well aware that this dimension was lacking in their lives, but had consciously decided to exclude it. Many informants also described the difficulty of making experience 'fit' as they tried to include the perspectives of others on what had taken place. Sometimes this was because they felt an uneasiness at the discrepancies of perspective and mismatches between accounts of experience from different members of the family. They might also be aware of distortions in their memories arising from the psychic distress they had experienced at times as children. Many informants spoke of events that were half remembered or shadows of events that had made an imprint on their minds but not necessarily in the original form. Some also said that they did not know if something was remembered, or if it was known to them because it had often been talked about.

A good example of how both memories themselves and the meaning of memories are contextualized in ways that lead to subtle shifts and new ways of thinking as the narrative unfolds comes from Gary Butler. His mother died when he was 7. He says he cannot remember his mother—'totally blocked'—and that he has never asked his father: 'it's the one thing I've never asked my father. Never.' However, later in the interview, after describing how he realized for the first time as a young adult that his mother had been cremated and where her ashes were located, he says: 'it's part of my life that I won't forget, but I won't bring it up.' A little later again he says, in response to being asked about the changes that happened when his mother died: 'these questions—to be honest—it's something now that I will ask. I will find out because I've never been one to ask. I wish I—but I would say I've been lucky with my stepmum. I've never needed to—I didn't need to, you know.' This last statement seems to hold a key to understanding his story about the past, for a dominant theme is that of mothers' replaceability, and the idea that having alternative attachment figures means the past does not need to be revisited:

And after she died, did your dad talk to you about her at all?
Not really because I'd got three more mums. . . . We didn't need to talk because I'd got a ready-made family again in that respect.

Asking questions about the past might therefore have been seen as disloyal or as lacking appreciation for the care he valued so much, especially from his stepmother. This in turn may have constrained him from thinking about his early years or valuing those memories he did have.

Because the shaping of a narrative depends so much on context, we need also to remember that coherence is not in itself necessarily good. Our sample is of people who have, to a greater or lesser extent, experienced fractured lives, and have had to make sense of contradictions, both past and present. Family transitions through divorce, death, single parenthood, and remarriage, not only involve loss, but also difficult challenges to generational boundaries and to social beliefs about the 'natural order of things'. One such belief is that the couple bond precedes the parent–child bond, both temporally and emotionally. This is succinctly expressed in the elision in common and professional parlance of 'marriage breakdown' and 'family breakdown'. When a child leaves home, even prematurely, this rarely evokes the same description of 'family breakdown'. Many of our informants have had to struggle with this contradiction between the social assumption that couple relationships are primary and their own lived experience that parent–child relationships are for them the most enduring. This had an effect both on how they made emotional space for an incoming step-parent, and how they carried forward beliefs about family when they married and had children themselves. In so doing they also challenge many conventional ideas about what constitutes a 'good' family life.

Two women both express this dilemma very clearly. Doreen Gower described how her mother always kept the two men she married after her first husband—the children's father—died, very separate from the children: 'they're nothing to do with us, they can't tell us what to do'. She herself found she could not sustain relationships with men, and she reflects on her unwillingness to leave her mother to live independently: 'See she's not like a mother, she's like a sister in a lotta ways. . . . I can do what I want, there's no—I just feel it'd be very hard for me get anything better, if you know what I mean. If I'm honest with myself, I don't think I ever will, and that frightens me sometimes.' Mandy Pope, who was brought up by her grandmother in a family where the women were also the breadwinners and there appeared to be very few reliable men, expresses a similar dilemma from her perspective as mother to a 12-year-old daughter: 'she's just always been with me for ever. I wouldn't know a life without her. In fact it will break my heart when she decides to marry and leave me.' Such statements are often contradicted at other points in the narrative, as a struggle between what is and what 'should be' emotionally gets played out.

Just as coherence itself is an insufficient concept, so reflectiveness alone is inadequate. We can identify several interviews where the informant clearly spent a great deal of time reflecting on the confusing and painful experiences in their lives, but whereas some had a sense of the dilemmas for different family members, others had a fixed and blaming view. There was a sense that some of these tangled beliefs were being endlessly replayed internally, rather than being modified or challenged by the development of present relationships. This process was most clearly seen in people who were socially isolated. Only one of these informants was in a stable relationship at the time of interview, and most did not have a stable or satisfying job. The part played by ongoing intimate relationships in creating new opportunities for a different way of viewing life, relationships, and family to be formed, was clearly crucial.[3] This was why so many informants saw their relationship with their spouses as the turning-point in their lives.

A reflective narrative which demonstrates many contradictions, and yet highlights both the ongoing struggle to make connections between past and present, and the ability to think differently in the context of having a close relationship in adulthood, is that of Jean Wheeler. She had a number of extremely adverse experiences after her parents split up, including her mother's remarriage to a man who was violent, lack of contact with her father, school problems, eviction from home, and an unsuccessful early marriage. She reflects in the interview on her developing sense of security in her present marriage, and also on her renewed sense of vulnerability following her second husband's recent unemployment.

I was living with him before I felt comfortable living with him. It took a long time. But yes, I'm still insecure. Deep down there's still that frightened little girl, afraid that at any moment something bad is going to happen, and her world is going to fall apart. But she's not important, there are other things that are not going to fall apart. So, even if the world as we knew it did, I'd survive. . . . It's a bad time, but we'll get through it, we always do. We're both survivors. So whether we survive with the house intact or not is another question, but we will survive.

Later on in the interview, she again appears overwhelmed by adverse experiences. 'It seems that every time I get everything settled, life itself kicks me while I'm down as well. We can't be the only ones in this situation. Half the world must be in the same situation, but it does tend to come down to being a bit personal.' The themes of adversity and deprivation, on the one hand, and strength and survival, on the other, evolve contrapuntally as she tells her life story and explores these themes in different contexts.

This does not mean that the narrative is incoherent; rather that each theme has the potential to become the dominant narrative, and so external contexts, including the response to her story by a researcher or therapist, have the potential to affect its development. One key question is to understand how far informants can override adverse contexts, or alternatively, how the context swamps any attempt to hold on to an untypical story. We also need to consider how far new contexts can either allow for the development of more flexible and hopeful stories, or rigidify existing ones.

Self-Esteem and the Survival of Adverse Experiences

What contributed to young people believing they had done well and that they had taken charge of their lives, and what contributed to persistent and ongoing poor self-esteem? Whereas the central and most predictable influence would cetainly be that of a secure relationship with a loving parent, we have throughout this book noted other factors promoting resilience, including the support of grandparents and other family members as well as friends, neighbours, and school. We are also concerned here with some less obvious contributory factors in the development of self-esteem. Although men and women were equally likely to talk about themselves in a self-critical or self-blaming way, it was women who tended to overtly address self-esteem, either commenting on their lack of it, or describing how they had developed it. Some linked it to being deprived of a sense of agency in their own lives. Men were less likely to describe these feelings of helplessness, and to link them to present feelings, they also seem to have less often found opportunities to experience a sense of agency which could connect them to a positive sense of having 'come through'. It was most often women who recounted clearly how, at different points in their lives, seemingly caught in a downward spiral, they had found a way of being an observer to this process, and hauling themselves out of the abyss.

Jean Wheeler thus describes her unhappiness after her mother remarried and her stepfather was violent. This led her to start truanting regularly. She recalls realizing the effect this was having on her life and going to see the headmistress, 'a real ogre, a real tartar', and telling her, 'I've got a problem, I've been truanting'. Reflecting on this, she says

I sort of got home and thought: 'Well, what, why am I doing this? This is not doing me any good, it's not doing anybody any good.' I have these flashes of inspiration where, all of a sudden, I think, coldly and calmly, I think, 'What have you been doing to yourself? And that was it.' Again, it took a lot of courage to stand up and say, 'I have been doing this.' I don't know where I found it from, but I did.

One possible source of strength for Jean may have been that, before her parents separated, she had already developed a strong attachment to her father, to whom she wrote letters regularly when he was away at sea, telling him about all her problems. Even though she had little contact with her father after her mother remarried, this childhood activity may have been crucial in enabling her to develop a reflective awareness about her life.

Ann Highfield, whose education was disrupted after her eldest sister suffered a crippling accident, and who had very poor relationships with both her stepmothers, talked about a period after she left home when she began drinking heavily. But she managed to see where this might lead her, and took herself to task. Although her father was extremely unsupportive, Ann had developed a relationship with a neighbouring couple who befriended her, and they may have conveyed to her some sense of her worth. Thus, while her childhood contained 'any sort of abuse someone in power can put on a child, and scare tactics and everything', she is able to assert at the end of her story, 'You know neither of us were really permanently damaged by anything that happened to us. . . . I'm proud of myself you know.' She adds, 'It just made me more determined to stick to one marriage and one family.'

Doreen Gower was more explicit about the effect of living with a stepfather she disliked. 'We'd lived altogether on our own after me dad died, and I felt we were all close together and I felt that a man was sorta intruding on us and I didn't like it. I didn't like the fact that my mum slept with him.' She describes herself as having very low self-esteem. 'I don't know if it's with having no father, I don't know, but I think it does affect you definitely. I've never had any confidence at all—none—in meself. Never. And that's held me back really.' Interestingly she connects her failure to develop independence to her mother's overprotectiveness, which was linked to a determination to keep stepfathers marginal. 'I think a man would have pushed us to do something a bit more. . . . Perhaps we've had it too easy. . . . We've had it done—everything's come too easy for us.' It may have been the combination of family changes over which she had no control and the lack of opportunity to demonstrate competence, and thus to feel that something was under control, which was so eroding of Doreen's self-esteem.

The connection between the ways in which children were able to maintain a sense of agency through times of family upheaval and the coherence and reflectiveness of their stories as adults is one that would merit further study. While it is often assumed that children suffer from being thrust into over-responsibility at an early age, the feelings of powerlessness that stem from being protected by exclusion from any helpful activity may be even more problematic.

Powerlessness indeed lies at the heart of the experience of trauma. A psychological trauma may be conceived of as an event or sequence of events which, in intense or violent ways, ruptures the protective layer surrounding the mind with long-lasting consequences for psychic well-being. Children feel traumatized when helplessness overwhelms them and they have no sense of mastery in a situation. They feel a failure of much needed protection, and the acute mental pain caused by the event re-creates itself in intrusive memories which replay repeatedly. This continual replaying and re-enactment of the uncopable event thrusts it into the present, through flashbacks triggered by reminders, and through dreams or nightmares. Such experiences were apparent in a number of the stories in which the trauma had become the only context for a life story, and, as if time had frozen: no other intervening experiences were able to soften its impact.

A few of those whom we interviewed were moved towards such memories in the process of recounting their story. Albert Black put it, 'the mind is like a video recorder, and it runs, you know, just constantly running and every now and again you get images, and every image is—too painful. . . . You have to block that part out.' For him the time in his life when he and his brothers and sister had to go into care stood as an example of how he had tried to exert some control and been overwhelmed.

I was 8 or 10, 9 or 10, I can't actually remember. That's a part of my life that is—that a part of my life where there's a lot of dark memories a lot of, a lot of hurt, a lot of pain, and a lot of crying, but I kept my family together. I fought and kept, I fought to keep myself, Steve and Jean together. . . . Yes, when we was in homes, yes. And I fought to keep the four of us together, because Gloria was still a babe in arms, and—

Paradoxically the experience of fatherhood created a new sense of connectedness to family for Albert, which both re-aroused the earlier experience of being disconnected from his family, and also presented a new possibility for connection. This did not correlate with stability in marriage, and it may be that his wife, who had recently left him, had felt overwhelmed by the strength of his emotions. 'The worst thing in my life is the memory of my grandfather crying. The best thing was watching new life come into the world, my son . . . the joy of watching him come from his mother. That is what has made the bond between me, Mandy, and Wayne so strong. It's an experience you cannot put into words.' For the interviewer, the experience of this interview was especially powerful, because Albert communicated, on the one hand, that he was desperate to talk, and, on the other, that she might too easily ask him a wrong question that would put his equilibrium and her safety at risk. It was an interview she was keen to end, but felt only able to end when he was in a calmer frame of mind.

Within a number of other accounts, traumatic episodes remained 'perpetually running' in people's heads. For Eileen Moriarty, the desertion by her mother was still something that it was very hard to think about clearly. 'I think when you are 7 you

probably don't know how to take things like that. You don't
believe people can go. People don't go do they, when you're 7?'
She adds later, 'You always wonder, will she turn up some day? I
can't imagine it, but it's always there.' She still felt that a taboo
barred any possibility of moving this thought on to a new position
through talking to her father. Traumatic memories remain stuck
when there is no opportunity to deconstruct them. In many
accounts this potent combination of trauma and taboo remained
as a powerful inhibitor to fresh thinking.

Where loss has remained as an overriding preoccupying factor
it can in itself affect the capacity to look forward. This can be
compounded by living with a parent also preoccupied with loss, or
where it had become incorporated into an unchallengeable family
story. Stephanie Rogers found it difficult to recover from her
father's death because of her mother's continued refusal to offer
her 'an answer', as to why he had died, but also because it was to
him that she had been closest. There had always been a poor
relationship between Stephanie and her mother, who was at times
physically violent towards her, in contrast to her remembered
close relationship with her much gentler and more indulgent
father. One of the effects of being locked into this embittered
relationship with her mother in her childhood was that she had
decided, after a long cohabitation, that she could not marry
anybody. 'I like me freedom, I do like me freedom and me own
space and being able to do what I want.' In looking at her account,
the question remains whether it was the single event of her
father's death which contained the kernel of her continuing rest-
lessness, or also her mother's preoccupation with her father's
death, even in the context of a second marriage: 'She's still like
me, wants an answer. She still wants to know why. Yes, she went
very very bitter—against life, against everbody in general—on the
verge of a nervous breakdown.'

For some children experiences of loss and transition were
compounded by further loss and traumatic life events. Two informants who had suffered the early loss of a parent, Ann Highfield,
whose mother had died and Richard Hammond whose mother
had left his father because of the latter's violence, had subsequent
experiences in their childhood of a close family member having a
serious accident. In each case describing this event appeared to be
the most affectively laden part of the interview, and in each case

the informant referred to it at the earliest opportunity. Richard Hammond's mother had a traffic accident when he was 7, and he was sent away to stay with relatives while she recoverd. Ann Highfield's sister was also knocked down by a car and she was even more seriously injured, suffering permanent brain damage.

The impact on these two informants' lives was, however very different. This may relate to how far for each a sense of agency was experienced. With Richard, who remained very close to his mother but unable to settle in a lasting adult relationship with a woman, his separation from his mother and the failure at the time to talk about the accident seems to have left him impotently insecure and so contributed to a lack of a sense of control over his life. For Ann Highfield, however, although her sister's accident was immensely traumatic, it meant that she had to give up her schooling to look after her. While this was clearly detrimental to her development at one level, the effect on her life seemed to have been a strengthening sense of self which gave her a great pride in her achievements. The story of strength and survival here triumphs over the story of adverse life events.

In families where there had been violent and abusive experiences the question of a family rule about what was to be remembered and what forgotten sometimes showed itself through fragmented memory and sometimes through a confusion of the original experience due to feelings of loyalty. For some children, loyalty was to the mother who had remained their primary parent, so that the confusion was around questions of how she could have chosen or remained in a relationship that the child saw as obviously bad. For others, the experience of loss was the overriding factor organizing memory, so subordinating the memory of the violence that had preceded a parent leaving. For others again, the loyalty had grown directly towards a stepparent over time, creating a commentary of contrast to the original violent experience between mother and father. However, in no case where a child had experienced violence from a stepparent towards themselves had this experience been superseded by more positive feelings and memories.

The impact of abusive domination, whether by parent or stepparent, is one that remains over time. It seems clear from different stories that where a child experienced themselves as having allies, whether siblings or an aunt or grandparent, the effects of a negative relationship with a parent were less dominant because they did not become the single powerful factor shaping the self-image of the child. Ann Highfield, whose first stepmother was violent to her had close relationships with her siblings and also had a local family who befriended her. Nevertheless the impact of the experience could operate in powerful ways in particular relationships. For some it consciously shaped attitudes to the upbringing of their own children. As Rosa Daniels, who had been bullied into a 'Cinderella' role throughout her later childhood, said:

I wouldn't want my kids to hate me like I hated her you know. . . . It affected me that way . . . I give in to her [daughter] a lot more you know, than what . . . I don't make her do half the things I had to do—I just keep thinking I don't want her growing up hating me you know. I want to be there for her because I didn't have anybody. You know I want to make sure that I'm there for her and I want her growing up knowing I'm there for her. Because like I say I didn't have anybody . . . I didn't have my dad. I didn't have a mum.

Others, who had experienced violence in their relationship with their parents but were now unable to remember it, were nonetheless aware of its presence in their lives. Rachel Colman, whose parents split when she was 7, and whose early childhood was characterized by a violence which made her mother put half the world between herself and her ex-husband, cannot consciously remember episodes she could describe. She is only aware of 'something I don't remember about my parents—my father and mother's marriage'. However she knew passionately that arguing made her physically sick, and that she had chosen a husband who also disliked arguments: 'We both tend if we feel an argument coming to change the subject.' Lily Beck, who is extremely happy in her marriage, nevertheless still has the shadows of her mother's abuse by her stepfather, and her own physical and sexual abuse by him strongly with her whenever her husband loses his temper. 'When he does get angry then look out—he makes me tremble in my shoes and it does sometimes bring back memories, you know. But it's silly because he never ever hit me.' Like Gill Deighton she is very clear about the fact that she would not tolerate violence: 'I've told him, if he did, we'd get divorced, because I couldn't, I think once a man has hit a woman then that's the start of the downhill I think.'

Lorna Maclean, who remained at the centre of sets of warring parental and stepparental relationships that had never resolved, was still caught in painful loyalty disputes. She also recounted her own ability to play the part of the aggressor in domestic violence as well as the abused. She and her husband married at 17. His parents had also been divorced. 'His father used to beat his mother up as well . . . I think he was worried that he was going to turn out the same as his father—and he does have a terrible temper which I provoke . . . I goad him a lot, but we never get to the stage where we come to blows.' The legacy of violence, which is something that they jointly share, has come out as a frightening factor primarily in relation to the children. She has learnt how to separate herself from her baby or toddler when they cry. 'I'm better down here—otherwise I can understand why some women who have to listen to a crying child all day go off their trolley. It's a hell of a thing to contend with, but I think I've still got enough sense up there to stop and to walk away.' Knowing as a result of her own training as a nurse that she has been in danger of 'bottling things up' too much, she was still anxious about exploding. Her husband also has to be checked from taking his hand to the children too strongly. In reflecting on the impact of their family histories on their own marriage, she says, 'maybe it makes us stronger as a couple—because we can understand what the other is going through'. She sees herself as remaining caught up in preoccupations with the unresolved conflicts between her ageing but still quarrelling parents.

The Past and Present in Parenting

More generally, it was in the context of bringing up their own children that many informants were determined that things would not be the same in the future as they had been in the past, and where stories about the past could be incorporated in a less negative way. 'The only thing I had in my mind was that in no way was she going to go through what I went through.' A conscious determination to prevent patterns from the past dominating the future often characterized accounts of present-day marriage and parenting. Questions about the future elicited thoughtful, reflective responses from most of our informants, perhaps because this is a theme which rarely evokes the need to stick to a rigid story.

For some it was expressed at a general level, by a blueprint of how family life should overlay former experience both in relation to partnership and to parenting. 'I try to think, "Well, that's happened, there's nothing you can do, you've got to get on and look forward, so I try not to dwell on the past"; we've seen what divorce does and its not nice and we don't want it.' For others, as Tom Rice succinctly put it, parenting offers 'a second chance based on your own experience; things you want to copy and things you don't want to—you definitely want to get away from . . . I don't think my parents showed enough affection to each other, so I never saw any kind of love being shown either between them, nor any consideration for others.'

Sometimes the patterns to be avoided were recounted as relating to discrete aspects of partnership and parenting which were remembered as negative, like poor communication; the absence of clear rule-setting or the setting of arbitrary and rigid rules, certain types of punishment, or the failure to develop a child's self-esteem. In talking about the long-drawn-out secrecies of her childhood, Eileen Moriarty describes a changing pattern in her own marriage, through which her children can develop stories different from her own. 'Brian always picks me up on when we don't actually say what we feel and what we want. We might say what we think the other person wants to say and that's what I sometimes do. I see my own dad and Jean sometimes doing it to please each other, and we've always said, "we'll always try to say what we wanted to say to each other."' Sylvie Higgenworth, who remembered a painful emotional disconnection from her mother, described a determination that she and her husband would operate as a pair on behalf of their children. 'We're very supportive with each other. We do nearly everything together . . . Pete is quite a secure person you know, and his mum and dad are very together and did everything as a family and—that's how I want it to be for, you know for my kids.'

For others the primary standpoint for change was clearer communication not only between the couple, but between the generations, coming across most clearly in relation to their own children. An emphasis on the importance of talking to children was characteristic of this group, many of whose parents had failed to prepare them in any way for the changes that had such profound consequences for their own lives and who were also only too aware of the emotional consequences for them of not being able to develop their own story. Emrys Hughes, for example, whose mother left home suddenly without preparing him at all, probably has a memory of his childhood vulnerability in mind when he stresses the importance of talking to his own children and encouraging them to be questioning and 'a bit more curious'. Similarly Wendy Johnson said:

I'm a bit more open with Sarah than what my mum was with me. I told her when we were gonna get engaged and I said to her, 'Dave and I want to get married', I said to her, 'What do you think about it.' I mean she was only 9, but she's a very intelligent girl. . . . She was thrilled to bits. I always said that if I met somebody that didn't get on with Sarah, I didn't want to know them.

For other parents the area of 'rule-making' was a key feature of better communication. Becky Armstrong remembers her mother and stepfather handling the unity of the two families very badly. 'We definitely could have been handled differently, with this feeling that we are not one family, even if that can't be thought, because obviously you're not one family, you're not one blood. I still think they should have agreed a set of rules for the children, which they both adhered to, for all the children. I think that was wrong, and that it didn't help.' For Emrys Hughes, by contrast, the 'imposition' of order he resented when his stepmother first joined the family changed as he came to appreciate the climate of order and routine she created; and the patience she showed with her stepchildren was a virtue which he listed as high on his own list of what good parenting is about. He described the ways that he and his wife try to provide for the children that were different to his own childhood experience: more openness, more communication, more questions, and more curiousity, as well as those features of stability and order which were the same.

Caroline Herbert distinguished her own attempts at discipline from those of her parents. 'I would never use the type of discipline that my father used which was really a psychological discipline but very strict really. . . . If ever I was going to tell them off for something, it would be that they were told off there and then and not linger. My punishment would go on for days with my father.' She has many ideas about encouraging her children that stem from her own belief that she was disqualified as a child. 'I wouldn't discourage them from wearing clothes which are fashionable, which my stepmother never let me do really. I always felt quite dowdy.' Like many other women she was very clear about the importance of self-esteem and the need for it to be actively developed in children. 'I suddenly realized how important it is to teach them how to make them feel good about themselves, which is something I never felt . . . and not to be frightened of showing affection for your children. I'll cuddle them often, whereas my dad he, it's not really until I had my own children that he's a bit affectionate with me.'

Others, on the other hand, had taken positive models from the families in which they grew up, and were incorporating aspects of care that had been part of their experience as children and which they had come to value. Mary Birch who had triumphed at sport as a child, had built a life with her husband which centred around their children's sporting activities. 'We spend an awful lot of time with our children. . . . Our lives revolve round them rather than them revolve round us you know. . . . We do everything as a family.' Gary Butler had married from and into a community in which he also wanted his children to grow. 'It were a very stable community, the same people all my life.'

Some informants whose childhood stories had included loyalty conflicts and feelings of an irreconcilable division between sets of parents, found in adulthood that they liked both of them and could incorporate ideas from both. As Caroline Herbert says, 'I never think of my mum and dad; it's always two separate families. But they are both my family.' Of her father and stepmother she says, 'they did work well together. Although I couldn't stand Gwen at times, they did work their relationship quite well.' Again the possibility of a more benign story as opposed to one which remained frozen and negative was probably enhanced by the experience of being connected to other important relationships: to spouse, parents-in-law, and children. This could allow the informant to escape from the sense of entrapment between two competing narratives. For others, the relationship with a child itself, and the positive belief in being themselves a good enough parent was a spur to re-evaluate the past. Sylvie Higgenworth expresses this when she reflects on her powerful feelings of resentment towards her stepsister, who continues in adulthood to receive more support from her mother than she does: 'It's took me a long time, but just my own maturity and being, I like to think, a good mum has helped me overcome the fact.'

The most serious difficulties in getting beyond the past seem to have been for those who had seriously lacked or lost intimacy as children. Intimacy in family life is hard to define, but the lack of it was sometimes expressed by both men and women in their accounts of their childhood lives. For many adults it was re-experienced particularly painfully as inhibiting closeness as parents to their own children. Mandy Pope, for example, expressed the distinction between a story of wished for intimacy and her inability to translate it into lived experience. In her family there was a three-generational tradition, whereby younger women continued to work while the older generation raised the children. She was proud of this tradition and she derived from it an identity that helped her to handle the breakup of her marriage. One concomitant of this pattern, however, was that it was not her mother who had shown her affection as a child; it was her grandmother to whom she went for cuddles. Now she herself found it hard to show affection to her own daughter, although she longed to do so; and she was worried that her daughter in turn would not know how to cuddle. 'I find that hard, to sit and cuddle . . . I just keep, I just keep telling her, "I love you", and then she'll shout, "I love you mum", as she's going upstairs. But she won't come downstairs and say, "I love you, mum". It's always as she's going upstairs. I think she's the same as me, doesn't show all that affection.' This difficulty with closeness had been acutely painful for Mandy when her daughter was a baby, 'when I could quite happily have picked her up and thrown her against the wall', but the power of this family story about mothers and daughters may have held her back from believing that her own experience could ever be different.

Wendy Johnson also talked about the connections between her childhood experience and her difficulty in showing affection despite her wish to show it. 'People put their arms round me now, it's the same with my husband. Affection is something I have great difficulty with, because, my grandmother always loved us, and she'd put her arms around me now and again, [but] my mum could never do it, very rarely did. My husband and I never did, I think I've grown up never really knowing affection.' Speaking of her daughter she says, 'She'll sit on my knees, and I hope that she's not going to grow up like I am. I've tried to be affectionate, but I find it hard. She'll sit on my knees, "Give us a cuddle, mum", and I can sit there for so long: and then I say, "Come on, off", you know. I hope she understands that I don't mean—I do love her, but I find it so hard.'

For those who had lost a parent by death, the acute pain of loss of intimacy was described especially poignantly when addressing key moments in their own development as parents. For Rosa Daniels and Carol Stevenson there were sleeper effects from the death of their mothers, which emerged with fresh pain as their own children were born and began to grow. Rosa believed she was going to die young as her mother did, and was depressed for the whole year leading up to the birthday when she reached that same age. 'I just kept thinking "What are my kids gonna do? Who's gonna look after them?" And I use to say to my husband, "If you meet somebody else, don't let them be nasty to my kids". And it was all just the fear of what I'd gone through.' Carol, who had lost her mother when she was 6 years old, remembered the loneliness of not having a mother; and the distinction between having a stepmother who had done her duty by her, and a mother with whom she believed she had had a special intimacy. Speaking of her stepmother she says, 'I will do anything for her, and I do appreciate what she did for us when I was younger. . . . If anything happened to her I would be upset because I do care about her, but I don't think I care about her like a mother, and I don't think I ever will.' In thinking about her own position as a young mother, she contrasted her story with those of friends from the antenatal clinic. 'All the others who had children at the same time say, "Oh, I'll go to my mum's and she'll show me what to do"—whereas I didn't have anybody: and also I was lonely.' Eileen Moriarty, whose mother was presumed still to be living, but whose loss was total, could not find a way of bringing her stepmother's experience and her own into a shared story at the key moment of her son's birth. Her stepmother had never been allowed by her father to have a child of her own, so Eileen felt this absence made their connection difficult when she was lonely and frightened as a result of a difficult Caesarian birth.

For other women, however, stories of lack of intimacy were

brought out afresh and amplified, not in the absence of a mother, but in the continuing experience of her presence. Perceptions of former and current lovelessness emerged afresh through experiencing a mother's lapses in relation both to herself as now a mother and to her own children as a grandmother. Especially through watching the paucity of relationships with grandchildren, an awareness of what they themselves had missed as children could be reactivated. As Becky Armstrong said, 'She comes up here, she doesn't really want to see them, she wants to see me, and I find that a bit difficult, because she pushes them away and I find that irritating you know.' She sees herself as definitely more affectionate as a mother. 'I tell them I love them, and I can't remember her saying anything like that to me.'

For yet others, the new presence of a mother-in-law heightened feelings of their own mother's inadequacy. Lily Beck suffered from a painful double awareness of her mother's absence, both as an emotional absence, and as the lack of a protective capacity:

She was never there. When I had both of them ill with chicken pox . . . she said, 'Oh well, let me know when, when they're better. I don't want to come round so that I don't get it, or any germs . . . '

Steve's mum is so different, which is how a mum should be; you know, when you're not well, you need your mum. And she's just not been there. . . . As my mum wasn't there for me, so I'm going to be there for my own children.

Later in her account she describes her mother as an 'empty shell—a woman without a core', and relates this to the effect of the relationship with her stepfather, who abused both her mother and herself physically and sexually over the years. Here we have another example of how a partner's family can become a source of strength as well as a model for family living: 'she's more of a mum to me than my mum. . . . I wanted to do things as much as possible like she had done them, because I really wanted to keep Steve for me.' The finding of such a crucial new source of strength not only through a partner but also in a partner's parents was recounted by many informants, and presented as a departure point for the development of their own stories of coping, strength, and development.

Actions not Words

Some of the young men in particular found it difficult to voice what it was the transitions and losses might bring to their parenthood of their own children. In some of their accounts we can sense them putting into action assumed but undescribed principles about what children need from father or stepfather. David Evans, whose own father had left him, saw fathering as 'just being there'. He sees his children as 'the best thing' in his life. He describes doing the 'feeding, washing and changing with kids—all the after-work bed-time stuff'; but for him the most important thing is 'just them having a father around'. His own childhood involved a mother and father who continued to fight long after the divorce, because his father wanted ongoing contact. His preferred model of a father was his peaceful stepfather, who he much admired, but had to lose in his teens when his mother divorced for a second time. Because of loyalty towards his father, he found it hard to express the obvious affection he had for his stepfather: 'it was more, he was more there for workwise'. But while he did not say this in words, his account of his adulthood suggested that he had taken this peaceful stepfather as a model rather than his own father.

Other men described learning from their wives how to adapt to the mysteries of fatherhood. Similarly many women described, with a slightly different emphasis, the process of involving their husbands in the early tasks of childcare as an important part of their own sense of growth as a couple. For many informants these accounts of everyday lived experience as adults implicitly revealed new strengths which could help overcome earlier childhood stories about failure or adversity.

In the narratives of some men a grandfather provided the model for developing a male role in the house, while the step-father although present had been absent as a parental influence: 'I can only think I was raised by my mother and influenced by my grandfather.' Other men's stories emphasized the lack of a male presence, even if largely symbolic. This lies behind regrets that there was nobody to push them harder at school and in their career plans: something they were determined to do differently for their own children. As Alex Plumber put it: 'I wish I'd had someone to drive me forward a little bit more and help me out, you know when you're perhaps leaving school. . . . You look back, and think—well I think how I am with my daughter you know and I want to devote a lot of time to her, and that's what I didn't get from him.' These accounts suggest a crucial difference between a stepfather who was easygoing but respected, and a man who was too disengaged to be seen as of any use at all to his stepchildren at key moments. For men especially, the awareness of the lack of male influence could reawaken a bitterness with fathers who had left the family and failed to play their part. In the context of their own adult choices many men found this less easy to forgive and their stories reflect this bitterness: 'I look back and think, if I had been him, I would at least have kept in touch with the kids and made sure I saw them now and again, but he never chose to. And I don't miss that, and I never have any desire to go and find out who he is and what he's like. Never have. Never will do, really.' In reflecting on stepfamily life, Alex Plumber speaks with regret about a quality that was missing in his stepfather: 'Even if his kids were his stepkids, [my father] would have loved the child the same, and that was definitely missing from my stepfather. . . . But I'm sure it could be like that and I'm sure a lot of families are like that—I'm sure I would have made more of a go of it with my family and been more positive.'

Gary Butler by contrast, who felt that there had been no 'push' from his father, nevertheless stresses how powerfully his father was always there for him. This is contextualized as intergenerational family stability: as his family was for him so Gary will be there for his own children. 'As long as they're happy, we're happy. . . . The most important thing is making sure they're all right, because at the end of the day that's—they're here and that's all there is to it.' His union was blessed by his father, their first flat being 'fifty yards up the road from where my mum [stepmother] and dad were, so he could keep an eye on us'. His adult story contains the same active family rituals as did his own childhood, such as going on holiday with the extended family, fourteen of them at a time, just as he did as a child; and his wife regards his family as closer than her own. But it is his stepmother on whom they first call if they need advice or help with the kids, and she is their chief babysitter. 'Everybody's always been together, so everybody is part of the family. If there's anything going on, we're together and that's it. To be honest we all belong as one unit.'

Staying Single

Among the informants who remained single, there were different evaluations of its meaning for them, which reflected their experience of their parents' marriage and breakdown or the death of a parent. Three contrasting statements by men show different degrees of personal expression of connection between past, present, and future.

Jack Finlay sees the explanation for his single status primarily as a reflection on himself and his own personality: 'I always thought of myself as maybe, younger than I am . . . maybe less mature or not as responsible, not responsible enough for raising a kid. My last girlfriend had a kid and I miss her. . . . It's maybe something to do with the shyness in me as well. I'm more introverted than other folk.' Richard Hammond, by contrast sees women as having let him down and is 'very bitter' about this. But his understanding of this is complicated by his mother's view of him, encouraging him to remain single and seeing him as the sensible one, because his sister has already been divorced and is now living with another man. Overlaying this again is the continuing bitterness and resentment which both Richard and his mother feel about his father's violent behaviour and a resulting suspicion that it may be safer not to enter into an intimate parnership.

Sid Western sees his single status as partly a positive choice and partly a reflection of his earlier life. 'Quite happy. I like the simple things in life.' Of marriage he says: 'No, I don't think it's for me. I think I shall stay single—I've always been happy on my own.' However, he also sees that his solitariness comes from 'the culmination of two things, moving down here and her [his mother] dying. They happened very quickly. I came down here, and I knew nobody, and then losing her, you had to be—certainly possibly I was on my own more than if she had been around.'

Thus while all three men were single and none believed himself likely to form a stable relationship soon, each of their different narratives about this aspect of their lives affected whether or not they were likely to continue single. Thus remaining single while trapped in a frozen narrative about the past, possibly out of loyalty to the remaining parent, as Richard Hammond was, would create a less favourable climate for developing relationships in the future than a sense of 'not being ready' or that a suitable partner simply had not come along.

Racism and Identity

The narratives of the three girls who were black or of mixed parentage make it painfully clear how for them racism was an additional stress factor. For them, the problem of how to develop a positive self-identity in a racist society emerges through complex and poignant details of relationships in their stories. Two of the girls found that they had to fight for pride in colour in the face of expressed ignorance or hostility at school. A strong connection with a peer group of the same ethnicity was an important protective element for one girl, but the other was painfully isolated within her community and integrated her mixed ethnicity as part of her identity once she was old enough to go and search for her father in another town, and subsequently marrying a man also of the same mixed ethnicity as herself.

Barbara Tizard and Ann Phoenix in their book *Black, White or Mixed Race?* conclude that, in relation to self-confidence, 'if the majority stigmatize one's colour then to be proud of it is likely to be a protective factor'. In their study, young people of mixed parentage spoke of racism at their primary school as the most painful thing. 'When you get called names when you're younger that can affect you for quite a long time, because you keep thinking about it and you get hurt easier then.'[4] In the same spirit Martine Brabourne remembered how her first experience of racism was from children in the school playground who weren't allowed to play with her, but looking at the open palms of her hands, commented, 'You're turning white, now I can play with you.' In relation to her teachers she described 'a two-fold kind of situation really. . . . You get a lot of teachers who by virtue of their racism just think that all, as a black child, that's all you're good at [running] and that's what they're prepared to push you in. And they won't encourage you academically.'

Martine's family originally came from Jamaica and several of her older women relatives seem to have remained inner resources into her adult development, particularly one aunt Lily.

She used to be a kind of special person for me and I was a daughter for her. . . . She was a very humorous woman and she used to be very joyful and sing a lot. . . . It comes to mind because my mum used to screech and wail. . . . And she used to play with her husband a lot. They used to play, pinch each other, silly little things like that—and I remember that kind of thing.

Her first stepfather, also from Jamaica, who she thought of as her dad, was also very important. He maintained a caring presence in her early teens even though he was no longer in the home. 'He was in charge of things, a foreman. Very very hard working, he saved a lot. As a young child . . . you could always look forward to getting something when Daddy came home—something from work he'd picked up that we'd like to draw on or some new crayons or paint or something.' Her dislike of her second step-father was also compounded by her awareness of how racism had defeated him. 'I find him really as a character, spineless. I feel that about . . . the way he had dealt with issues of racism, victimiza-tion of any kind really.' As a young adult, Martine said of herself: 'What you need to know about me now is that my culture, my identity as a black woman is important and that African culture is important to me. . . . That's something my parents never pro-moted and they've now recognized that I tend to hook up with people for.' As indeed with other aspects of stressful experience discussed in this study, such as suffering aggressiveness or mental illness, children learnt about racism by living it themselves and by witnessing the effects of it on others, including friends and parents.

Gill Deighton described confronting racism at levels of both heart and head. She had no memories of her Indian father, who had been thrown out by her mother when she was only 6 months old. She had never liked her stepfather, and only felt at home at her nan's where she would spend the week, joining her mother only at the weekend. In her late teens she undertook a search for her own father who had remarried to an Indian wife in another part of Britain. She gave a vivid account of her sense of wholeness when she found her fully Indian sisters: 'when I met Gazala, I felt they were like proper family'. Her choice of a partner also of mixed race also reflected this search for wholeness. 'I have no trouble at all [with racism now], but people do say things to Bill and I hate that.' The impact of race and racism in her life choices is referred to obliquely as well as overtly; in relation to the way that her mother experienced racism; being spat at for marrying a 'darkie'; and the way that Gill herself experienced it at school—'at one time, I wouldn't have told anybody, but this girl at school said she would tell everybody that I was a darkie, and I thought I was never going to have that over my head, that in future I would just tell everybody. It's nothing to be ashamed of.' Perhaps gaining in self-confidence following this confrontation, she later chose to challenge it as a student:

Once when I was at college, this girl was going on about coloured people all the time, and I said to her, 'Look, everybody's flesh and blood, do you like me?' And she said, 'Yes', and I said 'Well, I'm half-caste, and because I'm a different colour, you can't even tell the difference, and there's good and bad in everyone.' And she didn't believe me at first. I don't mind a joke, people at work saying 'coon'—I joke about it myself.

And although these few cases can only be suggestive, it seems possible that where young women had stayed more closely within the culture of families protected by a large extended network, the effects of racism were less likely to emerge as a theme of their narrative that was distinct from more powerful dramas continuing within the life of the family.

Images of Family

While all informants had the shared experience of growing up in a family configuration that departed from the biological two-parent norm, their narratives varied greatly in the extent to which these experiences had been incorporated into a mental map of family which informed their thinking as young adults. Whereas some demonstrated how they had absorbed ideas about complexity, diversity of life stages, and fluidity of boundaries, others seemed loyal to an image of the family as ordered by traditional stages, and boundaries which excluded non-residential parents and their extended families.

These notions were conveyed in various ways throughout the interviews, both in general in the language used to describe and explain family relationships, and also more specifically in response to certain key questions. One such question was, 'Who really belongs to your family today?' It is interesting to note that on this issue the Sheffield study found that less than a fifth of their stepfamily informants held 'pluralistic' views of the family.[5] Furstenberg's American research has compared the attitudes of members of intact families with those in stepfamilies. While one-fifth of intact family members exclude a sibling and one-twelfth exclude a parent, in stepfamilies two-fifths exclude a co-resident sibling and nearly one-third exclude a stepparent.[6]

In answering this question, our informants however, both men and women, presented a great variety of forms, from simple nuclear households to complex family trees including stepparents, stepsiblings, and in-laws. The more extended forms markedly predominated. There were some gender differences. Men were more likely to include their partner's family, and sometimes this was to the exclusion of their own family of origin: 'Jenny's family are family, like'. On the other hand, while most must have found the one-dimensional terms of 'family' belonging fitted awkwardly with their own experience, it was only two women who talked of a more ambiguously nuanced system with a household 'core' within a 'second tier', and a wider network beyond.

Many of the answers conveyed the impression that the confusing experiences of family transition in which adults might either seem to prioritize children's needs or to disregard them, left them clear that family membership was something that had to be earned rather than taken as given.[7] Family members who were felt to have failed informants could be replaced and in such instances connections maintained, if at all, only with the most important idividuals: 'Well basically—it's my mother on the top of the shelf. . . . My family's been relatively small and certain of them I don't get along with, so there's no point to it. And so in some respects, the family I haven't got has been replaced by Tracy's [wife's] family.' Another man described his family as 'only mother really: I don't even know if I could include my brother really'. Whereas in most cases parents were excluded from this definiton of family if they were out of contact, they might also be left out if either they or the informant were seen to have developed a strong allegiance to another side of the family. 'Pete and the kids, and really more Pete's mum and dad, you know, they—they're brilliant. I think everybody's looking to have somebody. Sharon [stepsister] always had my mum's support.'

If a parent was seen to be pursuing an unacceptable life course, they too might be replaced by a more satisfactory parental figure. 'The close side of the family is definitely my mother-in-law. I spend a lot of time with her and I'm very close to her. I don't see that much of my mother.' This mother is described as leading a 'hectic life with a toy-boy' and so not being available for her. However a once-estranged parent could re-enter the family fold: 'My immediate family, like my sisters and my mum—and I suppose my dad now as well, he's part of it now. Cos he's lost his family, you see in Canada, and I think he regrets a lot of what he did.'

The inclusion or exclusion of stepparents as family members depended more on the extent to which they were or continued to be emotionally close than on the length of time spent living with them: '[She was] only my dad's wife, not family'; 'I don't include his wife or either of my first two stepsisters. That's it. It's a really small family.'

Whereas some saw family in terms of a set of connections to a wider extended family, others identified the family unit as consisting of those who had been through the transitions together:

Still me sisters and me mum. That's as far as it goes really. We've always been a unit together, like a team. Me mum—I suppose Dave [stepfather] in a way. I s'pose Dave can be entered into it, yeh.
Had to think about that!
Yeh!

Some narratives reflected cumulative experiences of difference, as with a woman who was adopted: 'It was always very funny, our family, because we always knew we were adopted as well, so a bit more didn't make much difference.' Others dealt with ambiguity, hurt, or loss by defining a tight boundary around their new family of creation: 'Just husband and kids'; others transferred their attachment to the family of their spouse, and thus perhaps kept a map of a 'normal' family alive for themselves. For yet others, the boundary around the family was extended to include friends: 'my family are my family, but my best friend is my family as well. She is—she is more like my sister than my sister, so she is my family too.'

Of those who struggled to find a way of formulating a definiton of family that both made sense to them and could incorporate the different sets of relationships, perhaps the most eloquent was Caroline Herbert: 'I think if someone says my "family", I think of my husband and two children, and I think of my dad and Gwen [stepmother], and I think of my mother and stepfather. I never think of my mum and dad. It's always two separate families, but they're still both my family.'

Conclusion

We have explored some of the ways in which our informants could develop a version of their life story to live with, and in most instances, to form a positive identity for themselves. We believe it is important to stress that these stories are never fixed and are therefore hard to evaluate. They emerge in different forms in different contexts and in our own understanding are always evolving, particularly when changes are encouraged by new intimate relationships and by having young children of their own. Where narratives were unreflective, fragmented, contradictory, or locked in one frozen version, we could generally see one reason for this in the lack of more benign or stable contexts in the past or present.

These narratives are all to a greater or lesser extent memories of loss: loss through death, and loss through divorce and remarriage. Both the loss itself and the experience of successive stages of adaptation to new relationships require different stories to be available for the family; and for the child. In this respect, stories can be divided between dominant and marginalized versions; and different contexts may either bring out marginalized stories in positive ways, or confirm negative versions of self. For some, new relationships became progressively intimate leading to a more benign family environment, while for others they were increasingly dissonant, compounding or amplifying the earlier experience of loss, thus leading to very different developments of memory and narrative.

In some families the parents had used, and sometimes continued to use, 'public memories' for official purposes in order to retain their own sense of correctness of behaviour during times of stress and disequilibrium. In other families parents told stories of their own lives so fiercely contradictory that no sense of shared reality could be held by the child. This was especially problematic where physical violence was involved. The child's dilemma was then how to hold on to a sense of continuity of self over time. When other relational contexts were available, this could be maintained, whereas when they were not, there was a greater risk that confusion, self-blame, or destructive behaviour would persist into adult life. One reason for the power and complexity of the interviews is that the interview itself can provide an important context for self-exploration. As one researcher has commented:

The story format offers powerful possibilities to move between past, present and future. Characters can be easily moved through time, new ideas introduced, and endings reworked and/or changed. We can locate ourselves in different positions in stories in relation to how we appropriate and anticipate past, present and future. There is a resonance, an echoing of themes and issues that helps us to understand that in the present we are always carrying our past as well as imagining our future. The present is the pivot point connecting past and future.[8]

We are therefore left with the conclusion that, however sensitively a research interview is conducted, it constitutes an intervention into people's lives. We cannot escape the recognition that exploring narratives inevitably plays a part in constructing as well as describing those same narratives. When employing such evaluative terms as 'coherent' or 'reflective' of narratives, an understanding of the individual's changing family and social context helps to avoid using these terms in ways that oversimplify or fail to do justice to the richness and complexity of their lives.

9

Working with Stepfamilies:
Clinical and Legal Contexts

IT is one of the paradoxes of studying the long-term outcomes of stepfamily childhoods that by the time that they can be evaluated, there can have been such radical shifts in their typical context that it is difficult to predict from past experience into the future. What we say here about the future will therefore necessarily be less securely grounded than our interpretation of the past. Nevertheless we believe that there are indeed important messages to be learned from that past experience, both for social workers, therapists, and other professionals who work with stepfamilies, and also for the wider framework of social policy and the law. Here we shall discuss the more specific implications for working with stepfamiles and for the law separately. But let us begin with four general lessons which apply to both.

The first is to avoid over-simplified contrasts between 'ordinary' families and stepfamilies. Stepfamilies have always been very diverse in their demographic and emotional structures, depending on whether they have orignated from parental death or separation, are stepfather or stepmother families, were formed when the children were younger or older, include half-siblings and stepsiblings, resident or not. And while the 'ordinary' nuclear family of two parents and two children was certainly the typical family form in 1958, by the 1990s, because of the rapid rises in cohabitation, in births outside marriage, and in divorce, it has now lost its once clear dominance. As a result the stepfamily has to be set against a variety of other living arrangements, including both married and unmarried couples with or without children, same sex couples sometimes with children, and lone parents, some through choice, others not. Among this variety of forms the stepfamily, which in the 1960s was the childhood experience of a very small minority, is predicted by the end of this century to affect up to one in five of all children in Britain.

Secondly, not only has the typical structure of the family changed in the last thirty years, but so have some of the sources of stress which now face not only stepfamilies, but most young families in the 1990s. The stepchildren we have followed grew up with the double protection of full employment and the welfare state at its most generous. They were less at risk of suffering serious poverty, especially during the single-parent phase, than their successors today. Today the risks which confront the majority of families of all types with children include insecure employment, uncertain housing, and the retrenchment in family benefits (including support for their grandparental generation) through cuts in health and welfare expenditures. We would anticipate that a comparable study of current stepchildren would bring much more frequent mention of stresses from poverty and poor housing. Certainly recent research in north-eastern England has shown children after parental divorce suffering especially from frequent moves, forced to live either in unsatisfactory private rented accommodation, such as old terraces, or in the dwindling sector of public housing.[1]

The third lesson is the continuing need to reassess our theoretical concepts of child development. In the 1990s many of the concepts underlying the teaching about successful child development remain rooted in models of continuous and exclusive biological family life with attachments to one set of natural parents. Children who live in stepfamilies, however, are likely to have experienced more than one change of pattern in their key relationships, so that for them successful development may have depended on attachment to other parental figures and kin, sometimes of different generations from their parents alone. The role of older brothers and sisters as potential emotional supports or allies in dealing with family instability needs further research, as does the role of the wider kinship network of aunts, uncles, and grandparents. Some children may also have taken part in several household changes in their lives, or even come to regard moving between households as part of their normal everyday lives. Their life course will thus be markedly different from that of children growing up in intact families. We need to be better informed about these common differences resulting from divorce and subsequent family re-ordering; so that models of family life other than those of intact biological families inform professional thinking about child development, and form part of all professional training about the varieties of 'normal' family development.

Fourthly, in order to understand the experience of stepchildhood it is essential to remember that children only arrive in stepfamilies through a series of crucial transitions. These typically involve parental death or separation and, at least briefly, a phase of living in a single-parent family. Such transitions are likely to contain many losses which in themselves create cumulative stress. Whatever the possible future gains, the breaking up of a marriage or the death of a parent disrupts intimate relationships and patterns of stability and attachment. Today there are also an increasing number of children who go through more than one parental or stepparental break-up, and for them especially the cumulative losses may become harder to sustain without impairment in health or social and emotional development. In 1989 out of the total number of 150,872 divorcing couples with children there were 24,765 divorces where one of the adults had been divorced before, and 12,455 couples where both adults had been previously divorced. For some children therefore the process of such transitions will remain a part of their lives, even after their entry to a stepfamily. How far this might make it easier to accommodate to further change, or whether such successive change becomes itself a factor for accumulated stress leading to disturbance, is not yet sufficiently described and discussed.[2] Another question requiring more research is the best role which schools can play in responding to the needs of children for space and a time of lowered pressure while they assimilate family change during phases of transition.

What advantages can a family systems model bring to working with stepfamilies? By using the term 'family systems model' we are not confining our discussion to family therapy, or indeed any 'therapy', so much as putting forward a conceptual framework for understanding the complex processes that all practitioners encounter, however many members of the system they work with, or whatever the terms of their involvement are. Systemic approaches can provide conceptual tools for mapping and understanding complex sets of relationships in terms of their patterns, rules, and beliefs. Thus the process of engaging family members in drawing up a geneogram (family tree) can create the opportunity for looking at the entrances and exits from the system, exploring closeness and distance, and for noticing patterns that have repeated over generations. A more coherent picture can often emerge in which personal or relational conflicts can be seen as a part of difficulties or dilemmas within the wider system dilemmas, sometimes leading to them being experienced as less toxic, less blaming, and less overwhelming.

Gregory Bateson's celebration of the aesthetic qualities of complexity in his dictum that 'The world looks prettier as it gets more complicated'[3] can be hard to appreciate at the level of lived experience rather than intellectual interest. However, complexity tends to have a negative connotation only in so far as the world accords simplicity a more positive status; and in the case of families this makes some of the advantages of living within more complex structures less easy to notice.

Stepfamilies often span generations in ways that challenge conventional family norms or expectations. Brothers and half-brothers or elder sisters and stepsisters may sometimes be fifteen years or more apart, while stepchildren and stepparents will often have a much smaller age gap between them. This may result in much less polarization between generations within stepfamilies and encourage multi-positional beliefs about living arrangements, and greater skills in negotiation and in managing conflict as well as sharper lenses for challenging beliefs about family life and for scrutinizing the wider society. Stepfamily life is woven together out of more complex threads than is generally acknowledged in discussions about 'family life' in Britain today. Consequently a continuing dilemma for stepfamilies is that many of them still believe that they should 'show' themselves to be as similar to 'ordinary' families as possible, rather than celebrating the possibilities for healthy difference that diversity can bring. So therapists can help stepfamilies think about the advantages and disadvantages of these configurations, the new resources that are available as well as those that may have been lost and thus help family members to feel more confident about difference.

An example of this might be in relation to sibling position. Children who move between two households and have acquired half-siblings might be in the position of being the youngest child in one household but not in another; other children who have acquired stepsiblings might experience being the eldest in one household but not in another. These different experiences might be seen only negatively, in terms of being unsettling and leading to insecurity; but they could also be understood as an opportunity to experience differences between positions in family life that most other children do not share.

Working with the resources that a more complex system might bring thus means creating openings for stepfamilies to celebrate differences and thus feel more confident. But it does not entail dismissing difficulties. In the complicated and shifting sets of relationships that evolve around stepfamily formation, the potential hazards for practitioners who become involved with the part of the system that requests help are considerable, especially if they do not develop an understanding of the impact of their interventions on other parts of the system. For example, when post-divorce relationships are conflictual, sound and seemingly impartial advice given to one parent about a child's needs may be used as an opportunity to undermine the other's position. A grandparent who has been central to the functioning of a family in transition may actively disapprove of and try to undermine a helpful professional usurping their role in supporting a single-parent household. The dilemma and pain for a stepfather of being encouraged to offer active parenting to his partner's children when he is not in a position to do this for his own may not be appreciated if his own family experiences are not enquired about. Practitioners using the family systems approach should consider who else in the wider family system may have views or feelings relevant to the problem in hand, and should also reflect on the effect of any intervention on the family as a whole, regardless of however many family members they may actually see.

Another underlying issue concerns the typical nature of memory and communication with others in dealing with loss. The evidence of our own research and also of other studies suggests that professionals in both primary and specialist services ought to pay particular attention to the difficulties which adults are likely to have in communicating clearly with their children about events that have distressed them too. Such events include both natural losses such as death and also losses created by human misunderstandings and conflict such as divorce. In each case, adults frequently try to protect children and themselves from further pain by avoiding talk. But very many of our informants described extremely painful and often bewildering experiences of failure by their parents to communicate with them, and our clinical experience also suggests that children continue to suffer from inadequate or partial explanations for family breakdown and from the lack of opportunity to express their views about the arrival of new partners.

Family systems understandings of communication pay particular attention, not just to content, but also how the context of the communication affects its meaning. For example, a parent who felt guilty about remarrying might be at pains to stress the advantages to the children of this move, which might put children in a bind about any negative feelings they have and make it harder for them to communicate their objections. As we frequently found in our interviews, children's protectiveness of adults can act as a powerful barrier to their willingness to ask questions or express their own needs. Insufficient attention may be paid to the intense loyalty conflicts that constrain children from talking unless they are given clear permission and encouragement to do so, or their reasons for not wanting to do so are respected and acknowledged. Whereas other work has shown that children can make use of adults outside the family as confiding resources which operate as protective factors, especially in the case of adult mental illness,[4] the evidence from our study as well as a current study[5] suggests that this is less likely to happen where divorce or death takes place.

Our study has brought out the risks for emotional well-being in adulthood for those people who have not been able, as children, to develop a story for themselves about family changes. The likelihood of this being problematic is much greater for children whose parents have divorced because they are caught up in the competing narratives of their parents. This involves not just hearing two different versions of reality in relation to the divorce, but witnessing each parent rewriting their own story about the marriage in ways which may contradict the child's memories. At the extreme, we may find children giving up their own ability to think, with the inevitable consequences for their learning and development.

Individual sessions can therefore be extremely useful in providing a space for children to develop their own stories without having to contradict openly their parents' version of events. Groups for children can have the same advantage, with the added benefit of sharing experiences in a non-problematizing way. However, when children are seen separately, a family systems approach should pay attention to the importance of not undermining the parents' position, or of setting up further conflicts for the child between the professional and the parent. Helpful professionals may inadvertently exacerbate a parent's difficulty in coping if they focus on the child's needs in isolation from the adults. Memory and communication, in short, not only spring from the family system but help to shape it, so that here, as in so many aspects of stepfamilies, difficulties not only have to be addressed in themselves, but also as vital elements in the whole system.

Some Sensitive Issues

Other research into stressful life events and their impact on children[6] suggests that where children are able to witness a parent continuing to manage stressful events, they are more likely to be able to learn to manage their own. As a result of an experience of coping, they are better placed subsequently to manage further stressful life experiences themselves. Where by contrast a parent is visibly stressed, the child is less likely to manage well in the face of the same event. We are ourselves persuaded from the evidence of this study that one of the key negative impacts of divorce following the loss of the parent, was when the child had to witness the parent who remained suffering from extreme distress and losing the capacity to cope with daily life. For the majority of children in this study, parents were witnessed and experienced as coping. However, even when the remaining parent is temporarily struggling to function, it may be very important for professionals and others involved with children to be sensitized to the small but significant inputs, such as the maintenance of routines in some part of the child's life, that can help maintain a sense of agency for parents and children. Helping single parents lay down 'markers' of progress and achievement in what can seem like an overwhelming experience of hopelessness can be an important part of the practitioner's task. Groups for women in the post-separation phase can be of great benefit in providing the opportunity to share experiences and gain support without feeling pathologized.[7]

For children, too, an acknowledgement of their own contribution to the maintenance of household life can be crucial. There is some evidence from research[8] that children's resilience is fostered by their being given opportunities to participate and contribute to the household in meaningful ways, such as having their own tasks to carry out. While an excess of responsibility at a young age is clearly detrimental, the wish to protect children on the part of helpers and feelings of guilt on the part of parents may prevent them from highlighting the positive aspects of children's help and thus fail to foster a sense of agency. On the other hand, when a stepfamily is formed, the desire to relieve children of responsibilities may ignore the child's feeling of displacement. This appeared to be particularly the case for girls. The focus in the family systems approach on the gains and losses of changes for all family members can be helpful in this typically complex issue intertwining family practices with cross-cutting emotions.

When the parent unable to cope is a father, this may raise a further issue in the shifting character of socially accepted gender roles. The fathers reported on in this book were men of the 1950s and 1960s and the enormous difficulties which many of them faced as lone parents were in part a reflection of the generally stereotypical gender roles of the period. Since then what is publicly expected of men has changed somewhat, but nevertheless contemporary research also reveals how men may feel particularly challenged by the task of parenting on their own. Thus Sebastian Kraemer in his reviews of 'fathering' holds fast to the view that women continue to organize the context for the primary father–child relationship. Following divorce therefore a raw exposure to children can be more a shock than a privilege.[9] Michael Lamb has further observed how women have contributed to men's insecurity, suggesting that ambivalence about the dilution of their exclusive mother–child relationship may in many subtle ways create and maintain boundaries that inhibit men from sharing and learning what they might need to know.[10] Perhaps significantly a recent small study of fathers parenting alone in north London suggests that men usually manage better when they have themselves had fathers who shared in their parenting and are in touch with a network of other fathers for support.[11] Thus paying particular attention to the issues for men in parenting in the absence of a woman can be very important, as well as not underestimating the lack of confidence that may underlie some men's readiness to offload responsibility for their children onto a new female partner. It can be important to see the difficulties of many lone fathers both in terms of the shifting social expectations which they face, and of the transgenerational family models of parenting on which they can draw.

Moving now to the forming of the stepfamily, while recognizing that there are many variations, it may be helpful to highlight some key things which could help the relationship to start off positively. The first is preparation.

An ideal beginning would have been when the biological parent, whether mother or father, had prepared the child for the arrival of a new partner, and had spent some time letting the child and adult get to know each other; the children themselves had some wish for another adult in the house; and the incoming adult was well disposed towards the children. In the memory of many informants, however, none of these conditions were met. Typically stepparents were introduced with little or no preparation. The child frequently felt that the family was managing perfectly well without a 'missing' adult, and, particularly in the experience of girls, had often formed a very close relationship with their existing parent, which they resented being interrupted by a new partnership.

In one-fifth of the families the new stepparent was remembered as not being well disposed towards the children at all at the point of entry. For those who had already experienced a parental divorce the fears about an incoming stepparent were much higher than for those who had lost a parent by death. It took longer for these children to connect positively to their stepparents, and a higher proportion remained ambivalent or negative towards their stepparents throughout their growing up. However, in many families, this was clearly related to early fears about what might begin again in a new marriage, where quarrelling and also violence had been part of the child's pre-divorce experience in the original marriage. In a significant number of second marriages from adults who had divorced, these fears were confirmed as the marriages were again marked by quarrelling and violence. Professionals may be useful in helping to make these fears held by children explicit to parents, so that they may develop more attentive understandings of a child's reluctant behaviour.

Children who have established a particularly intimate relationship with a lone parent after divorce, coming to think of them almost as a sibling or a friend, are likely to have special difficulties in accepting the lessening of intimacy and power that the new adult-to-adult relationship implies. This can often be a painful process. Moreover it contradicts in itself the earlier emotional experience of both parent and child, that the enduring tie is not that of adults who separate, but of mothers and children who do not.

Once in the new stepfamily, the keystone is likely to be the remarried couple. With children from either or both partners, this couple is one of the most scrutinized relationships in Western family systems, watched by the children of each partner, by the parents of each partner, as well as the parents of their former partners, often still keenly involved grandparents, by the ex-spouses, where they wish to continue co-parenting and by friends, allies, and enemies on both sides of the new relationship. The couple may have huge expectations of their ability to get it right this time round. Yet their relationship is likely to have the shortest history in the entire system, so that attempts to make it the fulcrum for emotional connections may be unrealistic. In these circumstances, advice, guidance, and a friendly ear outside the family may be of enormous advantage. The Stepfamily Helpline, set up to respond to such situations has been constantly used,[12] but advice could similarly be offered by counsellors in general practice or in group formats where the vicissitudes of 'family life second time round' could be more openly acknowledged as a general life hazard rather than experienced as a personal failing.

Persistent unresolved quarrelling or violence between husband and wife in a second marriage where there are children from the first marriage as witnesses, inevitably has a partricularly bad effect on a child's potential relationship with a stepparent. In every family where a respondent remembered an acrimonious or violent relationship between their own parent and a stepparent, they described themselves too as having had a bad relationship with the stepparent.

Children who had already experienced a parental divorce were likely to fear an incoming stepparent more than those who had lost a parent by death. It took longer for these children to relate to their stepparents positively, and more of them failed to do so even in the long run. In many families, this was clearly related to early fears that quarrelling and even violence might re-erupt in a new marriage, and in some cases they were indeed to be confirmed. Professionals can help children make such fears explicit to parents.

Another important stress factor more openly described by the girls, although often anecdotally recounted by the boys, was the ongoing experience of the negative effects of living with a highly critical parent or stepparent, who was persistently running the child down. Where a parent already has a tendency to be critical towards a child, and is struggling to manage a family under difficult circumstances, such criticism is likely to be increased. Such negativity did not seem to diminish with remarriage. Only where the criticism came directly from a stepfather or stepmother were the negative effects directly related to the stepfamily itself.

For families undergoing cumulative stressful experiences, criticism may become a way of life. Criticism of children can often be linked to a parent's idea that they are not themselves good enough as a parent, and that they therefore could not have a good enough child. Such patterns can often be identified by families as recurring over generations. Through highlighting the 'vicious circles' that develop it may then become possible to stimulate contrastingly positive alternative stories in which everyone is 'trying their best'. Such alternative descriptions can be powerful and liberating interventions.

In situations where there are fewer extremes of behaviour, but the stepparent–stepchild relationship is nonetheless poor, it is important for practitioners to be aware of moderating factors which could be built up over time. Patterns of relationship can be developed where 'special moments' are notched up between stepparents and children. These may be of a practical nature as much as any direct manifestation of emotional closeness, such as having bikes mended, making things together, or doing the garden. Even in situations where particularly abusive relationships were described, positive moments were sometimes also vividly remembered. And in several of the marriages that contained violent episodes in the early days, the marriage endured, and the child came to know their stepparent in a different light in the later years of childhood. The advantages of seeing a parent contentedly settled with a partner can be more apparent for stepchildren as they become young people seeking their own independence outside the family home. A number of the girls described how their views on a stepparent were modified or reversed over the years when they reconsidered their story from the vantage point of their own adult life. Much of the violent hostility which they described themselves as displaying towards their stepparents while they were teenagers was reframed from the maturity of 30+ as 'part of adolescent behaviour'. It can be very helpful to a new stepchild to understand that step-relationships can grow if tolerated, and that succeeding in passing through a stage of temporary coexistence may be crucial if their relationship to their biological parent is to be maintained into adult life. And more broadly, the awareness that relationships change over time and in new contexts, if offered by a professional to a stepfamily in conflict, can be immensely reassuring when the participants experience themselves as embattled in a seemingly endlessly intolerable present.

However adversarial the beginning of stepfamily life could be, the ways in which the new adult in the family actually behaved over time, the small remembered details of daily activities, could slowly shape a changing atmosphere in the family as a whole, and play a part in the subsequent well-being of the stepchild. However stormy previous waters had been, a good relationship with a stepparent appeared to act as a moderating factor in terms of positive development into young adulthood, and making life choices. Conversely a bad relationship could amplify already existing vulnerabilities, increase low self-esteem and lead to reactive, rather than thought-out behaviour, on the young person's part. This makes it particularly important for professionals to make stepparents, and especially those who undervalue their role, aware of the important influence which they are likely to have on the future of their stepchildren.

A stepparent can act as a moderator of unhappiness in a family into which they enter in a number of ways which can amplify over time. Such changes can occur within the marital relationship and have a positive effect for children, as well as directly between a parent or a stepparent and children. It can also be observed in the relationship between the children in the household. It seems that even in the absence of an expressed positive attachment to a stepparent, the witnessing of a positive marital relationship in itself has beneficial effects over time. One effect appears to be that children are less likely to leave home in a dramatic and impulsive way, cutting off their connections with the family. Such a severance of links is likely to be particularly hazardous emotionally for young people who have already had their links with a parent disrupted following divorce.

In this respect our research helps to explain the process underlying the transitional hazards for stepchildren predicted by Kathleen Kiernan, of making a too early marriage ending relatively swiftly in divorce.[13] Such instances among our informants were associated with leaving home in anger, or being thrown out following a conflictful episode. Five out of the six women whose parents divorced and who themselves married young and had divorced by 30, had married in the context of an angry leaving home experience. In contrast, of the women in intact marriages at 30, eight out of ten had left home, to work or to train, with the approval of their parents. The pattern was much the same for women who had lost a parent by death. Similarly, all the men still in intact first marriages at 30 remembered positive relationships with their stepfathers or stepmothers. It may thus be important to distinguish early marriage as a risk factor from the quality of the young person's relationship with their family at the time of the marriage.

Thus a stepparent who exacerbates existing discord within a post-divorce family can therefore very much amplify risks for stepchildren, and precipitate them into a premature independence. This is made more of a danger by the present withdrawal of welfare benefits from young people of 16 and 17, who are presumed, if they are not working, to be supported by their parents, which in the 1990s has led to a serious increase in young people from discordant or abusive homes living on the streets.[14] An awareness of such possible consequences by professionals can help to highlight to parents the powerful emotional effects and potential dangers of continuing unresolved family discord.

Right from the moment of parental separation, the potential for discord comes not only from within any subsequent stepfamily but from outside it. Where the out-of-house parent and former spouse remain in active contact, the relationship between the sets of relationships, child to biological parent and spouse to former spouse, also has to be managed by each partner, not only emotionally in terms of tolerating the recognition of other intimate relationships impinging on the couple and family life, but also physically and structurally in terms of the arrangement of weekly life; timetables to be kept, plans that go wrong, feelings that are messed up, and result in angry and bitter outbursts. This forms much of the work of both Court Welfare Officers and Family Mediators, but also of social workers visiting families for other reasons, who could usefully be alerted to this dimension of family discord. Conversely, where former spouses are not parenting on a regular basis or where they have disappeared, it is important for the parent to help the child to construct an explanation in which the child feels that he or she is free from blame.

Studies of contact centres,[15] which were set up to further the development of relationships between parents and their children where the separation took place following marital violence, show how they have provided a forum for exploring the vulnerability of fathers who wish to maintain contact but do not know if they have the skills to do so. However, services are not currently geared to the recognition of this need. A small ongoing clinical study by one of us of families following divorce suggests that where violence has been intrinsic to family interaction, the development of positive parenting skills in fathers is a complex and challenging business. In a context where the communication between the parents is at worst openly adversarial and at best silently hostile the creation of a conflict-free milieu for the child on contact is probably an unrealistic goal. Indeed, such contact may also provide the opportunity for some violent men to continue to abuse their former parners.[16] Thus if therapeutic or mediating processes aim, on the one hand, to reduce both violence towards and the verbal undermining of the other parent, and, on the other, to develop men's self-confidence to be able to care practically for their child, a considerable persistence is essential in order to develop lasting changes in the patterns of relationship.

Since other British research has shown that fathers more often attempt to maintain contact where they have sons than where they have daughters,[17] it follows that boys are especially vulnerable to the effects of continuing parental rowing long after the divorce itself is over.

The patterns of loss and stress described by our women inform-ants were both more varied and articulated in more complex ways, which point to a need for professionals to attend to the loss factors experienced over a long span of development. Some of the women described themselves as having had a more intimate relationship with the parent who had gone than with the one who remained. More than one-third of the girls were not able to develop a close or confiding relationship with their mothers. They therefore experienced themselves as lacking intimacy and being less protected on two counts. In addition more women than men remembered worrying about the parent who wasn't there; and being preoccupied with whether and how he was managing away from home. This dimension of girls' experience needs espe-cially to be born in mind by practitioners, because an intense emotional preoccupation with a parent who is not around, and who may be believed by the family to have been 'replaced' by a stepparent may be much less obvious than the involvement of a child in an active 'tug of love'.

A final dimension of potentially sensitive problems both within and without the household comes from siblings. As we have seen, positive sibling relationships were likely to reflect the general emotional culture of the household, although there were a few instances where older siblings became quasi-parental figures, and provided the emotional support that parents were unable to give. Step and half-siblings could provide a range of different relation-ship experiences, and many developed a long-lasting closeness. Whereas brothers and sisters are potential allies and can provide a buffer against the stress caused by adults as well as create an alternative forum for processing emotional experience, they can also increase the isolation of a particular child, for example by relating better to a remaining or absent parent or to an incoming stepparent and stepsiblings. Siblings may end up replicating the divorce battles between the two parents. Hence therapeutic help can be of immense value in allowing their shared losses, gains, hopes, fears, and dilemmas to be voiced. In particular, the ways in which siblings take up positions in the new families can helpfully be viewed in terms of their interdependency. Thus a child who remains fiercely loyal to the non-residential parent may at some level be taking care of this relationship on behalf of a sibling (often younger) who may then be freer to connect to a stepparent.

A secondary set of problems arising from normal life events within the stepfamily might include the handling of stepsiblings. Where there are two sets of children, each with their beginning in different families, widely differing expectations, and constant disagreements, these relationships may themselves create stress. The arrival of new babies, half-siblings, can be a profoundly uniting event, as it was for many of our sample; but sometimes it may intensify existing disagreements about the handling of children. It is therefore a time when the adults may find antenatal classes or the advice of midwives who are sensitized to these issues to be of particular value. For boys, it seemed as though new babies exacerbated already existing feelings of dislocation set in train by their parent's death or divorce, which had not been picked up by the adults in their lives.

The other crucial members in the family scene who need to be taken into account are grandparents. Very many were not only an invaluable resource as providers of daily continuity of care, but also used by children as confidants, so playing a key part in the minds and daily lives of their grandchildren following the formation of the stepfamily. Their role in the family's life is, however, one that needs to be carefully observed, for occasionally they may be acting less as a resource and more as an adverse commentator or intervenor into the newly forming stepfamily. Thus grandparents of parents who died were sometimes burdened by their own grief; and while the grandchild became a favourite and much loved child, this was not always accompanied by attempts to help the child come to terms with the loss of their parent nor to facilitate the development of a new relationship between the living parent and a new partner.

Beyond the family household and the wider family, it is school which impinges most directly on a child's life. Perhaps because stepchildren were still relatively rare in the 1960s and 1970s, few schools were very positively remembered by our informants. Very few schools appeared to be aware of the stresses which children were experiencing at home, and indeed some contributed to the stress by creating embarassment about the new family form. We can be sure that schools now are much more likely to acknowledge diversity in family life and that there is usually a greater awareness of children's emotional needs, even if recently the formal arrangements for the pastoral care of troubled children have too often been victims of financial cuts. Equally regrettably, such economies also mean there may also be fewer opportunities for hobbies, clubs, and sports which can provide valuable alternative worlds for children outside their families. In the current situation of awareness of the stresses on children of family break-up, heightened dilemmas can arise between focusing on children's emotional needs and their educational development. Other step-family issues which schools will need to continue considering are how information is best provided for separated parents, and how to watch for potential conflicts between half or stepsiblings living in different households divided by continuing rivalries and conflicts.

Partly for the same reasons, other professionals played very little part in helping our informants or their families. While a few of their parents had contact with psychiatric or social services, no informant remembered a parent voluntarily consulting professionals at any stage of the post-bereavement, divorce, or second-family formation processes, and only six said they had themselves subsequently sought psychotherapeutic or counselling help. Nevertheless, on the basis of what they told us about their lives as well as from our own clinical experience, we believe there are some clear pointers to the issues that practitioners involved with families may need to attend to.

The Exeter study has emphasized the need which families feel for professional help to be available to parents and children once the decision to divorce has been taken.[18] Parents believed such help should be free of labels suggesting 'pathology', and should ideally be constructed as a primary service, accessible in the same way as is a general practitioner. Parents emphasized how, in the midst of the many changes involved in divorcing, they experienced their own decision-making abilities as undermined just when they were most in need of them. In the same way we suggest that primary health care should address itself to the need for a service offering advice and the opportunity to talk over the basic needs of children for clear communication and the development of explanations that help them understand why the family is changing, and what the implications will be for their own lives.

The professional services initially used by the Exeter families included their GPs, the Citizens Advice Bureau and, in a small number of cases, Relate. In the intermediate stage lawyers and mediation were used, while in the long run self-help asociations like Gingerbread or the Stepfamily Association were called upon as well as local child and family social and psychiatric services. Parents were not very clear about the role of the probation family court welfare service or about the possibility of using mediation.

Among the problems with which adults looked for help was in achieving better more reliable contact with the non-resident parent; and on how best to explain to their children about divorce and separation. Some families who had experienced violence said that they needed more information about how to use restraining injunctions and others said they needed a safer refuge than was then available.

How then can we summarize the most important points for professionals to keep in mind while working with stepfamilies?

First of all, stepfamily experience needs to be understood in two further contexts beyond that presented by the family in the room. The first is the context of all the previous transitions which they may have experienced, and their associated hazards to adult well-being and children's emotional development. The second is the extended family network and its patterns of relationship with the family in the room over time.

Secondly, communication in stepfamilies, and the way transitions have been discussed and explained, is of key importance to the well-being of children. Mismanagement ranges from ongoing acrimonious rowing between all adult parties, to evasion, silence, and lies. Children need to process information by repeating conversations over time, not through a single 'telling'.

Thirdly, the wider extended family may have been of crucial importance in supporting children and lone parents during transitional periods, and may therefore remain a presence for good or discomfort in the lives of subsequent family formation. Such kinship networks may hold more importance for children than adults give credit for. It is important to bear this wider network in mind in working with the child or family.

Fourthly, persistent unresolved quarrelling, violence, or abuse carry powerful legacies for children, and may require longer work to help them to untangle the effects on their own self-esteem and ideas about family management.

Fifthly, patterns of negative relationship in childhood exprience do not necessarily go away when children grow up. The same patterns may well continue into adult life and be part of adult experience. The effect of these patterns in all families who have experienced adversarial divorce may be an important component of disturbance in an individual presenting for psychiatric help, whether in the context of the divorce process, stepfamily life, or other forms of psychological distress.

Lastly, stepfamilies created by death are less common in our society, but may require the clinician to pay attention to how memories of the dead parent are allowed as part of the child's current experience. The attempt to deny a dead parent is likely to contribute to confusion in children; and also to negativity in current family relations.

Stepfamilies and the Law

Changes in divorce legislation over the period under consideration have both facilitated divorce in England and Wales, and followed a trend which has been evident throughout Europe, and beyond. The shame attached to divorce, and the secrecy surrounding it, gradually dwindled, reducing the self-consciousness of children caught up in the process. Whereas in the 1970s and early 1980s, few primary school children would have had separated or divorced parents, more recently a child in primary school is unlikely to be the only one in the class in this situation, and some will already have stepparents. Teachers are increasingly familiar with difficulties which may arise for children in the process or aftermath of divorce, even though the response of schools still often lags behind, for example in recognizing that a child may have more than one home, and a separated parent who plays an important part in the child's life, as well as a stepparent.

The attitudes of the courts, too, in the interpretation of the 'best interests of the child', also gradually changed over this period, though practice was by no means uniform, varying from district to district and also, with varying practices at the different levels of the court system. This was perhaps most obvious in the variability with which sole or joint custody of children was recommended, and the criteria on which this was based.[19] The assumption that contact with the non-residential parent after divorce is of fundamental importance to children lies behind current legislation, and has been highly influential in the courts since the implementation of the Children Act in 1991. However, the research evidence from an earlier period is not unequivocal,[20] perhaps partly because the various elements in the situation, including not only the child's developmental stage, and gender in relation to the absent parent, but also attachment status to each of the parents, and significant others; and the potential contribution, material, and/or emotional that an 'absent' parent might make to a child's life, have not been fully explored. Some studies have found that 'overall family functioning' is a better measure of outcome for a child than whether or not contact is maintained with the 'absent' parent.[21]

The Family Law Act (1996), which combines and updates current divorce and domestic violence legislation, but will not come into effect until 1 January 1999, has major implications for professionals caught up in helping those involved in the divorce process and its aftermath. As far as domestic violence is concerned, the Act recognizes the need for greater protection of children from an abusive home environment, as well as from the risk of direct abuse, for the first time specifically providing powers for courts to order the removal of a suspected abuser from the home, instead of having to remove the child. The major change introduced by the Act is to replace fault-based with time-based divorce, 'the fact that a marriage has broken down irretrievably being demonstrated by the passage of a period of time for reflection and consideration'.[22]

Under the Act, the parties to a divorce are required to attend an information meeting, conducted by a qualified person other than a lawyer, which among other matters explicitly considers the importance to be attached to the welfare, feelings, and wishes of the children, and how they might be helped to cope with the divorce. A new emphasis is placed in the Act on mediation, including the explicit consideration of how far each child should be invited to take part in the mediation process. It is, however, extremely questionable at the time of writing whether sufficient numbers of trained and qualified staff will be available to provide the marriage and mediation services which the Act specifies. It has also been pointed out[23] that the mediation process can be experienced as coercive, merely reinforcing unequal power relations between ex-partners in conflict. The absence of any mention of current partners or stepparents in this legislation is a particularly unfortunate omission, which may indeed have the effect of prolonging their already ambiguous, marginalized position in the legal process.

The aim of the Children Act (1989) was to bring the existing piecemeal legislation relating to children into one framework, with a simplified court system, and, in the case of children of divorcing parents, an interpretation of the 'best interests of the child' in terms of continuing joint parental responsibility following divorce. One of the effects of this legislation has undoubtedly been to empower the separated parent who can no longer be excluded from children's lives without a court order, a step which courts are reluctant to take even in the most extreme circumstances, for example, where there has been physical or sexual abuse of the child in the past. The Act makes clearly visible the social belief that a birth parent is for life. The Children Act also, for the first time, acknowledges the existence of stepparents and goes some way towards clarifying their legal status: whereas under previous legislation a stepparent had no legal status at all, and was in practice often excluded from court in proceedings relating to their partner, and the children of the household, stepparents (and others, such as unmarried fathers) are now often accepted informally in proceedings, and are entitled to apply through the courts for 'parental responsibility' which, if granted, gives them equal legal status to a biological parent. However, the Children Act certainly fails fully to take account of stepfamilies—indeed, mention of the stepfamily itself is altogether missing from the Act. Biological parents are assumed always to have primacy over stepparents, so that legal guidance in realtion to contact orders with separated parents has tended to be interpreted without taking account of the reality of the situation for some children in stepfamily situations, and thus not serving the 'best interests' of those children.

Another principle established in the Act is that in any matter related to the welfare of a child, that child's own wishes must be taken into account, according to their age and understanding. In relation to the complex and confusing issues that arise in stepfamilies, especially in the extreme case when biological parental conflict is being played out in court, the interpretation by professionals of a child's capacity to understand is a matter of fine judgement. The difficulty is frequently not sufficiently recognized by the professionals involved, who may lack training in developmental issues in relation to children. The resulting court decisions may lead to increased conflict, both within and outside the stepfamily, and so prove detrimental to the child's interests.

It is still too early to know what the longer-term effects of the Children Act on the outcome for children in relation to parental divorce will be. Thus the overarching notion of parental responsbility for life, enshrined in the Children Act in the place of the concept of parental rights, in principle provides a reference point to transcend the conflicts over which parental relationship should be given priority. But at the point of divorce in practice, however, the notion of responsibility is not linked in any formal way to the idea of how parents can develop a shared concept of how to manage that responsibility towards the child. The notion of a parental responsibility can thus either become a context for co-operative parenting, or a convenient catchphrase which allows each parent to act separately on the basis of different beliefs.

Hence though it might be hoped that the legislation will help to promote continuing parental cooperation in the interests of children, there are certainly some cases where this is unlikely to be true. Burgoyne and Clark, in their study of stepfamilies in Sheffield,[24] showed that the 'conscious pursuit of an ordinary family life', was the aim of many of those involved. This carried the belief that 'a man's responsibility was primarily to his new family'. More recently, the Newcastle study[25] has shown that the principle of continued parental responsibility may clash with the social and psychological needs of remarried parents and their children, who may need freedom from the potential threat of the intrusion of a previous partner, particularly if there has been violence in the past, to allow an opportunity for bonds between members of the new family to be developed and consolidated.

Moreover, as we have found in our own study, such adversarial patterns between the former partners often do not cease with divorce, and may last well into the child's adult life. Such conflict creates an inevitable tension for children between their wish and need to have an ongoing relationship with their biological parent and their need for stability and a sense of belonging in the new stepfamily. These tensions need to receive further public awareness and attention if they are not to perpetuate the illusion that a stepfamily is like a first-time marriage.

The authors of the Newcastle study argue that they found a widespread psychological need for ex-partners to apportion blame before being able to move on to the next phase of their lives. They conclude, as Burgoyne and Clark also suggest, that the aim of cooperative parenting is desirable but may be unrealistic. They show that the role of a non-custodial father requires a degree of personal sacrifice and flexibility which by no means all fathers can or wish to achieve.

At the same time, while the Children Act is notionally liberating for parents, freeing them to a greater degree than hitherto to come to their own arrangements without the interference of the courts, on the other hand, through it new and complex points of potential authority are introduced into the ongoing network of responsibility for children's lives, which may complicate the role of a stepparent. The Act gives much greater powers to members of the extended family to apply for orders in respect of children. However, stepparents are introduced as at an equal level with a number of others, without any special consideration being given to their key role in relation to their partner's children. Other applicants may be either family allies to the children, or indeed, contestants for them. As we have found in our study, the role of stepparents in relation to stepchildren may change over time: whereas they may initially be just another adult in a child's life, they may gradually come to play a much more central role, a change which at present has no reflection in the present law other than through adoption (which in itself may bring another set of difficulties). The extended family may also continue to have a powerful influence in the lives of stepfamilies and be a particular resource to children. Where such family members also take legal responsibility, what are the likely effects of this on the organization in a new stepfamily, which may well include new children and grandparents? How are stepfamilies themselves prepared to take relatives into account as part of the formal process of their own lives?

During the 1980s and 1990s, single parenthood has become increasingly a target of government opprobrium, with images of fecklessness linked with poverty. The Child Support Act (1993), concerned with the payment of maintenance by absent parents, has impinged forcefully on the role of some separated parents in relation to their children, their ex-partners, and to newly created stepfamilies. It translates into financial policy the principle of parental responsibility throughout childhood, whoever the child is living with. This could have offered more security to lone-parent mothers. But the Child Support Act, unlike the Children Act, which was based on over a decade of social policy research, was hurriedly cobbled together, in an attempt to achieve a reduction in the payment of state benefit, mainly to unsupported mothers. In practice, far from promoting the welfare of children, the Child Support Act has quite often been implemented to their detriment, and in contradiction to the intentions of the Children Act. Previously agreed, and established, financial arrangements between ex-partners have sometimes been overturned, creating stressful situations, and leading to harmful effects on the relationship between children and their separated parent, even in some well-publicized cases being implicated in the suicide of fathers.

This has made it considerably more difficult for stepfamilies to be sure of their financial position and liabilities, even when legally sanctioned financial arrangements were already in place. For a stepfather until recently there have been no reductions in the obligations to a first family even when he is financially responsible for stepchildren, unless their own biological father is dead or untraceable. And certainly the Child Support Act does not allow for the needs and wishes of dependent children themselves, as far as their age and maturity allows, an important principle running through the whole of the Children Act, to be taken into account. A detailed research study by five children's charities concluded: 'A year after the implementation of the Child Support Act, it is very difficult to find evidence of any benefit to the children concerned.'[26]

Time may well show that modifications of the Children Act are advisable, both in relation to non-residential biological parents, and to stepparents. Certainly, more scope for flexibility is needed in the interpretation of the interests of individual children; and legal acknowledgement of the existence of stepfamilies might help to form the basis for more reliable judgements in some complicated cases. As Erica De'Ath, Director of Stepfamily, pointed out at a London conference in 1994, 'legislation can only do very limited things and it usually can't do what stepfamilies want; which is to create some idea of cohesion, some formal framework for dealing with transitions, looking at change, adjustments, trying to sort out boundaries.' Attending to these needs as well as respecting the multiple loyalties adhered to by children in family transition, some of which may actively militate against just this search for cohesion, is an ongoing dilemma.

10

Conclusion

W E began the research which led to this book ten years ago with one overarching question, a question which then and now arises for all of us from personal and professional experience: if children are to grow up in stepfamilies, what is it that distinguishes the experience of those who fare relatively well and relatively badly? It was fundamental to our viewpoint that stepchildren, like human beings at any point in their lives, have an innate capacity for change, even for innovation, and that this can be crucial in helping them to overcome difficulties at any point in the life cycle.[1] We wanted to know whether the experiences of loss, transitions, and stepfamily living could bring them new strengths and skills as well as pain in the face of difficulties. And equally, we wished to understand better which aspects of their experiences most helped to protect their long-term well-being. In addressing these fundamental issues, we wanted to bring to bear the interdisciplinary insights of both therapists and clinicians and social science researchers. We were determined to draw on the best strengths of both quantitative and qualitative research. This was why we made certain that our own small-scale project avoided using a clinic sample and was instead based, like very few others, on a thoroughly reliable representative sample, and throughout our analysis it has been our practice, when interpreting our material, to test our intuitive hypotheses against hard figures. So how far have we reached with our quest? Can we answer those questions?

In researching this topic it becomes increasingly humbling to realize how elusive really firm answers must remain. This springs from the fundamental complexity of the topic at many different levels. Stepfamilies are very varied in themselves, depending on whether they are formed after a death or a divorce, whether or not they include half-siblings or stepsiblings, the age of the children, and so on. They also vary in important ways between cultures, and between historical periods. This means that even when—unlike the majority of British research on the topic—based on a reliable sample, if the sample is relatively small, which it must be if in-depth interviews are to be thoroughly analysed, the numbers will be insufficient to produce more than suggestive findings.

For the same reason, while such findings can be usefully contrasted with other studies, no certain deductions can result from this, because almost any other stepfamily study represents a different culture—most of it so far North American—and a different time period. Twentieth-century family cultures in Britain itself, particularly as regards child-rearing, have been diverse enough regionally to make any generalization from a single locality very rash,[2] so that to take either California, or Pennsylvania as representative of Britain is even more unwise. Similarly, in terms of economic context, of family structures, particularly as regards cohabitation and illegitimacy, and cultural attitudes, the 1960s were clearly an altogether different era.[3] Thus by the time that a long-term study has matured, its findings represent an original social context which has disappeared. This is fundamental to the unreliability of prediction in social research.

There is yet a further dimension to this 'methodological impossibilism' in the case of a study like our own which seeks to evaluate long-term outcome. It was with this in mind that we chose to work with the National Child Development Study cohort, which has been regularly documented since birth in 1958. But this in itself gives rise to further difficulties. The focus of research interest has shifted a lot since 1958, so that the earlier questionnaires (which are in any case no longer available) did not ask many of the questions which we would now wish. Thus in practice it has not proved easy to relate the qualitative with the quantitative in a detailed way in this long-term perspective. Moreover, because of the radical changes in British social attitudes to marriage and divorce in the last forty years, the context in which long-term outcomes were generated has changed, so that the explanations which applied to the 1958 generations may no longer be so relevant. Furthermore conceptually too, the longer timespan over which we seek to measure consequences, the weaker the associations must become. The intergenerational relationships between the attitudes and daily practices of parent and stepchild through their twin life cycles is constantly subtly changing over time. And as Sir Michael Rutter, who has investigated such issues more persistently and thoroughly than any other researcher, observes, the process of influence is far from straightforward: many of the most important protective factors in adversity operate 'through their effects, both direct and indirect, on chain reaction over time'. As he puts it, the quality of resilience, in how people cope with life changes 'is influenced by early life experiences, by happenings during later childhood and adolescence, and by circumstances in adult life. None of this is in itself determinative of later outcomes, but in combination they may serve to create a chain of indirect linkages that foster escape from adversity.'[4]

On top of this, in many respects 'resilience' may be demonstrated through a number of options, sometimes at the extreme opposites of a particular spectrum of choices. Thus while some stepchildren faced with relating to a mentally ill parent may successfully take on extra responsibilities, others may choose to distance themselves emotionally from a situation which they see as unalterably bad. So again in adulthood, some former stepchildren model their lives on their parents, while others wish to be different from them; some may react to memories of unsatisfactory parental marriages by marrying with high ideals of doing better, others by marrying very late with great hesitation if at all; some may try to be stricter with their children than their parents, others the reverse. Clearly it is extremely difficult to measure factors which are so indirect in their consequences, and all the more so when the links between cause and positive or negative effect are also unclear because the effects cannot be easily categorized as plus or minus until their consequences have in turn emerged further down the chain. Such behaviours thus cannot be measured 'objectively': they can only be understood in terms of their meanings as part of a sequence in each life.

With all these reasons in mind, we have had to accept more modest aims: to explore, in depth and with methodological rigour, the indirect linkages in one stepfamily chain. Too many recent post-divorce studies have been seized upon—usually briefly—as universally authoritative, offering general answers to policy issues. None could have justified such a reputation. It has become increasingly clear that we can never provide simple answers on stepfamily childhoods, either as to why yesterday's children have flourished or not, or as to which of today's children will flourish in the future.

Our study is based on memories of childhood. Like all remembered evidence, such recollections need to be interpreted both as accounts which allow us to reconstruct as far as possible what happened to the child, and also as expressions of the child's feelings. Inevitably these two sides to some extent interfere with each other, for feelings have particularly powerful effects in reshaping or suppressing memories. Nevertheless in practice the interviews provide abundant evidence, both 'objective' and 'subjective'. We found that the variations in memory were themselves particularly revealing. Thus some of our informants were continually haunted by traumatic memories: of loss, abandonment, homelessness, violence, physical and sexual abuse. Others by contrast found a strength in memory, rethinking their own past and the examples of their parents as a resource for their own adult lives.

There are intrinsic problems in family memories for many stepchildren, because their parents may be offering them conflicting versions of the past, or even cut out all memories of the other parent. We found marked differences in the abilities of men and women to present full and coherent childhood memories. Women's memories were typically fuller, richer, more reflective and open-ended, and they seemed more able to hold a multiplicity of viewpoints. It seems that daughters especially learnt to talk closely about family and personal questions from their mothers: and also that for women this was in turn a helpful factor in their own subsequent marriages.[5] Men by contrast much more often seemed to distance themselves from their memories, which were often relatively thin, and sometimes far from coherent. Half the men's wives joined in their interviews to help them, while no husband joined any of the women.

In our analysis we have drawn on a number of different theoretical strands. We have already hinted at two of them, gender and attachment, in discussing memory.

It has inevitably been a basic issue that we have considered how the attachment needs of children are met as families change, how far they have experienced a close relationship with at least one parent, and how this may have affected their adult lives.[6] This entails observing how far children have developed new attach-

ments to stepparents. Recent research on attachment has suggested a very interesting connection with coherence in presenting
one's story, and it could be very rewarding to follow this further
into adulthood. We have also felt anxious that the teaching of
child-development theory too often continues to assume the continuity of parenting from birth and ignores the now common
changes resulting from parental break-up and remarriage.

Gender has provided a still more pervasive viewpoint, crucial to
our understanding of stepfamily processes throughout.[7] Highlighting gender as a category also throws into question the idea
that forming a stepfamily can be seen simply in terms of a
straightforward change in family structure. The dominant role
played by women in handling family relationships undermines
any suggestion that remarriage in itself enables the crucial realignment of emotional attachments that is so often assumed. If we
take into account the wider context of gender, then we see that
relationships between mothers and children are generally the
most powerful and enduring; beyond that, the role of women as
carers to children and holders of emotional responsibility under-
lines, and is indeed strengthened by, family structural change.
Conversely, men's lack of experience in managing family relationships in the absence of women highlights the importance of
fathers' emotional ties to their children being demonstrated in
practical ways rather than being known in the abstract. The
problematics of gender, equally clearly revealed in men's and
women's differing reflections on childhood, suggests that further
research is needed on the specific vulnerabilities and resiliences of
boys and girls who face the stressful experiences of stepfamily
childhoods.

Equally important has been our understanding of 'family'. We
have been anxious to avoid the misleadingly fixed categories which
are too generally used in political or popular discussion, and even
to a disconcerting extent by some social scientists.[8] We see
families as complex systems, constantly in change, composed of
members who come and go, and who each have their own view of
their family and its meaning and ideals and its boundaries, and
who are linked by other members through relationships which are
social, material, and emotional. It is particularly important to
observe the role of wider kin and also the intergenerational
relationships in the family, above all in the key part played by

grandmothers. And just as each individual life follows a course with key transitions, so each family moves through a series of transitions, some predictable, others unexpected: each of which demands a renegotiation of relationships between members.

For this reason we would see any attempt to describe stepfamilies as if they were one single discrete and definable family form as highly misleading and limiting. There is no single pathway through divorce, nor recovery from death; no set sequence of stresses or procedures to be gone through that is common to all stepchildren. Nor is there any logical timescale for the resolving of unhappy past events, or the acceptance of new sets of relationships in the place of those lost. Our informants' lives did not bear out the contemporary 'blueprints' which some writers have offered for moving from a first to a second marriage.[9] One particularly common situation in which the dangers can be seen is the overemphasis on the stepfamily as a 'new' or 'second' family along with the very widespread beliefs of families themselves that they can make a 'fresh start' after a divorce when a stepparent joins them. This can in itself exacerbate the difficulties of the non-resident parent in retaining a caring parental role and also provoke more severe loyalty conflicts in the children.

The intergenerational dimension is an equally important part of this family systems approach. Our evidence demonstrates that repeating family patterns, whether of a protective or a stressful nature, could be as salient in our informants' lives as their direct experiences of family breakdown and reconstitution. Some of these repeating patterns reflect the wider social context, the most obvious examples being poverty, racism, and gender differences; others represent the traditions, culture, and practices handed down within particular families.

This then was our approach. But before turning to our findings we should explain how, for our own rough guidance, we measured 'outcome' in adulthood. This outcome, we must emphasize, should be seen as an indicator rather than as a firm 'finding'. We chose three criteria. The simplest was occupation: upward or downward mobility or the same level of occupation as compared with parents (we did take into account the mother's position as well as the father's). The second, more complicated, was marriage and its quality, to which we also gave three ratings: for this purpose we took a more conventional view than in our qualitative interpretation, giving no approval to cohabitations and invariably disapproval to divorces, a conventional quantitative position now seeming increasingly anachronous. Lastly, we deduced a measure of psychological well-being from a self-administered questionnaire, supplemented in a few cases with evidence from the interviewer.[10]

We then looked at the group as a whole in terms of these measures of adult outcome, dividing our informants in terms of gender, social class, age of entry into a stepfamily, and whether they lost a parent through divorce or death.[11] In terms of overall occupational mobility, we found no gender differences, but those who lost a parent from divorce did better than those whose parent died. There was, however, a very particular gender difference when we looked at upward mobility.[12] It appears that upwardly mobile men move at the expense of relationships, while for women the pattern is reversed; or to put it another way, marriage and upward mobility correlate for women, but not for men. This is a finding which fits well with the evidence of one major American longitudinal family study for a cohort born thirty years earlier, who experienced role-divided marriage at its peak.[13] A different effect may emerge, as has been suggested by another British study, when more of our cohort are divorced, for while men are most often held back occupationally by marital dislocations, for women, especially those with middle-class aspirations married to a working-class man, divorce can be a crucial release which sets them free for upward mobility.[14]

It is also striking that those, mainly men, who are upwardly mobile without successful marriage relationships are overwhelmingly working class, presumably because they felt most driven to overcome childhood material deprivation; but it is interesting that few women shared this priority, relationships always remaining equally salient.[15] Conversely, of the five who are downwardly mobile in occupation but successful in their marriage, four are middle class.[16] It looks as if those brought up in relative material comfort were more likely to put fulfilment in relationships first of all.

When we examine measured outcome in terms of marriage, no differences appear related to social class, but there is again a clear gender distinction. Men were more likely to remain single; but of those men and women who did marry, it was the women who had experienced more serious relationship difficulties.[17] There is also an intergenerational effect: the children of divorced parents have worse marital problems than those who lost a parent through death. On the other hand, more of those whose parent died never married. This may partly reflect the slightly greater tendency of those whose parents died to suffer from psychological difficulties. Such difficulties were also more prevalent with women than with men, and with the working-class informants. Not surprisingly, those with such psychological difficulties less often had successful marriages.[18]

We also looked to see whether there were any clear effects of the timing of entry into a stepfamily. Perhaps surprisingly, the briefer transitions of two years or less between parental loss and stepfamily formation were no more likely to lead to psychological problems,[19] or to affect marriage or mobility. There were clearer consequences of the age of entry into a stepfamily. Psychological difficulties were least with those who entered latest and most with the youngest entrants, who also suffered more relationship problems. Those with teenage entry, on the other hand, seemed to be slightly disadvantaged in terms both of marriages and occupations.[20]

With these overall patterns as a background, let us go on now to summarize our more detailed findings. We shall do so by following the thread of the life course.

Let us begin therefore with the intact family. Those who had memories of this stage of their childhoods portrayed a full range of family relationships, from the gentle to the harsh or violent, and from the garrulous to the laconic. There were general tendencies for working-class families to use harsher discipline with less intimate communication between parents and children, and for fathers in general to be much less communicative than mothers. An interesting caution in over-interpreting this difference—as has been done, perhaps, in the very important work of John and Elizabeth Newson[21]—is the recognition that in contrast to the predominantly feminine and middle-class ideal of closeness through intimate verbal communication, there is also another model, more male and more working class, and sometimes powerfully successful in fostering parent–child attachment, of caring through doing and intimacy through physical toughness, including even harsh discipline.

In terms of the future it was particularly interesting to note that while as regards discipline there was no difference between those whose parents were to die or to separate, there was at this stage (although not necessarily later) somewhat less good parent–child communication, as well as markedly more cases of quarrelling and violence between the marital couple, in the families which were to be broken by divorce. This seemed indeed to be one of the key differences between the two groups. Two-thirds of those whose parents parted remembered their sustained quarrelling, and at least half of these also recalled episodes of violence, despite often being very young when the split occurred. By contrast, under one-third of those who lost a parent through death had similar memories.[22]

The point is especially important. It was very clear from their accounts that the experience of violence between their parents before their divorce had a very lasting impact. For boys it seems to have made a good relationship with a stepfather less likely. And it frequently left both men and women with legacies which they carried forward into their own decisions as adults in relation to marriage and partnership. In other words, from the child's per-spective the family's difficulties did not begin with the divorce, but preceded it; and indeed some of them directly experienced the divorce as a relief from them. For this generation, when of course divorce was a rarer and more drastic step, there may therefore have often been considerable justification in a divorcing parent seeing the marital separation as a help for the children as well as for themselves. Our evidence reinforces the tentative observations of some other more recent researchers who have also shown that children's familial difficulties typically precede rather than begin with a divorce.[23]

What seemed to moderate the ways in which a child's life was dramatically changed as the result of the loss of a parent? One key factor, as with subsequent transitions, was communication between the remaining parent and the child. However, very much as with Ann Mitchell's Edinburgh study of divorcing families in the 1980s,[24] three-quarters of our informants recalled problems in communication, ranging from silence and evasions to down-right deception. The most confused were the youngest, not one of whose curiosity was met. Some parents already secretly had a lover, so that the child was simultaneously catapulted into a stepfamily. Linked to this was the particularly startling finding that one-fifth of parents had at some point succeeded in misdescribing the basic family situation to the NCDS interviewers, so that they were originally misclassified in our sample.

For some families, deception over a single event of fact such as a child's parentage could create a culture of evasion which pervaded all aspects of family life. For others lack of communication about death, divorce, or the entry of a new adult into the household was part of a more general family culture of not talking. With few exceptions, our informants had an opposite aim, a 'corrective script'[25] for communication in their adult lives, attaching especial importance to talking openly to their partners and to their own children. Because we did not interview the parents who were deemed to have failed to communicate, we cannot know what their view was about whether they had talked enough to their children. However, clinical experience suggests how often there is a gulf between an adult's idea about what they have communicated to a child, often in a single conversation, and a child's need to process the information through repeated conversations over time. While our informants grew up at a time when divorce and remarriage had a far lower public profile and parents may therefore have been more given to secrecy, clinical experience again leads us to conclude that adults still frequently fail to give children a convincing reason for family breakdown or remarriage.

The silence was particularly complete where it was a mother who had left. Only in one such case was the mother's reason for leaving the child even hinted at. For none of these children was the loss of their mother moderated by any attempt at explanation by the father. It seemed that fathers had been unable to construct any self-respecting explanation, and had not attempted to enter into the loss for the child because they could not bear their own pain. They resorted instead to either blame or to silence, including the destruction of photographs and any of her possessions which remained in the house. This double loss, of a mother and of any understanding of her disappearance, can be described as contributing to lasting trauma[26] for at least three of our informants.

Nor was this failure in communication limited to those whose parents parted. To our surprise we also found that two-thirds of those whose parent died were also further disadvantaged by silences, the destruction of physical reminders, and even deceptions, and the absence of a place where death could be discussed. Few children were allowed to attend their parent's funeral. Even later they felt that death was a 'taboo' subject which they could not broach with the remaining parent. It was in fact somewhat easier for the children whose parents had parted to talk in later years about how and why this had happened.[27]

Linked to communication, but distinct from it, is closeness between children and parents. Closeness to the parent who remained was undoubtedly one of the most important factors in helping children through the transitions which followed the loss of a parent. Two-thirds of all our informants maintained a close relationship with one parent throughout, whatever the reason for their loss of the other, and this was their most important single source of support.

During the single-parent phase there was a general tendency for a shift towards much gentler disciplining of children and more intimacy between parent and child, both of which often helped to soften the child's losses. There was, however, also a new added danger in the possibility of the remaining parent failing to cope, either—especially for men unused to household responsibilities—practically, or, for both men or women, emotionally. In contrast to the dramatic pictures painted by some other researchers of the aftermath of divorce,[28] only three of our informants described a parent as 'going to pieces', and a further seven as visibly suffering extreme distress or briefly 'breaking down'. Boys and girls tended to react differently to such troubles, boys expressing concern through some form of practical helping, while girls, as well as trying to look after a distressed parent, also often worried helplessly about them. On the whole, however, informants emphasized the strength and determination of the parent with whom they remained to keep the family going and the aid which was given to them by their extended family. Other research into stressful life events and their impact on children has suggested that where a child is able to witness a parent continuing to cope, they are themselves more likely to learn how to manage stressful events and in turn to cope well through their own subsequent life difficulties. Where a parent is visibly stressed the child is less likely to manage in face of similar events.[29]

We now reach the point of entry into the stepfamily itself. Although there were many variations in how the complex new relationship was recalled as beginning, certain key points seemed to help towards a positive start. These were that the biological parent, whether mother or father, had prepared the child for the arrival of a new partner, and had given some time for the child and adult to get to know each other; that the child too had some wish for another adult in the house; and that the incoming adult was well-disposed towards the existing children.[30]

We intended the age of entry to a stepfamily in our sample to be only between the ages of 7 and 16, but due to the misinforming of early NCDS interviewers by some parents, our informants did include ten who were already stepchildren by the age of 6. However this revealed interesting consequences. Half of these early entrants suffered severe psychological problems, far more than the others; and this seems most likely to be accounted for by the parental deception involved, rather than by the timing in itself. Conversely it is also noticeable that the last group, who entered stepfamilies as teenagers, when they were able to argue and even to fight with adults, and as a last resort to leave home, remember in contrast much more open communication and negotiation with parents over the transition.

In general, while the new arrival was awaited by some children with fear and some with anticipated delight, most tended to be somewhat apprehensive. This seemed to be more problematic for those whose parents had divorced.[31] Also at any age there was a marked distinction between the typically greater skills of mothers than fathers in introducing a new partner. Mothers usually introduced a stepfather slowly, and at first simply as a friend, and over a half clearly explained the situation and even asked the child's consent to the new marriage. When the children were teenagers there might even be some collective negotiation over house rules. Fathers showed none of this skill in introducing their new partner. This meant that right from the first moment stepmothers usually had a more difficult task than stepfathers.

Nevertheless, once the stepfamily was formed, for the child the most fundamental point remained their relationship with the remaining natural parent. Looking at the whole period, it is clear how vulnerable many were rendered by this. At one extreme, almost one-third remembered being 'very close' to at least one parent. But at the other, one-third received at best only material care, some with parents hard even to the point of violence; so that if they were deprived as children, it was above all because of the intrinsic quality of parental care which they received, rather than as a consequence of entering a stepfamily. In between the two extremes at least one-third felt ambivalently about parents who, although 'always there', were often difficult to get close to.[32] Again these contrasts to a considerable extent also reflected gender differences.

Next in importance was how, over time, the child came to regard the stepparent. Half of our informants either thoroughly disliked their stepparents, or regarded them as marginal figures, irrelevant to their own emotional circle. For the other half, memories were either partly or wholly positive. It is very noticeable that four-fifths of those with positive feelings towards a stepparent also remembered their parents as supportive, or had good memories of the lost parent who had died. Thus a good relationship between a child and stepparent was much more likely to reinforce good parenting, than to compensate for the lack of it.

For a stepparent to be fully accepted in the long run the quality of the new marriage was especially crucial. Quarrelling and violence between husband and wife in a second marriage had in every case a particularly bad effect on the child's view of the stepparent. It is very noticeable that remarriages after death are much more often remembered as successful than those after divorce.[33] This was a very important reason why children from divorced families slightly less often felt warmth towards a stepparent.[34] When the first parental marriage had been violent, boys were especially unlikely to get close to a stepfather.

Much more striking, however, is the general difference in attitudes to stepfathers and stepmothers. Positive feelings were much more likely towards stepfathers, while strong hostility was almost entirely confined to stepmothers.[35] Altogether stepmothers were actively disliked by two-thirds of children, both girls and boys; while stepfathers were disliked by only one-third, who were mostly girls. The explanation for the difference lies principally in the very different expectations held of stepparents of each gender.

Relatively little was expected of a stepfather, beyond caring for the mother and bringing an increased income to the household—both obvious gains for the child to see. He was otherwise essentially a marginal figure, more like an uncle, perhaps helping the children or playing with them, such as mending bikes, gardening, or making things together, but not responsible for them. Discipline remained the mother's prerogative. Only five stepfathers seem to have been accepted as a full substitute father. With a small number of girls some sexual jealousy of the newcomer was remembered. However, conflict between stepfather and child typically arose precisely when they aimed at this, either by asserting discipline or by trying to change the household routine, which usually continued with minimal disturbance. Our informants give very powerful testimony that for their generation a successful stepfather was very different from their expectations of a natural father.

For a stepmother the expectations were much more complex. In contrast to the role of stepfather, they were expected to fulfil the role of a full substitute mother; yet precisely because of this, resented by a child whose grief at losing a mother was still raw. A stepmother was expected to provide the children with love, to take over responsibility for their discipline, and to assume all household responsibilities. The gender role assumptions of the period made it seem natural that a woman should give up work and take over her new family. For the same reason men's typical lack of domestic and caring skills meant that they were sometimes willing to offload these tasks onto a thoroughly unsuitable woman, whom they would then leave unsupported and floundering. In the background, looming threateningly as a vindication of hostility as soon as a child felt ill at ease with a stepmother, hovered the myth of the wicked stepmother. Stepfathers could be uncaring, even violent, but they were scarcely ever as hated and vilified as stepmothers could be. When the difficulties of the task are understood, it becomes impressive that one-third of all children nevertheless came in time to accept or even like their stepmothers.

What of the role of the parent who had died or was lost once the stepfamily had formed? For many children, this loss has remained throughout their lives the 'worst thing' that has happened to them.[36] In this respect it is interesting that those who had lost a parent through death, and therefore finally, more often suffered psychological difficulties.[37] Half of those whose parent had died had scarcely any memory of them at all, and another six of those whose parent had left had no memories either. These were the most absolute losses. It was an especially serious blow when the absent parent had been the child's favourite. And for all of them the weight of that loss continued to be felt in changing ways as life unfolded. Boys above all yearned for shared activities, girls missed the sharing of intimate feelings. Later on some of those whose parent had totally disappeared set out in adulthood to find them, or at least traces of them, a photograph or the semblance of a voice.

Where there were discernible memories, for those who had died the images were usually positive, even if idealized, and sometimes could provide a positive inspiration in life. The earlier memories of those who had left were much more varied, ranging from the idealized to the thoroughly disliked, and with very few exceptions, even when there was no contact, these absent parents did have some discernible influence on the development of a child's life, even if it was primarily to avoid making the same kinds of mistakes.

In half the families where a parent had left, some contact was retained at least for a period. It was not strongly encouraged by the courts at this time, and was typically irregular and sparse.[38] There was less contact where the break had been very early, or the ex-partners remained hostile, and it depended upon the mutual willingness of the child and the absent and caretaking parents. Because fathers were more negative towards contact and more often bitter towards partners who had left them, mothers were more liable to be cut off completely than were fathers. It is not clear that continuing contact was always in the child's overall interest: it is noticeable that boys who were in contact less often formed a good relationship with their stepfather, perhaps partly because of their exposure to conflict between their parents. Also, at that time there was a complete lack of guidance as to how to succeed as an absent parent. Nevertheless it is certain that contact ensured that the absent parent remained an important if peripheral figure in the child's life. Quite often even when unsatisfactory it could be helpful in getting to know the missing parent as a real person, perhaps with serious failings, and so to understand why the parental split had taken place. Most important of all, by maintaining the thread of communication it opened up the later possibility, which for some could prove very important, of help at the transition into adulthood, for example in getting a job or a home.

Within the family there were two more important potential protective resources for a child: first, brothers and sisters; and secondly, grandparents and other kin.

Although we included good confiding relationships with an elder brother or sister as a possible resource for a child, we found that only half our informants remembered siblings as having been helpful. A sibling could be important in moderating stress, by providing both a buffer from adult hostility and another forum in which emotional experience could be shared. On the other hand, there may often be sharp differences between how different siblings relate both to the remaining parent and to the step-parent. For example, at the extremes one may be regarded as the favourite and another as the problem; and in the latter case this will exacerbate rather than modify stress. In general, good relationships between siblings, probably because they were encouraged by parents, seemed closely tied to good parent–child relationships. Nevertheless there were seven children who lacked a close supportive relationship with a parent, and did find one with a sibling.

We found that variations in attitudes to siblings ranged from intense love to hatred, but they were three times as likely to be loved as disliked. The range of feeling was strongest with full siblings and least with stepsiblings. Intense hostility, which was common among full siblings, was thus rare among half-siblings or stepsiblings. With half-siblings, relationships were almost always positive, and when they lived together they would usually bond as full siblings.

Relationships with stepsiblings were in general much less close, and when they lived in different homes there was typically little or no contact between them. There were twelve families with co-resident stepsiblings. In most of these, relationships were good, but in three they were seriously conflictual. A key factor in successful stepsibling relationships was whether both of the parents in the home were able to treat each half of the family with equal fairness. When a biological parent was perceived as taking sides with a new partner against their own children, this was felt as particularly unfair. In such a situation stepsibling relationships could be an ongoing discordant element in a child's life, amplifying anger and negativity in other relationships.

The role of grandparents was much less ambivalent, and it provides a striking counter to suggestions of the declining role of the extended family in contemporary Britain. It is true that because of the split in the family resulting in most instances of divorce, and also surprisingly often after a death, the number of relatives who were seen regularly fell sharply. But at the same time a much closer relationship was likely to develop with those who continued to be seen. In the lives of forty-four children an important role, in practical caring or emotional support or both, was played by a member of the extended family: most often a grandmother, but also quite often a grandfather, aunt, or uncle. (At that time, in contrast to today, a stepgrandparent was only rarely very significant.) During the single-parent phase, it was quite common for a grandmother to live with the child in the same home. This meant that typically memories of those who had lived with a 'lone parent' were less those of a truncated family unit but rather of being embedded within a wider extended family network. Altogether there were sixty such supportive relatives recalled, and the child had felt closely attached to three-quarters of them. After a close supportive relationship with their remaining parent, this was the single most important protective factor for which a child of this generation could hope.

Beyond family relationships, it also mattered whether the child could retain a familiar and supportive physical and social environment. For most children their house provided a safe and secure world, and for those away from the more impersonal neighbourhoods of London and the south-east there could also be a helpful continuity in a known community of neighbours and friends. Individual long-standing friends were in fact only mentioned in two instances before the stage of boyfriends and girlfriends, but the wider peer group was often an important source of fun and relaxation. Moving home could threaten all this; and it was made still worse when the move was into an inferior house. In fact only fifteen children moved more than three times; but it seems likely that for these, such frequent moving was in itself an amplifier of their stress.[39]

Lastly, this generation of children had enjoyed strikingly little positive support from professionals. Most did not suffer any disruption of their schooling, but as many children strongly disliked school as those who liked it, and only four remembered school as a helpful refuge from their family difficulties. Twelve children became rebellious or truanted. Teachers showed a general lack of understanding or sensitivity towards the stepfamily situation. Only six children had strongly positive memories of a teacher. Most left school as early as possible, and only six later moved socially upwards through education. And as to other professionals—doctors, social workers, or therapists—none were remembered as having given significant help to them as children.

A stepchild's life does not stop evolving with the end of childhood. Nevertheless the majority of studies of stepfamilies misleadingly give the impression that it is possible to predict with a high degree of certainty that suffering at a certain point in childhood, or apparently rash choices made at the onset of adulthood, will inevitably and permanently shape a life. This makes far too little allowance for the quality of resilience, of the continuing capacity for change, which is so strongly characteristic of human societies and individual men and women. Our evidence reveals powerfully how often young adults are able to find compensatory experiences for themselves, new anchor points around which to rebuild their lives, most often through work or through new relationships and attachments.

In evaluating which aspect of their own lives had given them most fulfilment, although most mentioned both family and work there were often important differences in emphasis between the women and the men. On the one hand, children appeared salient for only one-fifth of the men, but for one-third of the women: and for two, the keystone of life, 'all I had'. On the other hand, with regard to work, while some women were certainly ambitious, even these tended to speak of their achievements dismissively, while men were much more likely to describe work as 'great'. And at the extreme one-third of the men, including four who never married, but only one woman, focused on work to the exclusion of relationships.

Apart from the mothers of pre-school children, only one of our fifty informants was not in work, a strikingly low level of unemployment which in itself contrasts with the gloomy reports which have come from some other studies.[40] Similarly, very few had been frequent job-changers: typically they had been working in up to three jobs over a period of fifteen years. Their achievement was, moreover, remarkably impressive, for even at this stage in their lives more than twice as many were working at a level above their parents than below it.[41] It is important to notice, since this would be much less easy today, that those who rose rarely achieved this through a formal educational path.[42] Most had left school at the earliest opportunity, and not one went on to complete a university degree. A minority did indeed return to further education in their twenties, but somewhat fewer than was normal for their generation.[43] In other words, they worked their way up essentially on the spot, through the energy and adaptability which they threw into the job they had found. This makes what they made of the situation all the more impressive. Ten of these risers were men from working-class family backgrounds, who seemed to have put success and fulfilment through work ahead of relationships.

It seems important at this point to recall that the contemporary aim at a balanced life including fulfilment in both work and family, equally for men and for women, which we share ourselves, is a goal very particular to our own period. It was not prevalent when our informants were growing up, nor had it been normal at any point in British society for at least the last four hundred years. For centuries, indeed, women in Britain have made an essential social contribution above all through their roles in the family. In the same way some of the most important male contributions to society have been made by men fixated on work to the exclusion of intimate relationships, often themselves stepchildren, such as— to take the extreme instances, in which obsession became genius—Leonardo da Vinci or Isaac Newton.[44] We need to accept the multiplicity of viable paths both to personal fulfilment and to social usefulness.

In terms of relationships our own informants had on the whole followed patterns typical of their generation. They were as likely to have married and more likely to be on their own. None said that they were in same-sex relationships. A group of women had followed a pattern of serial cohabitation, but their numbers were very few.[45]

More strikingly, three-quarters of those who had married were still married, for up to seventeen years, almost as many as for their generation as a whole, and many appeared to be very close to their partners.[46] It was indeed quite clear that a strong and successful marriage, by providing a new intimate relationship in adulthood, could enable a young adult to put the difficulties of childhood behind them and give them strength even to survive an adversity as harrowing as the death of their own child.

This puts into a different perspective the tendency towards marriage at a slightly earlier age which earlier researchers had found among stepchildren in the NCDS cohort, and which aroused considerable anxiety because of the general tendency for early marriages to more often result in divorce. Indeed, beyond this it would seem that for our informants in difficult home situations early marriages could be used as a context in which to grow and develop more self-confidence about relationships. When such marriages ended in divorce, a much sharper distinction needs to be made than is at present between those marriages which had resulted in children and those which did not. Socially the latter can be understood as in many ways closer to first cohabitations by somewhat older couples; and indeed today even young couples would be more likely to test out their relationships by cohabiting rather than marrying.

When we try to understand the underlying differences between those who stayed married and those who did not, neither marriage nor starting relationships at a young age emerge independently as notably important.[47] There were three other predisposing factors which did seem to be very influential. The first, for both girls and boys, was the manner of leaving home. While those still in intact marriages had normally left home, either to train or to work, with their parents' approval, those who had divorced had usually left home in anger, or been thrown out of it.[48] Closely linked to this, because it was basic to whether or not the stepfamily home was conflictual, was the quality of the parent's new marriage, and equally, the child's own relationship with the stepparent.[49]

The third predisposing influence towards divorce was the familial inheritance which had been transmitted to the young newly-married from earlier generations, typically through childhood experiences. Children whose parents had divorced were twice as likely to separate themselves as those who had lost a parent through death. And interestingly, the pattern of marital break-ups could often be traced back to the grandparental generation.[50]

Of course the importance of this should not be exaggerated, because the intergenerational 'transmission' of divorce was a minority pattern, so that it cannot explain the wider social growth of divorce as a general practice.

Finally, four-fifths of our stepchildren had themselves become parents: a significantly higher proportion than their generation as a whole, which in itself may be taken as a symbol of their wish to create new and better lives for themselves as adults.[51] And as parents it is striking how so many of them used the understanding of the vulnerabilities of children which had come from their own childhood difficulties, determining to stay together as parents, and bringing up their children with a gentler discipline and more communication than they had known themselves. This could be problematic for those who lacked a childhood model of physical or emotional intimacy. It was noticeable too how often men learnt to be parents from their wives, or from the grandparental generation. This could bring new bonds, including with step-grand-parents.

Nine of our fifty stepchildren—markedly more than the national average—had themselves already become stepparents,[52] and although only one was living with his stepchildren in a stepfamily household, this in itself had brought many of them to reflect on their own memories of childhood. For some, passing through similar experiences, from the perspective now of an adult rather than a child, especially helped them to review how they felt about their own stepparents and to evaluate them more benignly. So the wheel had turned full circle.

To sum up: what do these memories suggest is most important in helping the child of a stepfamily to surmount the challenges that this can pose both in childhood and in adulthood?

1. The quality of the parental marriage: the absence of acrimony, quarrelling, or violence between the child's parent and partner.

2. The quality of the child's relationship with the remaining caretaking parent: a close, intimate relationship between the child and the parent, including open talking, and also that parent's own positive emotional well-being, whether single or married. Con-

versely, an absence of any physical violence between parent and child.

3. The handling of change by parents with sensitivity towards the child's feelings, gradualness, and clear and repeated explanations.

4. Support, both practical and emotional, from grandparents and the extended family.

5. The child's compatibility with the stepparent.

6. The child's good relationships with siblings, half-siblings, or stepsiblings.

7. Continuity and security in housing, school, and local friendships.

8. After leaving school and home, continuing positive contact with the family.

9. And finally in adulthood: finding fulfilment in work or in strong close emotional relationships.

Such is our own distillation of these fifty life stories. Like all memories, they can be read in many different ways: for information, for interpretations, for myths. One of the strongest messages which came across to us in these stories was the power of these earlier memories in shaping people's lives and self-understanding. They conveyed to us equally vividly how the past can hang as a dark shadow over a life or provide recurrent strength, and how crucial reflection can be in turning the experiences of the past into an enabling force for the future. It is in this spirit that we have tried to understand them ourselves, in the hope that our interpretations may help their successors, the stepchildren of today and of the future.

NOTES

Preface

1. Haskey (1994); Hansard, Written Parliamentary Answer (9601), 17 Jan. 1996; *The Family Law Bill* (London: Family Policy Studies Centre, 1996).
2. Wallerstein and Kelly (1980).
3. Furstenberg and Spanier (1984); Hetherington et al. (1978, etc.); Ochiltree (1990).
4. Burgoyne and Clark (1984).
5. Cockett and Tripp (1994).

Chapter 1

1. De'Ath (1992); Haskey (1994).
2. For an exhaustive review, see Robinson and Smith (1993).
3. De'Ath (1992).
4. Ibid.
5. Walker (1992).
6. Santrock and Warshak (1979). Cowen, Pedro-Campbell, and Gillis (1990) also found that the degree of social support from adults outside the family was related to children's adjustment.
7. Wallerstein and Kelly (1980); Furstenberg and Spanier (1984). Johnson (1988a): three-quarters were in weekly contact, and 89 per cent helped with babysitting, 75 per cent with economic help, and 22 per cent with regular income maintenance. Slightly different calculations are given in Johnson's book (1988b).
8. Wallerstein and Kelly (1980); Guidobaldi and Cleminshaw (1985); and Kiernan (1992).
9. An outstanding relatively early instance is Visher and Visher (1978).
10. Ferri (1984); Emery and Forehand (1994).
11. Wallerstein and Kelly (1980); Wallerstein, Corbin, and Lewis (1988); Wallerstein and Blakeslee (1989); Wallerstein (1991).
12. Most of the findings of the Exeter study are in line with those of other research, but any concerning stepfamilies which are out of line

could be results of the form of sampling used. The study is based on children aged 9–14 attending local schools. Families were identified through a screening questionnaire sent out by schools, which had a rather low response rate (62%). More seriously, the fact that the questionnaires were sent by the schools must have exaggerated the normal reluctance of families which felt themselves less 'respectable' to participate, and indeed the proportion responding appears to have somewhat over-represented intact families—and in the case of those sending their child to private education, markedly so. On this basis a final sample was selected, with a further fall-out of 5% refusals, resulting in interviews with 76 intact families and 76 with various types of reordered families, including 33 from stepfamilies (30 with stepfathers and 3 with stepmothers). In nearly all the families both resident parents and children were interviewed, and also 27 of the 76 absent parents.

Unfortunately, given the small numbers involved, particularly for stepfamilies, the information from the project has so far been largely presented in an inappropriate statistical manner, only occasionally illustrated by brief quotations from the children. The project has thus not met its declared 'major intention', which was 'to listen carefully "to the voice of the child"' (Cockett and Tripp 1994: 6, 77).

13. Wadsworth (1979: 39)—there were altogether 2,196 boys, of whom 280 experienced broken homes, and 82 remarriage; the girls were not analysed for this study of delinquency, but certainly would have shown much lower rates; Wadsworth et al. (1990); Wadsworth (1991); Maclean and Kuh (1991).

14. Ferri (1984).

15. Kiernan (1992).

16. The study was based on a sample of 1,000 young people who are part of the West of Scotland Twenty-07 Study, which consists of three age cohorts. The work forms part of the Transitions to Adulthood project with Martin Richards and Virginia Morrow (University of Cambridge) and Kathleen Kiernan (London School of Economics): Social Policy Research 95: Findings, Joseph Rowntree Foundation.

17. The fuller picture of the cohort at this point is summarized in Ferri (1993).

18. 'Research on children's functioning after a parental divorce identifies many factors associated with risk but little research related to resilience': Emery and Forehand (1994).

19. Emery and Forehand (1994).

20. Furstenberg (1988); Furstenberg et al. (1983); and Furstenberg and Nord (1985).
21. Kruk (1992); Hart (1993); c.f. Walker (1992).
22. Hetherington (1988, and 1989*a* and *b*); Hetherington, Cox, and Cox (1978, 1985); Hetherington and Anderson (1987); Hetherington and Furstenberg (1989).
23. Isaacs, Leon, and Donahue (1987).
24. Lund (1984).
25. Emery and Forehand (1994); Maccoby and Mnookin (1992).
26. Emery (1982); Emery and Forehand (1994); Grych and Fincham (1990).
27. Emery (1988).
28. Walker (1992).
29. Maclean and Kuh (1991); Wadsworth (1991); Everett (1991).
30. Ochiltree (1990).
31. Wadsby (1993).
32. Ochiltree (1990).
33. Mitchell (1985).
34. Walczack and Burns (1984).
35. Wallerstein and Blakeslee (1989).
36. Elliott et al. (1990).
37. Ochiltree (1990).
38. Amato and Ochiltree (1987).
39. Ochiltree (1990).
40. Rutter (1971); Rutter and Quinton (1984).
41. Elliott and Richards (1992).
42. Jenkins, Smith, and Graham (1988).
43. Clingempeel et al. (1984, 1986, and 1988); J. Anderson and White (1986); Hetherington, Cox, and Cox (1985).
44. Bray (1988).
45. Brand and Clingempeel (1987); Hetherington (1988 and 1989*a* and *b*).
46. Furstenburg (1987).
47. Walker (1993); Simpson, McCarthy, and Walker (1995).
48. Ochiltree (1990).
49. Clingempeel and Segal (1986), and Santrock and Sitterle (1987), have shown how the quality of the stepmother–stepchild relationship is related to the frequency of visits from the non-resident biological mother. In our samples there were no such instances.
50. Amato (1986), Amato and Ochiltree (1987), and Hetherington

(1989*a* and *b*) have all looked at the way that self-esteem is connected to the quality of the child's relationship to incoming stepfathers and have suggested that boys do better than girls. However, this may vary depending on what is being assessed. Whereas boys who tend to have a worse time in the post-divorce single-parent phase when they are living with their mothers but then settle down and benefit from stepfathers, girls continue to give them a hard time over a longer period.

51. Early studies of stepfamilies, Yahraes and Bohannon (1979) and Burgoyne and Clark (1984), showed that stepfathers did not rate themselves as highly as biological fathers. Mothers rated them more highly than either they did themselves, or than stepchildren did. Stepfathers were reported to use a more autocratic style of parenting based on enforcing rules and traditional values. This was not the predominant reporting of the respondents in our study, although it did tend to characterize fathering that was not going well.

52. In Ochiltree's study (1990) only 25 per cent of children in stepfather families saw their stepfather's as the 'boss' in the household, unlike intact biological families where two-thirds of children thought their father was the boss. More children in stepfather families thought that both parents were the boss than they did in intact families. Children generally described their biological parent as a more effective agent and powerful figure in their own lives.

53. Hetherington (1988).

54. Kolvin et al. (1988).

Chapter 2

1. Whitehead (1993).

2. Dominian et al. (1991); Ni Brochlain (1992)

3. Giddens (1991: 12–13) commenting on the effects of highly publicized research such as Wallerstein and Blakeslee's study on children of divorce, *Second Chances* (1989).

4. Giddens (1991: 9).

5. Main and Goldwyn (1994).

6. An earlier connection was provided by the American school of family sociology led by Reuben Hill (1971), which developed a

family systems approach to research with cross-influences on American social work (Cheal 1991).

7. Thompson (1988); Plummer (1983).

8. Tonkin (1992).

9. Mishler (1986).

10. Bertaux and Thompson (1993); Bertaux and Thompson (1997); Chamberlain (1994).

11. Examples in the family therapy literature of descriptions of families which could be called reductionist are to be found in Walsh (1982), or in the research project on families carried out by Lewis et al. (1976).

12. Examples of such critiques can be found in Goldner (1985, 1988) and Walter et al. (1988).

13. Family myths and their regulatory functions have been written about by Ferreira (1968) and Byng-Hall (1979, 1988, and 1995). Ideas about family belief systems form an integral part of many approaches but have rarely been written about separately. Myths are also an important concern of life story sociologists and oral historians (Samuel and Thompson 1990).

14. Key texts on family systems approaches include: Gurman and Kniskern (1991); Burnham (1986); and E. Jones (1993).

15. Two key texts which develop a family life cycle approach are Carter and McGoldrick (1988) and Falicov (1988).

16. For example, Robinson (1991) and Robinson and Smith (1993).

17. Keith and Whitaker (1988: 447).

18. Research studies which highlight these qualities as fundamental to family functioning include: Lewis et al. (1976) and Olson et al. (1989).

19. As well as the research already mentioned, some of the work on expressed emotion in the families of schizophrenics carried out by Julian Leff and his colleagues would fit this description (Leff and Vaughn 1985).

20. Key influences in constructivism have been the biologists Humberto Maturana and Francisco Varela (1980, 1987), and in social constuctionism, the social psychologist Kenneth Gergen (1991). See also paper by Lynn Hoffman (1990).

21. Narrative approaches to systemic family therapy can be found in the work of Harlene Anderson and Harry Goolishian (1988) and of Michael White and David Epston(1989).

22. Bruner (1986: 143).

23. Backett (1982); Mansfield and Collard (1988).
24. This literature includes work by Kenneth Gergen, John Shotter, and Anthony Giddens.
25. Bruner (1986: 143).
26. See e.g. Campbell and De Carteret (1984) and Asen et al. (1991).
27. Such as Reiss (1981).
28. Shotter (1986).
29. Giddens (1991: 6).
30. Ainsworth et al. (1978).
31. Main and Cassidy (1985: 90–1).
32. Main, Kaplan, and Cassidy (1985).
33. The interviews are tape-recorded, transcribed, and coded with specific rating scales and overall classifications. Scoring relies on the organization of content even more than on the content of the experiences described.
34. Adult attachment classifications have been shown to be indicative of adaptive parenting. Concordance rates between adult classifications by the adult attachment interview and classifications of infants through the strange situation test, administered concurrently, are relatively high, around 65 to 75 per cent. Thus, at the one extreme, parents classified as 'autonomous' are likely to have infants classified as 'secure', whereas at the other, parents classified as 'unresolved' are likely to have infants classified as 'disorganised' (Zealah and Emde 1994).
35. Rutter and Quinton (1984).
36. For example, Ferri (1984); Kiernan (1992), etc.
37. Of our fifty cases, eleven seemed to have been misclassified by the original NCDS interviews. At age 7, nine children were already living with stepparents, but this was not revealed to the interviewers (until age 11 or 16); six of these had been stepchildren for several years. Two other children were misclassified for other reasons. One had a stepfather at 16, but did not live in his household; he lived with his grandmother. Another had been illegitimately conceived when her mother was married to another man; she was now living with her true father, but he was presented as her stepfather.
38. Vaughan (1987).
39. Hareven (1982).
40. Stone (1990); M. Anderson (1983).
41. Burgoyne and Clark (1984).

42. Litwak (1959); Thompson, Itzin, and Abendstern (1990).
43. Burgoyne and Clark (1984) describe graphically the difficulties in obtaining a sample.
44. Originally we had hoped to interview equal numbers of men and women, and of those living in stepfather and (the rarer group) in stepmother families. This did not prove fully possible, but by prioritizing men and those in stepmother families in each region we successfully reduced the imbalances.

Altogether 29 of the informants were women and 21 were men. 32 lived in stepfather families, and 18 in stepmother families (including three who at other times lived with a stepfather).

Ten had entered stepfamilies up to the age of 6, including one anomalously in a pseudo-stepfamily (see above, n. 37); 21 between the ages of 7 and 11; and 19 subsequently (including one who did not actually live with his stepfather).

21 had lost a parent through death, and 29 through divorce. This proportion (death 42%) compares with 34% in the main cohort.

Age of entry	Stepmother family		Stepfather family		Total
	Women	Men	Women	Men	
0–6	1	—	7	2	10
7–11	5	2	9	5	21
12–16	2	8	5	4	19
Totals	8	10	21	11	50

Interviews were carried out in London, the home counties, and East Anglia; the south-west and South Wales; the Midlands; Lancashire, Cheshire, Yorkshire, and Durham; and central Scotland.

A subsequent analysis by NCDS showed that those who were interviewed by us before their most recent wave were more likely than others to agree to be re-interviewed for the main study, presumably because they found the experience of a life story interview rewarding. This is a very encouraging finding for researchers seeking to attach qualitative in-depth research to panel or longitudinal studies.

45. One indication of this probability is the slight over-representation of stepfamilies following a parental death rather than a divorce (42% as against 34% of stepfamilies in the main cohort). On the other hand, we did not find that there was much difference overall in outcomes

between the two groups (Ch. 10). Moreover, since one of the key difficulties in making contact with men was that they were away for their work, so that interviewing more of such men would not have resulted in less optimistic information on occupations: men or women who were not working were more likely to feel themselves available for interview. It should also be noted that by deliberately raising the proportion of those brought up in stepmother families, we also increased the numbers of informants who had got on badly with their stepparent.

46. Bertaux and Thompson (1993); Bertaux and Thompson (1997).

Chapter 3

1. Most notably the studies by J. and E. Newson in Nottingham (1963, 1968, 1976), which cover the period in which our informants were children. It is commonly assumed that child discipline was more severe in the past because parents are much less likely to report harsh discipline than children. Contemporary information from the Exeter study suggests that smacking (18%) and shouting (50%) are almost equally common in intact and other families. In contrast, physical violence between partners is reported in only 3% of intact but 26% of reordered families (Cockett and Tripp 1994: 30–1).

2. Richards and Dyson (1982); Lund and Riley (1984).

3. Mitchell (1985) reported, from an Edinburgh study carried out five years after parental legal separation, that only half the children could remember being given any explanation by their parents. Still fewer of the parents claimed to have explained the change to their children. Similarly, McCredie and Horrox (1985: 6), in a non-sample television study of London children after divorce, commented that 'one theme stood out above all others in the interviews: the lack of communication between parent and child. At best, the children were told only misleading half-truths.'

4. Many clinicians have noted unresolved mourning due to the speed of change as a special problem in entering a stepfamily: e.g. Robinson (1991: 152–3). We were therefore surprised that in our own sample swift transitions do not appear in general to have affected long-term outcomes for the worse: those who entered stepfamilies two or less years after losing a parent were not subsequently more vulnerable to

severe psychological difficulties, nor did their patterns of marriage or work mobility differ from those of the others.

5. For striking American parallels, see Simon (1964: 144).

6. American studies have particularly emphasized the negative consequences of marital break-up on the custodial parent. Wallerstein and Kelly (1980: 36, 47, 103) highlighted examples from their clinic study of children supporting depressed or suicidal parents, worrying about them, and providing them with advice and company as 'parents for their own parents'. Weiss (1979) also remarked on children who were parenting their parents in the single-parent phase. Hetherington (1989a and b) reported from her sample survey that it was typical of post-divorce parents to become 'more anxious, depressed, angry, rejected, and incompetent'. Parents 'communicated less well, tended to be less affectionate, and showed marked inconsistency in discipline' (pp. 157, 163). This was, however, normally a brief phase of less than two years.

7. American studies have typically noted changes in parental discipline as a further problem, rather than an adaptation which might have brought benefits to a child needing comfort, and sometimes reflected a need to combine roles previously split between mother and father. Thus Hetherington, Cox, and Cox (1978: 164) comments disapprovingly that 'the divorced mother tried to control her child by being more restrictive and giving more commands which the child ignored . . . The divorced father wanted his contacts with the child to be as happy as possible.' Wallerstein and Kelly (1980: 111–12) claim from their clinic study that over half of the mothers found it hard to take over discipline, and in general, 'fearing rejection, women tried to please and placate'.

8. Ochiltree (1990) found in Australia in a cross-age sample that while the children who entered stepfamilies at the youngest age were initially more vulnerable (in this case, most knowing that they were stepchildren), in the long run they could form the closest relationships with stepparents. Burgoyne and Clark (1984: 151) also suggested that their Sheffield stepparents felt closest to the stepchildren whom they had known longest.

9. Of 10 early entry families, 2 had stepsiblings and 9 had half-siblings; of 21 middle entry, 10 had stepsiblings and 12 half-siblings; of 19 late entry, 14 had stepsiblings and 9 half-siblings.

10. Burgoyne and Clark (1984: 152) in their Sheffield study noted how 'remarried parents of older children tended to think more carefully

about the everyday conduct and decisions involving the children, pursuing a course of what we have called "conscious parenthood"'.

Similarly in American research, Chase-Lansdale and Hetherington (1990) reported adolescents as better able to understand divorce and quicker to adapt to it, while Kurdek and Siesky (1980), in a study of 132 white US children, note how the older children were more often given a two-sided explanation of their parent's divorce, and to accept it.

11. Burgoyne and Clark (1984: 82) noted similar distaste by children living with sexually expressive remarried couples in their Sheffield families.

12. Chase-Lansdale and Hetherington (1990) reported that in their American sample pre-adolescent girls were especially likely to resent a man with a 'companionable' relationship with their mother.

13. It may be that on this point there is an important difference between social expectations in Britain and the USA. For example, Wallerstein and Kelly (1980: 287–8) wrote of the men in their clinic sample that 'with a few exceptions, they expected to assume the role of parent to their wives' children. Encouraged by their women, most men took this responsibility seriously and moved quickly into the role of the man of the household with the prerequisite prerogatives, and authority traditionally accorded this position. . . . Only a few men appeared sensitive to the need to cultivate a relationship with the child gradually.' Other American clinical and research studies typically assume that stepfathers should aim to assume full parental authority including a disciplinary role, but should do so gradually over a period of up to two years (e.g. Stern 1978; Visher and Visher 1978; and Hetherington, Cox, and Cox 1985: 528)—'the most successful stepfathers are those who establish a positive relationship with the child before taking an active role in discipline and decision-making.'

Our findings also differ from those of Burgoyne and Clark (1984) in whose Sheffield families the stepfather was assumed to be taking on a full paternal role, including the exercise of authority. This is most likely to reflect local child-rearing patterns which are typically harsher in the oldest British industrial towns (Thompson 1993a: 56–63).

14. As Burgoyne and Clark (184: 146–7) observed of their Sheffield families, the role of a stepmother is more difficult because the

role of a mother is more clearly defined than that of a father, 'at once more specific and more encompassing'.

15. The tendency of stepchildren to focus hostility on a stepmother and the prevalence of the wicked stepmother myth have frequently been noted in earlier American and British literature (e.g. Visher and Visher 1978; Santrock and Sitterle 1987; Ferri 1984), although Ochiltree (1990: 12) remarks that few Australian children were aware of the wicked stepmother myth. The myth is well set out by D. Brown (1982).

   Robinson (1980) sees the myth as allowing the child to split naturally ambivalent feelings towards the parent by polarizing an idealized lost parent against a wicked incoming stepmother. Hughes (1991) examined the impact of the myth through participant observation of five British stepfamilies in which both parents were stepparents. None of the fathers felt 'wicked', but all the mothers were aware of this as a danger for themselves. She suggests that the myth is a way of legitimizing feelings of dislike, but is most potent with non-custodial stepmothers where it is less challenged by 'direct contact'. The subtle interaction between myth and personal experience is explored for an earlier generation by Burchardt (1990).

Chapter 4

1. The term 'illegitimate' was made redundant by the Family Law Reform Act 1987 and has gradually dropped out of common usage. In the 1960s and 1970s when these children were growing up, 'illegitimacy' still carried a significant social stigma. For further consideration of the effects of illegitimacy in the 1958 cohort, see Ferri (1976) and Crellin, Kelmer-Pringle, and West (1971).

2. 'Attachment' is a concept first developed by Bowlby (1980): see above, Ch. 2. For further discussion see e.g. Holmes (1993) and Rutter (1995).

3. Waldvogel (1982); Spencer and Flin (1990). Waldvogel is reprinted from 'The frequency and affective character of childhood memories', *Psychological Monographs*, 62, no. 291: a classical questionnaire study of early childhood recollections.

4. D. Jones (1987).

5. A decade or so earlier, such attitudes are described in Gorer (1965).

6. Parkes (1986); Abrams (1995).

7. Burchardt (1989).

8. See e.g. Brown, Harris, and Bifulco (1986); and Saler and Skolovick (1992).

9. Eekelaar et al. (1977). Most subsequent studies have found that between one-third and one-half of non-residential fathers lose all contact within five years, although the proportion of fathers currently remaining in contact with their children has now almost certainly increased. Bradshaw and Millar (1991) found that just over half their non-residential parents maintained contact; Bob Simpson, McCarthy, and Walker (1995) found a similar proportion in their study of non-residential parents.

10. Quoted in Mnookin (1979: 50).

11. McFarlane, Bellissimo, and Norman (1995: 859). Among our own fifty stepchildren, those who had lost a parent through death were more likely to make successful marriages in adulthood. On the other hand, they did worse in terms of occupation, and slightly worse in terms of psyche as measured by the health questionnaires.

Chapter 5

1. Davidoff (1995); Dunn and Kenrick (1982).

2. Pasley and Ihinger-Tallman (1987) include a chapter entitled 'Sibling and step-sibling bonding in stepfamilies', but this contains very little information; nor does the statistical analysis of Zill (1988). L. White (1994) on 'family solidarity' concludes that sibling relationships are strengthened rather than weakened by entering stepfamilies. Wallerstein and Kelly (1980: 45) confine themselves to the clinical observation that 'although children did not acknowledge the help of siblings, they huddled together with them and conferred frequently'.

It is symptomatic of the general neglect of the issue that NCDS information gained during the childhood of our informants failed to distinguish full siblings from half and stepsiblings (Ferri 1984: 30).

The Exeter study simply notes that there were only 'one or two cases' of 'serious' sibling rivalry in reconstructed families: somewhat fewer instances than might have been expected (Cockett and Tripp 1994: 29).

3. This is a higher proportion than one would expect from survey information based on one year only, and indicates that longitudinal information provides a fuller picture. Of the 202 stepfamilies in the

General Household Survey sample, 52% have at least one co-resident joint child and 8% a stepchild, but 40% none at all.

4. Bumpass (1984) estimated that of American children who enter step-families under the age of 5, half gain a half-sibling, the proportion declining to only 16% of those who enter stepfamilies aged 10–13. This is because younger children are more likely to have younger parents and fewer full siblings. Conversely, older children are more likely to have older parents and stepparents, so that the remarriage is less likely to produce new children but more likely to bring with it stepchildren.

5. Mitchell (1985: 168) noted that in her Edinburgh families resident half-siblings were regarded as full siblings, and 'none showed any jealousy. The younger ones were very much loved.' Burgoyne and Clark (1984: 160) found that their Sheffield remarried parents hoped that a joint child would make them an ordinary family again: 'they cement a marriage.'

   One American statistical study of 88 families also found that the presence of half-siblings had a strikingly positive effect, both on relationships between stepchildren and stepparents (78% good in contrast to 53% good without half-siblings) and also on relationships between stepsiblings (44% good with, 19% good without) (Duberman 1973).

6. Mitchell (1985: 168) similarly found that stepsiblings who lived away were not known, and not regarded as siblings—'definitely not in my family'.

   The tendency of stepfathers' earlier children to be non-resident remains typical of stepfamilies. In the General Household Survey 86% of stepchildren resident in stepfamily households are the wife's children.

7. She has a full brother and sister to whom she is not close, and a half-sister to whom she is.

8. In Britain, research on grandparents and stepfamilies has only just begun. Mitchell (1985: 71) again notes shrewdly from her Edinburgh families that for the children of separating parents the grandparents, and especially the grandmothers, were 'often the best-known, best-loved, and most available adults apart from the parents'. The Exeter study collected information on contact with and caring by both maternal and paternal grandparents, but this is disappointingly used. Six different patterns after divorce are described, but it is not clear which are more prevalent; allowance is not made for the different kinds of transitions involved, or for differences between grandfathers and grandmothers; and the only clear conclusion is

that, not surprisingly, contact with the absent father's parents typically diminished. The most interesting suggestion is that step-grandparents were likely to be a positive gain (Cockett and Tripp 1994: 32–3).

The American evidence is conflicting, probably because of regional contrasts between areas where kin networks are more or less rooted. In their rural Pennsylvanian sample study Furstenberg and Spanier (1984: 128, 148–9, 157) found that after parental separation, 90% of children saw their grandparents on the side of the custodial parent regularly, nearly half weekly. Grandparents could act as 'emotional intermediaries between children and their separated parents' and they would 'often represent the interests of the absent parent'. Furstenberg comments that 'in coping with transitions, children are frequently sustained by relations outside the nuclear family. Grandparents, in particular, are often figures of stability' (Pasley and Ihinger-Tallman 1987: 58). Even higher levels of support were reported by Johnson's (1988a and b) much smaller study of white middle-class families in the San Francisco Bay area (Ch. 1 above, n. 7).

This makes it particularly surprising that among their Californian clinic families, by contrast, Wallerstein and Kelly (1980: 43–4, 222) found that 90% received no help from either kin or their local community. For many, no kin were available, but only one-quarter of those who did have kin received help from them. In the few cases where grandparents were nearby and regular visitors, the children 'appeared to benefit considerably'. Other children 'told us about loving, devoted grandparents who kept them in mind, and provided summer vacations for them, telephone calls at frequent intervals, and an ongoing relationship'.

9. Thompson, Itzin, and Abendstern (1990).
10. Burgoyne and Clark (1984).
11. This was the finding of Burgoyne and Clark (1984).
12. In three-quarters of those 15 households where relatives co-resided, this followed the death or departure of a parent.
13. Thompson, Itzin, and Abendstern (1990: 175).
14. Cf. Furstenberg (1987).
15. Half of the Exeter schoolchildren in stepfamilies reported receiving 'good support' from their new step-grandparents (Cockett and Tripp (1994: 32).
16. Ochiltree (1990) found that Australian children in stepfamilies moved on average three times during childhood, as opposed to twice for those in intact families.

17. Wallerstein and Kelly (1980: 165) remark on the tendency of girls to confide in friends. However, the role of friendships with other children has been ignored in most stepfamily studies. Because of the rapidly shifting patterns of girls' friendships, it is possible that they seemed more important at the time than they remain in memory.

18. Earlier NCDS data give teachers' ratings of children's social adjustment at school. At 11, children living in stepfamilies were reported as being worse adjusted, but at 16 there was no difference from those in intact families (Lambert and Streather 1980; Ferri 1984).

    Ochiltree (1990) found that among Australian children, 16% of those in intact families and 33% living in stepfamilies disliked school. The Exeter study (which was conducted through the assistance of the local schools, and therefore has an in-built positive bias towards education), found that the feelings of children from reordered families towards teachers were more positive, and only 15% found school 'difficult'. On the other hand, the number of families mentioning truanting had risen to 26% (compared with 14% of our own informants) (Cockett and Tripp 1994: 24–5). However, this needs to be seen in the context of the much more general steep rise in truanting over the last decade.

19. The NCDS study at 16 showed that this was particularly true of boys (Ferri 1984: 106). This was to show up later in the higher proportion of middle-class boys from stepfamilies than intact families who left school before 18.

20. Here the contrast with the present is striking. The Exeter study reported that 'nearly six out of ten children from re-ordered families said that their teachers knew about their changed family circumstances and nearly a third had talked about it to their class teacher' (Cockett and Tripp 1994: 23).

Chapter 6

1. Bernard (1973).
2. Burck and Daniel (1995b).
3. Chodorow (1978).
4. Daniel and Thompson (1996).
5. These discrepancies have been noted by Backett (1982) in her study

of mothers and fathers negotiating parental behaviour and Brannen and Moss (1991) in their study of dual-earner households.

6. The dilemmas for family relationships when creating a stepfamily household involves the new partner being drawn into a gender-stereotyped replacement role are described in Walters et al. (1988).

7. For a lively commentary on this topic, see Smith (1990); also Burch-ardt (1990).

8. Frosh (1995) provides one theoretical exploration of the problematics of masculinity.

9. Such attitudes link with an interesting commentary by Serra et al. (1993) where they put forward the idea that men are given moral stature for choosing to be non-violent whereas women are not seen to be exercising a moral choice because they are physically less likely to be able to intimidate men.

10. Jordan et al. (1991) provide an analysis of women's psychological development which points to the importance of reaching maturity through connectedness rather than through differentiation and autonomy. While this approach can have the disadvantage of reinforcing stereotypes about women's emotional development, it provides an important antidote to psychological work (e.g. that of Erikson 1959, 1965) which take male development as the norm.

11. For example, Ross and Holmberg (1992) looked at the differences between husbands' and wives' memories of events in their mutual pasts and found that the women's memories tended to be more vivid and affect-laden than men's; see also Daniel and Thompson (1996).

12. Burck and Frosh (1993).

13. For further elaboration on the social construction of gender roles, see Burck and Daniel (1995a).

Chapter 7

1. The health questionnaires consisted of 24 questions, such as, 'Are you scared to be alone when there are no friends?' The great majority of informants, 28 out of 45 who returned the questionnaires, gave no more than six 'yes' answers. We classified informants who gave seven or more 'yes' answers as having psychological problems, and compared the test outcomes with our own subjective evaluations from the interview transcripts, which in most cases concurred. There were however a few men who did appear from

the transcript to have serious psychological problems, and were also deniers of their feelings past and present, who had returned the questionnaire with a complete set of 'no' answers; these we classified with the 'problems' group. Altogether we thus classified 13 as having problems, of whom eight had completed more than six 'yes' answers.

This group with psychological problems included an over-representation of women, of those from a working-class back-ground, or of stepchildren by parental death.

2. Kiernan (1992).

3. Of our 43 ever-married informants 31 were still married: that is 72%, little different from the 75% in the whole NCDS sample still in first marriages. Both figures refer to marriages contracted at any age (Ferri 1993: 18).

4. Wallerstein (1985: 548).

5. Wadsworth et al. (1990) found downward mobility among children whose parents had divorced or separated, but not of those who had died, which they explained in terms of the disruption of education. However Elliott and Richards (1992) found effects in the NCDS cohort only among stepchildren from middle-class families, among whom the boys tended to leave school early, and the girls under-performed occupationally.

6. 24 were in occupations classified above the level of their parents, 16 on the same level, and only 10 below.

7. This is one fewer than would have been predicted, for in the NCDS cohort as a whole at 33, 4% were unemployed and currently seeking work; three times as many of these unemployed were men as women (Ferri 1993: 84).

8. This gendered contrast in concerns with family and work appears to reflect those of the main sample (Ferri and Smith 1996).

9. Of the whole NCDS cohort, 70% went on to some kind of post-school education up to the age of 23, and 34% aged 23 to 33, and 4% were awarded degrees at a university (Ferri 1993: 38–41). Our informants thus continued to have markedly lower educational levels than their age group as a whole.

10. In the whole NCDS cohort, 17% never married (although under 10% had never lived with a partner), and of those who did marry, 75% were still in their first marriage (Ferri 1993: 17–18); of our informants, 14%, and 72% respectively.

11. Wallerstein and Blakeslee (1989).

12. There were children from six of the fourteen early marriages which did break up.

13. In the whole NCDS cohort, of those who had divorced 35% were now remarried, 25% cohabiting, and 40% were living without a partner (Ferri 1993: 18).

14. Of our informants, 18% were childless (10% of the women, 31% of the men); in the NCDS cohort as a whole, 33% were childless (Ferri 1993: 19).

15. In addition one man's wife had a child by another man, leading to their break-up. This could be seen as a stepchild relationship but we have excluded it. In the NCDS cohort as a whole 12% (19% of the women, 6% of the men) were stepparents and 3% living in step-family households—compared with 18% and 2% respectively of our informants (Ferri 1993: 24).

Chapter 8

1. Main (1992).

2. Fonagy et al. (1991); Fonagy (1993).

3. Rutter and Quinton (1984); Rutter (1987).

4. Tizard and Phoenix (1993). See Bentovim (1995) for an account of the effects of trauma.

5. Burgoyne and Clark (1984: 194).

6. Furstenberg (1987: 50).

7. The idea that sterner criteria for family membership are applied by the children of separated parents than those living in two-parent families is suggested by O'Brien, Alldred, and Jones in their study of children's constructions of family and kinship. They found that children in nuclear families were more likely to argue for family membership on the basis of consanguinity, whereas 'children who had experienced some form of parental separation in their lives argued that parents, particularly fathers, needed to show caring contact with children before they could be considered part of a family' O'Brien, Alldred, and Jones (1996: 92).

8. Roberts (1994).

Chapter 9

1. Bob Simpson and McCarthy (1991).
2. Judy Dunn is currently mounting a large-scale study of stepfamilies from which it is hoped that some answers to these questions of cumulative transition and what creates the conditions for successful adaptation will emerge.
3. Bateson (1989).
4. Rutter (1966).
5. Gorell Barnes and Dowling (forthcoming).
6. Garmezy and Masten (1994: 203).
7. Burck, Hildebrand, and Mann (1996) give an account of a systemic approach to groupwork with mothers, post-divorce.
8. Benard (1992).
9. Kraemer (1994).
10. Lamb, Pleck, and Levine (1987).
11. Gill Gorell Barnes and Mary Bratley, research in progress.
12. Batchelor, Dimmock, and Smith (1994).
13. Kiernan (1992).
14. G. Jones (1994: 3).
15. Bratley (1995); Simpson, McCarthy and Walker (1995).
16. Bratley (1995); Gorell Barnes and Dowling (forthcoming).
17. Bob Simpson, McCarthy, and Walker (1995).
18. Cockett and Tripp (1994).
19. See e.g. Eekelaar (1984) and Murch (1980).
20. Ganong and Coleman (1986); Adams, Milner, and Scepf (1984); Wallerstein and Kelly (1980).
21. McFarlane, Bellissimo, and Norman (1995).
22. Payne (1996); Bieker (1997: 187).
23. Eekelaar (1996).
24. Burgoyne and Clark (1984).
25. Bob Simpson, McCarthy, and Walker (1995).
26. Children's Society (1994).

Chapter 10

1. On the same issue, see Thompson, Itzin, and Abendstern (1990) and Thompson (1993b) on older people, and Thompson (1984) on childhood and work.

2. Thompson (1993*a*: ch.4).

3. The risks in assuming an unchanged context of course increase further as one goes back in time: one may instance the positive social approval which was once given to marriage between cousins, and the battle over whether men should be legally permitted to marry their deceased wife's sister, which created as much parliamentary excitement as the abortion issue in recent decades. On the other hand, we would want to emphasize that provided allowance is made for these differences in social context, there is much to be learnt from the past, and a need for more research on British stepfamilies especially from the 17th to the mid-19th centuries, for which ample unexploited resources are available.

4. Rutter (1985: 608).

5. This shows up particularly among the girls whose parents had divorced. Of the 10 still in intact marriages, 8 had talked closely with a parent; of the 6 who had married and themselves divorced, only 2.

   Clausen (1993) reports of the Berkeley cohorts that all the women but only half of the men said that they were influenced by their parents' marriage in shaping their own.

6. See esp. Ch. 2, pp. 35–7.

7. But see esp. Ch. 6.

8. Such as most notoriously historical demographers of the Cambridge school, who because of the limitations of their sources have tried to identify the family with the physical household.

9. Bohannan (1970); Papernow (1984).

10. This applies mainly to a small number of men who seemed clearly disturbed, but handed back questionnaires denying any symptoms at all.

11. The numbers in this table refer to the number of informants in each category. The informants are either divided as male or female; or as those who were children in stepfamilies formed after death or divorce; whose parents were in manual or non-manual occupations (working or middle class), or one parent in each (intermediate class); or from our whole sample. Three kinds of outcome are measured, each in terms of upward or downward movement or stability (+, −, or =).

   The first outcome is in terms of occupation, compared with those of both parents.

   The second, in terms of marriage, was more problematic to

measure because of the changing social meaning of marriage and cohabitation. We decided to rate as + all those in marriages of over five years' duration, with the exception of two in unstable marriages, of which one was childless (both of which we rated as =). We rated as − all those who had remained single without partners, those women who had had children outside marriage, all but two of those who had separated or divorced, and one recently married woman who had previously had a series of unsuccessful cohabitations. We rated as = three women who had happily remarried after unsuccessful first marriages, and also one recently married man.

The third outcome, in terms of psychological state, was based on self-evaluations through the health questionnaire, adjusted in the light of the interview evidence (for the method used, see Ch. 7 n.1).

	Job	Outcome Marriage	Psyche
males			
death	3+ 5= 1−	4+ 1= 4−	3−/9
divorce	8+ 1= 3−	6+ 6−	2−/12
ALL	11+ 6= 4−	10+ 7= 4−	5−/21
females			
death	5+ 4= 3−	8+ 4−	4−/12
divorce	8+ 6= 3−	7+ 2= 8−	4−/17
ALL	13+10= 6−	15+ 2= 12−	8−/29
all death	8+ 9= 4−	12+ 1= 8−	7−/21
all divorce	16+ 7= 6−	13+ 2= 14−	6−/29
all males	11+ 6= 4−	10+ 7= 4−	6−/21
all females	13+10= 6−	15+ 2= 12−	10−/29
working class		13+ 1= 12−	9/26
Intermediate		5+ 3−	1/8
middle class		7+ 2= 7−	3/16
TOTAL	24+26= 10−	25+ 3= 32−	11/50

12. Upwardly mobile men: of 11, marriage, 4+ 7−, and 3P−; Upwardly mobile women: of 14, marriage, 8+ 4−, and 3P−.

13. In his analysis of the Berkeley cohorts, which date back to 1928, Clausen (1993) found striking differences in the sources of success between men and women. Men depended partly on social background, partly on their own intelligence and ability; for women,

physical appearance (which can only be slightly manipulated) was as important as intelligence (which can be radically developed), and what counted most of all was their choice of spouse and the success or otherwise of their own children. They were also much more influenced by their family memories. Thus in many fundamental ways men seemed to have been much freer to make their own destinies. This cohort of course not only suffered the 1930s depression as children, but also the heyday of gender role-divided marriage as young adults.

14. Bertaux and Thompson (1997: ch. 2, 'Women, Men, and Transgenerational Influences in Social Mobility', 32–61).
15. Of 12, 10 are working class (6 men, 4 women).
16. 2 men, 2 women.
17. Never married, of 7: 5/21 men, 2/29 women; 5/21 death, 2/29 divorce.
18. Of 13 with psychological problems, 5 had successful marriages and 8 not.
19. Five out of sixteen cases, a little above average.
20. Early entry (10): more psychological (5P−) and relationship problems (3+ 6−); middle entry (21): normal psyche (7P−), slightly better marriages (13+) and jobs (14+, 4=, 4−); late entry (19): better psyche (4P−), but less good marriages (9+ 3= 9−) and slighlty less upward mobility.
21. Newson and Newson (1963, 1968, 1976).
22. Parental quarrelling and violence: death 6/21; divorce 19/29.
23. Jenkins, Smith, and Graham (1988); Elliott and Richards (1992).
24. Mitchell (1985); cf. Walczack and Burns (1984).
25. Byng-Hall (1988, 1995).
26. Bentovim (1992).
27. Still not possible to talk to parent about the past: death 16/21; divorce, 18/29. The difference is stronger when it is remembered that the divorce group also includes those who were intentionally deceived from birth; more typically, over half of them were able to talk with their parents.
28. Wallerstein and Kelly (1980); Wallerstein and Blakeslee (1989).
29. Garmezy and Rutter (1983). Since lone fathers tended to cope less well than lone mothers, boys were more likely than girls to experience a same-sex parent in difficulties.
30. One-fifth of incoming stepparents appeared to be not well disposed towards the children.

31. Fear at entry of stepparent: death 11/21; divorce 23/29.
32. 14 very close; 18 ambivalent; 18 material care only.
33. Parents happy in second marriage: 16/21 death; 12/29 divorce.
34. Felt warmth towards stepparent: 11/21; divorce 11*/29 (*but another 4 were on balance positive).
35. Positive feelings; stepfathers 22/32; stepmothers 3/18.
36. As also Lund and Riley (1984).
37. Serious psychological problems: divorce 6/29; death 7/21.
38. Some contact with absent parent: 16/29.
39. The Exeter study similarly reported that 35% of their children in stepfamilies had moved more than three times since birth. This compares with about one in ten children from intact families (Cockett and Tripp 1994: 12–13).
40. Wallerstein and Blakeslee (1989); Kiernan (1992).
41. 24 risers; 16 level; 10 fallers.
42. Only six instances out of 24 risers.
43. Among our informants, 13/50 (26%) undertook further training or education in their twenties; in the whole NCDS sample 34% took further courses aged 23 to 33 (Ferri 1993: 40).
44. Isaac Newton's mother remarried when he was aged 3. He felt ambivalently towards her, and bitterly resented his stepfather. From childhood he seems to have retreated into a mental inner world, always seeming abstracted, playing with things rather than with other children, and making ingenious mechanical models. He always found personal relationships somewhat difficult and never had an intimate sexual relationship. Leonardo was illegitimate, at first brought up by his single mother, then moving to his grandmother and finally to a stepmother. He too was a famous creator of mechanical toys, while the ambiguous smile on the faces of his women has been thought to reflect his insecure relationship with his carers (Storr 1989: 83–104, 154–5).
45. 43 (86%) of our informants had married, compared with 83% of the whole NCDS sample; 13 of our informants were currently single (26%) compared with 21% of the whole NCDS sample (Ferri 1993: 18). Four of our informants reported three or more live-in relationships (8%), and this was more than the main cohort (4%) (Ferri 1993: 18).

The median age of our informants at first marriage was 21 (of women, 20: cf. average age our women informants 22.7, in whole NCDS women from stepfamilies by divorce 21.1, by death 23.0).

The lack of same-sex relationships seems surprising: so far there has been no published evidence on this in the main cohort.

46. Of our 43 informants ever-married, 31 were still married (72%); in the whole NCDS cohort 76%. Interestingly, NCDS found that both men and women in second marriages were significantly happier in second than in first marriages (Ferri 1993: 18–19). In this respect our informants have fared somewhat better than the other stepfamilies in the NCDS cohort at 33, of whom 65% of those ever-married were still married. The difference is probably principally due to our higher proportion of stepfamilies resulting from parental deaths.

47. Obviously the longer a marriage, the more it was likely to have broken, but this was not significantly intensified with the earliest marriages.

48. Women still married, 8/10 left home approved, 2/10 in conflict; separated, 1/6 left home approved, 5/6 in conflict. Men still married, 6/9 left home approved; separated, 1/5 approved, 4/5 in conflict.

49. Of those informants who had remained married, three-quarters remembered their parents as having good second marriages, in contrast to two-thirds of those informants who had separated; of those who remained married, two-thirds had got on well with their stepparent, in contrast to half of those who had separated.

50. Ever-married informants who separated: divorce 11/29; death 3/21. 9/29 stepchildren by divorce had grandparents who also divorced; 2/21 by death.

51. 41/50 (82%) had children, compared with 67% of the NCDS cohort as a whole. Only three of the ever-married had no children (Ferri 1993: 19). This also was a higher rate of parenting than of the whole NCDS stepfamily cohort at 33 (67%). The principal reason is likely to be that women at home with children felt more able to be interviewed.

    Our informants had also had more children than was typical of the NCDS cohort as a whole: an average of 1.62 in contrast to 1.35.

    Two of the never-married were lone single mothers, while three other married women were now also single parents living alone, and one father was living apart from his children: 12%, well above the 7% of currently single parents in the NCDS cohort as a whole (Ferri 1993: 19–21).

52. Nine (18%) of our informants were stepparents, 12% of the main

NCDS sample (Ferri 1993: 24). On the other hand, only one of our informants (2%) was living in a stepfamily with his partner's children, compared with 3% reported for the whole project. This makes one question whether the formal interviews carried out for the NCDS survey at 33 may have under-reported the number of step-children, as they did in the earlier phases of the study.

BIBLIOGRAPHY

ABRAMS, REBECCA (1995), *When Parents Die* (London: Thorsons).

ADAMS, PAUL L., MILNER, JUDITH R., and SCEPF, NANCY A. (1984), *Fatherless Children* (New York: Wiley).

AINSWORTH, MARY D. SALTER, BLEHAR, MARY C., WATERS, EVERETT, and WALL, SANDRA (1978), *Patterns of Attachment: A Psychological Study of the Strange Situation* (Hillsdale, N.J.: Lawrence Erlbaum).

AMATO, PAUL R. (1986), 'Family processes in one-parent, stepparent and intact families: The child's point of view'. *Journal of Marriage and the Family*, 48: 327–37.

—— and OCHILTREE, GAY (1987), 'Child and adolescent competence in intact, one-parent and stepfamilies: An Australian study', *Journal of Divorce*, 10: 75–96.

ANDERSON, HARLENE, and GOOLISHIAN, HARRY (1988), 'Human systems as linguistic processes: Preliminary and evolving ideas about the implications for clinical theory', *Family Process*, 27: 371–93.

ANDERSON, JUDITH Z., and WHITE, GEOFFREY D. (1986), 'An empirical investigation of interaction relationship patterns in functional and dysfunctional nuclear families and stepfamilies', *Family Process*, 25: 407–22.

ANDERSON, MICHAEL (1983), 'What is new about the modern family: An historical perspective', Office of Population Censuses and Surveys Occasional Paper 71.

ASEN, KARL, BERKOWITZ, RUTH, COOKLIN, ALAN, LEFF, JULIAN, LODER, PETER, PIPER, ROBIN, and REIN, LORRAIN (1991), 'Family therapy outcome research: A trial for families, therapists and researchers', *Family Process*, 30: 3–20.

BACKETT, KATHRYN (1982), *Mothers and Fathers: A Study of the Development and Negotiation of Parental Behaviour* (London: Macmillan).

BATCHELOR, JANE, DIMMOCK, BRIAN, and SMITH, DONNA (1994), *Understanding Stepfamilies: What Can Be Learned from Callers to the Stepfamily Telephone Counselling Service* (London: Stepfamily).

BATESON, GREGORY (1989), 'The pattern which connects', in Fritzjof Capra (ed.), *Uncommon Wisdom: Conversations with Remarkable People* (London: Rider and Co.), 73–92.

BENARD, BONNIE (1992), 'Fostering Resiliency in Kids: Protective Factors in the Family, School and Community', *Prevention Forum*, 12: 1–16.

BENTOVIM, ARNON (1992), *Trauma and Organised Systems* (London: Karnac Books).

BERNARD, JESSIE (1973), *The Future of Marriage* (London: Souvenir Press).

BERTAUX, DANIEL, and THOMPSON, PAUL (1993) (eds.), *Between Generations: Family Models, Myths, and Memories* (International Yearbook of Oral History and Life Stories, 2; Oxford: Oxford University Press).

—— —— (1997), *Pathways to Social Class: A Qualitative Approach to Social Mobility* (Oxford: Oxford University Press).

BIEBER, JOHN D. (1997), *If Divorce is the Only Way* (Penguin Books: Harmondsworth).

BOHANNON, PAUL (1970), *Divorce and After* (New York: Doubleday).

BOWLBY, JOHN (1980), *Attachment and Loss: Loss* (New York: Basic Books).

BRADSHAW, JONATHAN, and MILLAR, JANE (1991), *Lone Parent Families in the UK* (London: HMSO).

BRAND, EULALIE, and CLINGEMPEEL, W. GLENN (1987), 'Interdependencies or marital and stepparent–stepchild relationships and children's psychological adjustment: Research findings and clinical implications', *Family Relations*, 36: 140–5.

BRANNEN, JULIA, and MOSS, PETER (1991), *Managing Mothers: Dual Earner Households after Maternity Leave* (London: Unwin Hyman).

—— and O'BRIEN, MARGARET (1996) (eds.), *Children in Families: Research and Policy* (Brighton: Falmer Press).

BRATLEY, MARY (1995), 'Parents' Experience of a Contact Centre'. M.Sc. in Family Therapy: Practice, Teaching and Research (Tavistock Centre, London).

BRAY JAMES H. (1988), 'Children's development during early remarriage', in E. M. Hetherington and J. D. Arasteh (eds.), *The Impact of Divorce, Single Parenting and Stepparenting on Children* (Hillsdale, N.J.: Erlbaum), 279–98.

BROWN, DIANA (1982), *The Stepfamily* (Norwich: University of East Anglia monograph).

BROWN, GEORGE W., HARRIS, TIRRIL, and BIFULCO, ANTONIA (1986), 'Long term effect of early loss of parent', in Michael Rutter, Carl Izard, and Peter Read (eds.), *Depression in Young People* (New York: Guilford Press), 251–96.

BRUNER, EDWARD (1986), 'Ethnology as narrative', in V. Turner and E. Bruner (eds.), *The Anthrology of Experience* (Chicago: University of Illinois Press), 139–55.

BUMPASS, LARRY (1984), 'Some characteristics of children's second families', *American Journal of Sociology*, 90: 608–23.

BURCHARDT, NATASHA (1989), 'Structure and relationships in stepfamilies in early twentieth century Britain', *Continuity and Change*, 4(2): 293–322.

—— (1990), 'Stepchildren's memories: Myth, understanding and forgiveness', in Raphael Samuel and Paul Thompson (eds.), *The Myths We Live By* (London: Routledge), 239–51.

BURCK, CHARLOTTE, and DANIEL, GWYN (1995a), *Gender and Family Therapy* (London: Karnac).

—— —— (1995b), 'Moving on: Gender beliefs in post-divorce and stepfamily process', in C. Burck and B. Speed (eds.), *Gender, Power and Relationships* (London: Routledge), 185–201.

—— and FROSH, STEPHEN (1993), paper to Institute of Family Therapy seminar, Apr. 1993.

—— and SPEED, BEBE (1995) (eds.), *Gender, Power and Relationships* (London: Routledge).

—— HILDEBRAND, JUDY, and MANN, JUDY (1996), 'Women's tales: Systematic groupwork with mothers post-separation', *Journal of Family Therapy*, 18: 163–83.

BURGOYNE, JACQUELINE, and CLARK, DAVID (1984), *Making a Go of It: Stepfamilies in Sheffield* (London: Routledge).

BURNHAM, JOHN (1986), *Family Therapy* (London: Tavistock).

BYNG-HALL, JOHN (1979), 'Re-editing family mythology during family therapy', *Journal of Family Therapy*, 1: 103–16.

—— (1988), 'Scripts and legends in families and family therapy', *Journal of Child Psychotherapy*, 12(2): 3–13.

—— (1995), *Rewriting Family Scripts: Improvisation and Systems Change* (New York: Guilford Press).

CAMPBELL, DAVID, and DE CARTERET, JOHN (1984), 'Guidelines for clinicians considering family therapy research', *Journal of Family Therapy*, 6(2): 131–47.

CARTER, ELIZABETH, and McGOLDRICK, MONICA, (1988), *The Changing Family Life Cycle: A Framework for Family Therapy*, 2nd edn. (New York: Gardner Press).

CHAMBERLAIN, MARY (1994), 'Family and identity: Barbadian migrants to Britain', in Rina Benmayor and Andor Skotnes (eds.), *Migration and Identity* (International Yearbook of Oral History and Life Stories, 3; Oxford: Oxford University Press), 119–36.

CHASE-LANSDALE, LINDSAY, and HETHERINGTON, E. MAVIS (1990), 'The impact of divorce on life span development: Short and long-term effects', in P. B. Baltes, D. L. Featherman and R. M. Lerner (eds.),

Life Span Development and Behaviour, (Hillsdale, N.J.: Lawrence Erlbaum), 105–50.

CHEAL, DAVID (1991), *Family and the State of Theory* (London: Harvester).

Children's Society (1994), *Losing Support: Children and the Child Support Act* (London).

CHODOROW, NANCY (1978), *The Reproduction of Mothering: Psychoanalysis and the Sociology of Gender* (Berkeley: University of California Press).

CLAUSEN, JOHN (1993), *American Lives: Looking Back at the Children of the Great Depression* (New York: Free Press).

CLINGEMPEEL, W. GLENN, and SEGAL, SION (1986), 'Stepparent–stepchild relationships and the psychological adjustment of children in stepmother and stepfather families', *Child Development*, 57: 474–84.

—— and WOODWARD, KATHRYN BOWEN (1988), 'Family relationships and children's psychological adjustment in stepmother and stepfather families', in E. M. Hetherington and J. D. Arasteh (eds.), *The Impact of Divorce, Single Parenting and Stepparenting on Children* (Hillsdale, N.J.: Erlbaum), 299–324.

—— IEVOLI, RICHARD, and BRAND, EULALIE (1984), 'Structural complexity and the quality of stepfather–stepchild relationships', *Family Process*, 23: 547–60.

COCKETT, MONICA, and TRIPP, JOHN (1994), *The Exeter Family Study: Family Breakdown and its Impact on Children* (Exeter: University of Exeter Press).

COWEN, EMERY, PEDRO-CAMPBELL, JOANNE, and GILLIS, LINDA ALPERT (1990), 'Relationships between support and adjustment among children of divorce', *Journal of Child Psychology and Psychiatry*, 31: 727–35.

CRELLIN, EILEEN, KELMER-PRINGLE, MIA and WEST, PATRICK (1971), *Born Illegitimate: Social and Educational Implications* (Slough: National Foundation for Educational Research).

DANIEL, GWYN, and THOMPSON, PAUL (1996), 'Stepchildren's memories of love and loss: Men's and Women's narratives', in Selma Leydesdorff, Luisa Passerini, and Paul Thompson (eds.), *Gender and Memory* (International Yearbook of Oral History and Life Stories, 4; Oxford: Oxford University Press), 165–85.

DAVIDOFF, LEONORE (1995), 'Where the stranger begins: The question of siblings in historical analysis', in L. Davidoff, *Worlds Between: Historical Perspectives on Gender and Class* (Cambridge: Polity Press), 206–26.

DE'ATH, ERICA (1992), 'Stepfamilies in the context of contemporary family life', in E. De'Ath (ed.), *Stepfamilies: What Do We Know and What Do We Need to Know* (Croydon: Significant Publications), 5–18.

DOMINIAN, JACK, MANSFIELD, PENNY, DORMOR, DUNCAN, and MCALLISTER, FIONA (1991), *Marital Breakdown and the Health of the Nation* (London: One plus One).

DUBERMAN, LUCILE (1973), 'Step-kin relationships', *Journal of Marriage and the Family*, 35: 283–92.

DUNN, JUDY (1984), *Sisters and Brothers* (London: Fontana).

—— (1996), *Stepfamilies: Who Fares Well, Who Fares Badly* (Hillsdale, N.J.: Erlbaum).

—— and KENRICK, CAROL, (1982), *Siblings: Love, Envy and Understanding* (London: Grant McIntyre).

EEKELAAR, JOHN (1984). *Family Law and Social Policy* (London: Weidenfeld and Nicolson).

—— (1996), 'The Family Law Bill: The politics of family law?' *Family Law*, 26: 45–8.

—— CLIVE, ERIC, with CLARKE, KAREN, and RAIKES, SUSAN (1977), *Custody after Divorce* (Oxford: Centre for Socio-Legal Studies).

ELLIOTT, JANE, and RICHARDS, MARTIN P. M. (1992), 'Children and divorce: Educational performance and behaviour before and after parental separation', *International Journal of Law and the Family*, 5: 258–76.

—— OCHILTREE, GAY, RICHARDS, MARTIN, SINCLAIR, CHRISTINA, and TASKER, FIONA (1990), 'Divorce and children: A British challenge to the Wallerstein view', *Family Law*, 20: 309–14.

EMERY, ROBERT E., (1982), 'Interparental conflict and the children of discord and divorce', *Psychological Bulletin*, 92: 310–30.

—— (1988), *Marriage, Divorce and Children's Adjustment*, (Beverly Hills, Calif.: Sage).

—— and FOREHAND, REX (1994), 'Parental divorce and children's well-being: A focus on resilience', in R. J. Haggerty, L. R. Sherrod, N. Garmezy, and M. Rutter (eds.), *Stress, Risk and Resilience in Children and Adolescents: Processes, Mechanisms and Interventions* (Cambridge: Cambridge University Press), 64–99.

ERIKSON, ERIK (1959), *Identity in the Life Cycle* (New York: Norton).

—— (1965), *Childhood and Society* (Harmondsworth: Penguin).

EVERETT, CRAIG A. (1991) (ed.), *The Consequences of Divorce: Economic and Custodial Impact on Children and Adults* (Binghampton: Haworth Press).

FALICOV, CELIA (1988), *Family Transitions: Continuity and Change over the Life Cycle* (New York: Guilford Press).

Family Law Act, 1996 (1996), Highlight 146 (London: National Children's Bureau).

FERREIRA, ANTONIO (1968), 'Family myths and homeostasis', in N. W. Bell and E. F. Vogel (eds.), *A Modern Introduction to the Family* (New York: Free Press), 541–8.

FERRI, ELSA (1976), *Growing Up in a One-Parent Family,* National Foundation for Educational Research (NFER) (Windsor: Nelson).

—— (1984), *Stepchildren: A National Study,* NFER (Windsor: Nelson).

—— (1993), *Life at 33: The Fifth Follow-up of the National Child Development Study* (London: National Children's Bureau).

—— and SMITH, KATE (1996), *Parenting in the 1990s* (London: Family Policy Studies Centre).

FONAGY, PETER (1993), 'Psychoanalytic and empirical approaches to developmental psychopathology: Can they be usefully integrated', *Journal of the Royal Society of Medicine,* 86: 577–81.

—— STEELE, MIRIAM, STEELE, HOWARD, MORAN, GEORGE, and HIGGITT, ANNA (1991), 'The capacity for understanding mental states: The reflective self in parent and child and its significance for security of attachment', *Infant Mental Health Journal,* 12 (3): 201–18.

FROSH, STEPHEN (1995), 'Unpacking masculinity: From rationality to fragmentation', in C. Burck and B. Speed (eds.), *Gender Power and Relationships* (London: Routledge), 218–31.

FURSTENBERG, FRANK F. (1987), 'The new extended family: The experience of parents and children after remarriage', in Pasley and Ihinger-Tallman (1987), 42–61.

—— (1988), 'Child care after divorce and remarriage', in E. M. Hetherington and J. D. Arasteh (eds.), *The Impact of Divorce, Single Parenting and Stepparenting on Children* (Hillsdale, N.J.: Erlbaum), 245–61.

—— and NORD, CHRISTINE (1985), 'Parenting apart: Patterns of child-rearing after marital disruption', *Journal of Marriage and the Family,* 47: 893–905.

—— and SPANIER, GRAHAM, (1984), *Recycling the Family: Remarriage after Divorce* (Newbury Park: Sage).

—— NORD, CHRISTINE, PETERSON, J. L., and ZILL, NICHOLAS (1983), 'The life course of children of divorce: Marital disruption and parental contact', *American Sociological Review,* 48: 656–68.

GANONG, LAWRENCE H. and COLEMAN, MARILYN (1986), 'A comparison of clinical and empirical literature on children in stepfamilies', *Journal of Marriage and the Family*, 48(2): 309–18.

GARMEZY, NORMAN, and MASTEN, ANN S. (1994), 'Chronic Adversities', in Sir M. Rutter, E. Taylor, and L. Herson (eds.), *Child and Adolescent Psychiatry: Modern Approaches*, 3rd edn. (Oxford: Blackwell).

—— and RUTTER SIR MICHAEL (1983), *Stress, Coping and Development in Children* (New York: McGraw Hill).

GERGEN, KENNETH (1991), *The Saturated Self* (New York: Basic Books).

GIDDENS, ANTHONY (1991), *Modernity and Self-Identity: Self and Society in the Late Modern Age* (Cambridge: Polity).

—— (1992), *The Transformation of Intimacy* (Cambridge: Polity Press).

GOLDNER, VIRGINIA (1985), 'Feminism and family therapy', *Family Process*, 24: 31–47.

—— (1988), 'Generation and gender: Normative and covert hierarchies', *Family Process*, 27: 17–31.

GORELL BARNES, GILL and DOWLING, EMILIA (forthcoming), *Going through the Divorce Process: Working with Children and Families* (Basingstoke: Macmillan).

GORER, GEOFFREY (1965), *Death, Grief, and Mourning* (London: Cresset Press).

GRYCH, JOHN H., and FINCHAM, FRANK (1990), 'Marital conflict and children's adjustment: A cognitive–collective framework', *Psychological Bulletin*, 108: 267–90.

GUIDOBALDI, JOHN, and CLEMINSHAW, HELEN (1985), 'Divorce, family health and child adjustment', *Family Relations*, 34: 35–41.

GURMAN, ALAN, and KNISKERN, DAVID (1991) (eds.), *Handbook of Family Therapy*, ii (New York: Brunner-Mazel).

HAREVEN, TAMARA (1982), *Family Time and Industrial Time* (Cambridge: Cambridge University Press).

HART, BRUCE (1993), 'Gender role self perceptions and attitudes of single fathers', M.Sc. in Family Therapy (Tavistock Clinic, London).

HASKEY, JOHN (1994), 'Stepfamilies and stepchildren in Great Britain', *Population Trends*, 76: 17–28.

HETHERINGTON, E. MAVIS (1988), 'Parents, children and siblings six years after divorce', in R. Hinde and J. Stevenson-Hinde (eds.) *Relationships within Families* (Cambridge: Cambridge University Press), 311–31.

—— (1989a), 'Coping with family transitions: Winners, losers and survivors', *Child Development*, 60: 1–4.

—— (1989b), 'Marital transitions: A child's perspective', *American Psychologist*, 44(2): 303–12.

—— and ANDERSON, EDWARD R. (1987), 'The effects of divorce and remarriage on early adolescents and their families', in M. D. Levine and E. R. McArney (eds.), *Early Adolescent Transitions* (Lexington, Md.: D. C. Heath), 49–67.

—— and FURSTENBERG, FRANK F. (1989), 'Sounding the alarm', *Readings*, June 1989: 4–8.

—— COX, MARTHA, and COX, ROGER (1978), 'The aftermath of divorce', in Joseph H. Stevens and M. Mathews (eds.), *Mother/child Father/child Relations* (Washington, D.C.: National Association for the Education of Young Children), 149–76.

—— —— —— (1985), 'Long term effects of divorce and remarriage on the adjustment of children', *Journal of American Academy of Child Psychiatry*, 24(5): 518–30.

HILL, REUBEN (1971), 'Modern systems theory and the family', *Social Science Information*, 10(5): 7–26.

HOFFMAN, LYNN (1990), 'Constructing realities: An art of lenses', *Family Process*, 29: 1–12.

HOLMES, JEREMY (1993), *John Bowlby and Attachment Theory* (London: Routledge).

HUGHES, CHRISTINA (1991), *Stepparents: Wicked or Wonderful? An In-Depth Study of Parenthood* (Aldershot: Avebury).

ISAACS, MARLA BECK, LEON, GEORGE, and DONAHUE, ANN MARIE (1987), 'Who are the "normal" children of divorce? On the need to specify a population', *Journal of Divorce*, 12: 107–19.

JENKINS, JENNY, SMITH, MARJORIE, and GRAHAM, PHILIP (1988), 'Coping with parental quarrels', *Journal of American Academy of Child and Adolescent Psychiatry*, 28: 182–9.

JOHNSON, COLLEEN L. (1988a), 'Post-divorce: The organization of relationships between divorcing children and their parents', *Journal of Marriage and the Family*, 50: 221–31.

—— (1988b), *Extra Familia: Grandparents, Parents and Children Adjust to Divorce* (Brunswick, N.J.: Rutgers University Press).

JONES, DAVID P. H. (1987), 'The evidence of a three-year-old child', *Criminal Law Review*, 677–81.

JONES, ELSA (1993), *Family Systems Therapy: Developments in the Milan-Systematic Therapies* (Chichester: Wiley).

JONES, GILL (1994), 'The Cost of Moving Out', *Family Policy Bulletin* (September).

—— (1995), *Family Support for Young People* (London: Family Policy Studies Centre).

JORDAN, JUDITH, KAPLAN, ALEXANDRA, MILLAR, JEAN, STIVER, IRENE, and SURREY, JANET (1991), *Women's Growth in Connection* (New York: Guilford Press).

KEITH, DAVID and WHITAKER, CARL (1988), 'The Presence of the Past: Continuity and Change in the Symbolic Structure of Families', in Falicov (1988), 431–47.

KIERNAN, KATHLEEN (1992), 'The impact of family disruption in childhood on transitions made in young adult life', *Population Studies*, 46: 213–34.

KOLVIN, ISRAEL, MILLER, FREDERICK J. W., FLEETING, M., and KOLVIN, PHILIP (1988), 'Social and parenting factors affecting criminal offence rates: Findings from the Newcastle Thousand Families Study, 1947–1980', *British Journal of Psychiatry*, 152: 80–90.

KRAEMER, SEBASTIAN (1994), 'What are fathers for?', in Charlotte Burck and Bebe Speed (eds.), *Gender and Power in Families: New Developments* (London: Routledge).

KRUK, EDWARD (1992), 'Psychological and structural factors contributing to the disengagement of non-custodial fathers after divorce', *Family and Conciliation Courts Review*, 30: 81–101.

KURDEK, LAWRENCE, and SIESKY, ALBERT (1980), 'Children's perceptions of their parents' divorce', *Journal of Divorce*, 3(4): 339–76.

LAMB, MICHAEL, PLECK, JOSEPH, and LEVINE, JAMES (1987), 'Effects of increased paternal involvement on fathers and mothers', in Charles Lewis and Margaret O'Brien (eds.), *Re-Assessing Fatherhood; New Observations on Fathers and the Modern Family* (London: Sage),

LAMBERT, LYDIA, and STREATHER, JANE (1980), *Children in Changing Families: A Study of Adoption and Illegitimacy* (London: Macmillan).

LEFF, JULIAN, and VAUGHN, CHRISTINE (1985), *Expressed Emotion in Families: Its Significance for Mental Illness* (New York: Guilford Press).

LEWIS, JERRY, BEAVERS, W. ROBERT, GOSSETT, JOHN, and PHILLIPS, VIRGINIA (1976), *No Single Thread: Psychological Health in Family Systems* (New York: Brunner-Mazel).

LITWAK, EUGENE (1959), 'The use of extended family groups in the achievement of social goals: some policy implications', *Social Problems*, 7: 177–87.

LUND, MARY (1984), 'Research on divorce and children', *Family Law*, 14: 198–201.

—— and RILEY, JENI (1984), 'Schools caught in the middle: Educating the children of divorce', *Journal of the National Association of Primary Education*, May 1984, 3–5.

MACCOBY, ELEANOR E., and MNOOKIN, ROBERT (1992), *Dividing the Child*, (Cambridge, Mass.: Harvard University Press).

MCCREDIE, GILLIAN, and HORROX, ALAN (1985), *Voices in the Dark: Children and Divorce*, (London: Allen and Unwin).

MCFARLANE, ALLEN H., BELLISSIMO, ANTHONY, and NORMAN, GEOFFREY (1995), 'Family structure, family functioning, and adolescent well-being: The transcendent influence of parental style', *Journal of Child Psychology and Psychiatry*, 36: 847–64.

MACLEAN, MAVIS, and KUH, DIANA (1991), 'The long-term effects for girls of parental divorce', in M. Maclean and D. Groves (eds.), *Women's Issues in Social Policy* (London: Routledge), 161–78.

MAIDMENT, SUSAN (1984), *Child Custody and Divorce* (London: Croom Helm).

MAIN, MARY (1992), 'Metacognitive Knowledge, Metacognitive Monitoring and Singular (Coherent) versus Multiple (Incoherent) Models of Attachment: Findings and Directions for Future Research', in C. Murray Parkes, J. Stevenson Hinde, and P. Mains (eds.), *Attachment across the Life Cycle* (London: Routledge), 127–59.

—— and CASSIDY, JUDE (1988), 'Categories of response to reunion with the parent at age 6', *Developmental Psychology*, 24: 415–26.

—— and GOLDWYN, RUTH (1994), 'Predicting rejecting of her infant from mother's representation of her own experience: Implications for the abused–abusing intergenerational cycle', *International Journal of Child Abuse and Neglect*, 8: 203–17.

—— KAPLAN, NANCY, and CASSIDY, JUDE (1985), 'Security in infancy, childhood and adulthood: A move to the level of representation', in Inge Bretherton and Everett Waters (eds.), *Growing Points of Attachment Theory in Research* (Monographs of the Society for Research in Child Development, Serial No. 209, Vol. 50 i–ii), 66–104.

MANSFIELD, PENNY, and COLLARD, JEAN (1988), *The Beginning of the Rest of Your Life? A Portrait of Newly-Wed Marriage* (London: Macmillan).

MATURANA, HUMBERTO, and VARELA, FRANCISCO (1980), *Autopoiesis and Cognition* (Dordrecht: Reidel).

—— —— (1987), *The Tree of Knowledge* (Boston: New Science Library).

MISHLER, ELLIOT (1986), *Research Interviewing: Context and Narrative* (Cambridge, Mass.: Harvard University Press).

MITCHELL, ANN (1985), *Children in the Middle: Living Through Divorce* (London: Tavistock).

MNOOKIN, ROBERT H. (1979), *Bargaining in the Shadow of the Law*, Working Paper 3, Centre for Socio-Legal Studies, (Wolfson College, Oxford).

MURCH, MERVYN (1980), *Justice and Welfare in Divorce* (London: Sweet and Maxwell).

NEWSON, JOHN, and NEWSON, ELIZABETH (1963), *Infant Care in an Urban Community* (London: Allen and Unwin).

—— —— (1968), *Four Years Old in an Urban Community,* (London: Allen and Unwin).

—— —— (1976), *Seven Years Old in the Home Environment* (London: Allen and Unwin).

NI BROCHLAIN, MAIRE (1992), 'Longterm effects of divorce: Fact or fallacy?', *ESRC Data Archive Bulletin,* 50: 12–13.

O'BRIEN, MARGARET, ALLDRED, PAM, and JONES, DEBORAH (1996), 'Children's constructions of family and kinship' in J. Brannen and M. O'Brien (eds.), *Children in Families* (Bristol, Penn.: Falmer Press), 84–100.

OCHILTREE, GAY (1988), 'The effects of marital disruption on children: An overview', *Family Matters,* Australian Institute of Family Studies, 22 (Dec.): 6–11.

—— (1990), *Children in Stepfamilies* (Melbourne: Prentice Hall).

OLSON, DAVID H., MCCUBBIN, HAMILTON, BARNES, HOWARD, LARSEN, ANDREA, and WILSON, MARC (1989), *Families: What Makes Them Work,* rev. edn. (Beverly Hills, Calif.: Sage).

PAPERNOW, P. (1984), 'The stepfamily cycle: An experimental model of stepfamily development', *Family Relations,* 33: 355–63.

PARKES, COLIN M. (1986), *Bereavement: Studies of Grief in Adult Life,* 2nd edn. (Harmondsworth: Penguin Books).

PASLEY, KAY, and IHINGER-TALLMAN, MARILYN (1987) (eds.), *Remarriage and Stepparenting: Current Research and Theory* (New York: Guilford Press).

PAYNE, LISA (1996), *Highlight 146* (London: National Children's Bureau).

PLUMMER, KEN (1983), *Documents of Life: An Introduction to the Literature and the Problems of a Humanistic Method* (London: Unwin).

REISS, DAVID (1981), *The Family's Construction of Reality* (Cambridge, Mass.: Harvard University Press).

RICHARDS, MARTIN, and DYSON, MAUREEN (1982), *Separation, Divorce and the Development of Children: A Review* (Cambridge: Child Care and Development Group).

ROBERTS, JANINE (1994), *Tales and Transformations: Stories in Families and Family Therapy* (London: W. W. Norton).

ROBINSON, MARGARET (1980), 'Stepfamilies: A Reconstituted Family System', *Journal of Family Therapy*, 2: 45–69.

—— (1991), *Family Transformation through Divorce and Remarriage* (London: Routledge).

—— and SMITH, DONNA (1993), *Step by Step: Focus on Stepfamilies* (Brighton: Harvester Wheatsheaf).

ROSS, MICHAEL, and HOLMBERG, DIANE (1992), 'Recounting the past: Gender differences in the recall of events in the history of a close relationship', *Journal of Social and Personal Relationships*, 2: 191–204.

RUTTER, SIR MICHAEL (1966), *Children of Sick Parents: An Environmental and Psychiatric Study* (London: Oxford University Press).

—— (1971), 'Parent–child separation: Psychological effects on the children', *Journal of Child Psychology and Psychiatry*, 12: 233–60.

—— (1985), 'Resilience in the face of adversity: Protective factors and resistance to psychiatric disorder', *British Journal of Psychiatry*, 147: 598–611.

—— (1987), 'Psychosocial Resilience and Protective Mechanisms', *American Journal of Orthopsychiatry*, 57: 316–31.

—— (1988), 'Functions and consequences of relationships: Some psychopathological considerations', in R. Hinde and J. Stevenson-Hinde (eds.), *Relationships within Families: Mutual Influences* (Oxford: Oxford University Press), 332–53.

—— (1995), 'Clinical Implications of Attachment Concepts: Retrospect and Prospect', *Journal of Child Psychology and Psychiatry*, 36: 549–71.

—— and QUINTON, DAVID (1984), 'Long-term follow-up of women institutionalised in childhood: Factors promoting good functioning in adult life', *British Journal of Developmental Psychology*, 18: 225–34.

—— TAYLOR, ERIC, and HERSOV, LIONEL (1994), *Child and Adolescent Psychiatry: Modern Approaches*, 3rd edn. (Oxford: Blackwell).

SALER, LAUREN, and SKOLOVICK, NEIL (1992), 'Childhood parental death and depression in adulthood: The roles of the surviving parent and family environment', *American Journal of Orthopsychiatry*, 62: 504–16.

SAMUEL, RAPHAEL, and THOMPSON, PAUL (1990) (eds.), *The Myths We Live By* (London: Routledge).

SANTROCK, JOHN, and SITTERLE, KAREN (1987), 'Parent–child relationships in stepmother families', in Pasley and Ihinger-Tallman (1987), 273–99.

—— and WARSHAK, RICHARD (1979), 'Father custody and social development in boys and girls', *Journal of Social Issues*, 35: 112–35.

SERRA, PIERA (1993), 'Physical violence in the couple relationship: A contribution towards the analysis of the context', *Family Process*, 32: 21–33.

SHOTTER, JOHN (1986), *The Cultural Politics of Everyday Life* (Buckingham: Open University Press).

—— and GERGEN, KENNETH (1989) (eds.), *Texts of Identity* (London: Sage).

SIMON, ANNE W. (1964), *Stepchild in the Family* (New York: Odyssey).

SIMPSON, BOB, and MCCARTHY, PETER (1991), *Issues in Post Divorce Housing: Family Policy or Housing Policy?* (Aldershot: Avebury).

—— —— and WALKER, JANET (1995), *Being There: Fathers after Divorce, An Exploration of Post-Divorce Fathering*, Relate Centre for Family Studies, University of Newcastle-upon-Tyne.

SIMPSON, BRIAN (1994), 'Access and child care centres: An ethnographic perspective', *Children and Society*, 8: 42–54.

SMITH, DONNA (1990), *Stepmothering* (Brighton: Wheatsheaf Harvester).

SPENCER, JOHN R., and FLIN, RHONA H., (1990), 'The child witness, ingenious or ingenuous? A review of the psychological evidence', in *The Evidence of Children: The Law and the Psychology* (London: Blackstone Press), 285–336.

STERN, PHYLLIS N. (1978), 'Stepfather families: Integration around child discipline', *Issues in Mental Health Nursing*, 1: 50–6.

STONE, LAWRENCE (1990), *Road to Divorce: England 1530–1987* (Oxford: Oxford University Press).

STORR, ANTHONY (1989), *Churchill's Black Dog and Other Phenomena of the Human Mind* (London: Fontana).

THOMPSON, PAUL (1984), 'The family and childrearing as forces for economic change: Towards fresh research approaches', *Sociology*, 18: 516–29.

—— (1988), *The Voice of the Past*, 2nd edn. (Oxford: Oxford University Press).

—— (1993a), *The Edwardians: The Remaking of British Society*, 3rd edn. (London: Routledge).

—— (1993b), '"I don't feel old": The significance of the search for meaning in later life', *International Journal of Geriatric Psychiatry*, 8: 685–92.

—— ITZIN, CATHERINE, and ABENDSTERN, MICHELE (1990), *I Don't Feel Old: The Experience of Later Life* (Oxford: Oxford University Press).

TIZARD, BARBARA, and PHOENIX, ANN (1993), *Black, White or Mixed Race?* (London: Routledge).

TONKIN, ELIZABETH (1992), *Narrating Our Pasts: The Social Construction of Oral History* (Cambridge: Cambridge University Press).

VAUGHAN, DIANE (1987), *Uncoupling: Turning Points in Intimate Relationships* (London: Methuen).

VISHER, EMILY B., and VISHER, JOHN S. (1978), *Stepfamilies: A Guide to Working with Stepparents and Stepchildren* (New York: Brunner-Mazel).

WADSBY, MARIE (1993), 'Children of divorce and their parents', Linkoping University Medical Dissertations, 405 (Department of Child and Adolescent Psychiatry, Linkoping University, Sweden).

WADSWORTH, MICHAEL (1979), *The Roots of Delinquency: Infancy, Adolescence and Crime* (Oxford: Martin Robertson).

—— (1991), *The Impact of Time: Childhood, History and Adult Life* (Oxford: Clarendon Press).

—— MACLEAN, MAVIS, KUH, DIANA, and ROGERS, BRYAN (1990), 'Children of divorced and separated parents: Summary and review of findings from a long term follow-up study in the UK', *Family Practice*, 7(1): 105–9.

WALCZACK, YVETTE with BURNS, SHEILA (1984), *Divorce: The Child's Point of View* (London: Harper and Row).

WALDVOGEL, SAMUEL (1982), 'Childhood memories', (1953), reprinted in Ulric Neisser, *Memory Observed: Remembering in Natural Contexts* (San Francisco: Freeman and Company, 1982), 73–6.

WALKER, JANET (1992), 'Divorce, re-marriage and parental responsibility', in E. De'Ath, *Stepfamilies: What Do We Know and What Do We Need to Know?* (Croydon: Significant Publications), 19–30.

—— (1993), 'Co-operative parenting, post-divorce: Possibility or pipedream?' *Journal of Family Therapy*, 15: 273–93.

WALLERSTEIN, JUDITH (1985), 'The long term effects of divorce on children: A review', *Journal of the American Academy of Child and Adolescent Psychiatry*, 30(3): 349–60.

—— and BLAKESLEE, SANDRA (1989), *Second Chances* (London: Bantam).

—— CORBIN, SHAUNA B., and LEWIS, JULIA (1988), 'Children of divorce: A ten year study', in E. M. Hetherington and J. Arasteh (eds.), *The Impact of Divorce, Single Parenting, and Stepparenting on Children* (Hillsdale, N.J.: Erlbaum), 197–214.

—— and KELLY, JOAN (1980), *Surviving the Break-up: How Children and Parents Cope with Divorce* (London: Grant McIntyre).

WALSH, FROMA (1982), *Normal Family Processes* (New York: Guilford Press).

WALTERS, MARIANNE, CARTER, BETTY, PAPP, PEGGY, and SILVERSTEIN, OLGA (1988), *The Invisible Web* (New York: Guilford Press).

WEISS, ROBERT (1979), 'Growing up a little faster: The experience of growing up in a single-parent household', *Journal of Social Issues*, 35: 97–111.

WHITE, LYNN (1994), 'Growing up with single parents and stepparents: Long-term effects on family solidarity', *Journal of Marriage and the Family*, 56: 935–48.

WHITE, MICHAEL, and EPSTON, DAVID (1989), *Literate Means to Therapeutic Ends* (Adelaide: Dulwich Centre Publications).

WHITEHEAD, BARBARA DAFOE (1993), 'Dan Quayle Was Right', *Atlantic Monthly*, Apr. 1993, 47–84.

YAHRAES, HERBERT, and BOHANNON, PAUL (1979), 'Stepfathers as parents', in *Families Today*, i. *A Research Sampler on Parents and Children* (Washington, D.C.: US Department of Health, Education, and Welfare and National Institute of Mental Health), 347–62.

ZEALAH, CHARLES H., and EMDE, ROBERT M. (1994), 'Attachment disorders in infancy and childhood', in Michael Rutter, Eric Taylor, and Lionel Hersov (eds.), *Child and Adolescent Psychiatry: Modern Approaches*, 3rd edn. (Oxford: Blackwell), 493–5.

ZILL, NICHOLAS (1988), 'Behavior, problems, and achievement among children in stepfamilies', in E. M. Hetherington and J. D. Arasteh (eds.), *The Impact of Divorce, Single Parenting, and Stepparenting on Children* (Hillsdale, N.J.: Erlbaum), 325–68.

INDEX

absent parents, loyalty to 115–
16; images of 113, 118–
19, 121; and new
stepfamily 113–16; term 88–
91; worry about 255
adoption, by stepparents 263
affection 164, 227, 228–30
agency, sense of, professional help
and 247–8; and self-esteem 217–
24
aggression 12
Ainsworth, M., Blehar, M., Waters, E.,
and Wall, S. 35
alcoholism 102, 187
Amato, P. 20
Amato, P., and Ochiltree, G. 16, 20
Anderson, J., and White, G. 19
Atlantic Monthly 24
attachment, 'Adult attachment
interview' 36, 293; caretaking
parent 117; and caring through
doing 273–4; cross-
gender 113; to
grandparents 131–2; and
narrative coherence 269–70; and
reflective abilities 209–10; to
work 180; *see also* intimacy
attachment theory 33, 35–7, 293, 298
aunts and uncles 132, 133–8, 282
Australia, 'Children in Families'
study 13, 16; research 11, 13–
14
avoidance 30–1

Backett, K. 33
Bateson, G. 244
Bertraux, D., and Thompson, P. 45
birth, impact on parents 193–4
Bowlby, J. 35
Brand, E., and Clingempeel, W. 20
Bray, J. 19
Britain, divorce rates v, 1; National
Child Development Study vi–vii,

7–8, 38, 44–5, 267; research 17–
18
Bruner, E. 33, 34
Burgoyne, J., and Clark, D. 21, 41, 262,
263, 296–8; *Making a Go of It* vi

Canada 13
careers and work, attitudes to 179–83,
272, 283–4, 304
caretaking parents, memories of 122–3
change, capacity for, effect of
marriage 200–2; and repeated
break-ups 243; reworking old
relationships vii, 22, 202–8, 212,
252, 266, 283; *see also* resilience
Chase-Lansdale, L., and Hetherington,
E. 297
child development, models and
norms 242–3
Child Support Act (1991) 88, 263–4
Children Act (1989) 3, 260, 261–2, 264
Citizens Advice Bureau 257
class, and attitudes to careers and
work 180–1; and discipline and
communication vii, 50, 51, 273–
4; and narrative coherence 210;
and occupational mobility 272
Clingempeel, W., Ievoli, R., and
Brand, E. 19
Clingempeel, W., and Segal, S. 20
Cockett, M., and Tripp, J. 289, 301,
302
cohabitation 191–2, 284, 308
coherence in narratives 209–10, 213–
17; and attachment 36, 269–70,
293
communication, after death of
parents 110–13, 245–6; avoiding
negative patterns 225–
6; between parents after
divorce 12; and class 273–
4; explanations to children 14,
19, 47, 54–61, 110–13, 258, 287,